Caribbean Examinations Council®

Law

CAPE®

CXC®

UNIT 1

for self-study and distance learning

OXFORD
UNIVERSITY PRESS

Great Clarendon Street, Oxford, OX2 6DP, United Kingdom

Oxford University Press is a department of the University of Oxford. It furthers the University's objective of excellence in research, scholarship, and education by publishing worldwide. Oxford is a registered trade mark of Oxford University Press in the UK and in certain other countries

Originally published in 2010 by the Caribbean Examinations Council in association with The Commonwealth of Learning.

This material was originally developed by the Caribbean Examinations Council with assistance from The Commonwealth of Learning.

This edition first repackaged and distributed by Nelson Thornes Ltd in 2012

British Library Cataloguing in Publication Data
Data available

978-1-4085-1702-4

10 9 8 7 6

Printed and bound by CPI Group (UK) Ltd, Croydon, CR0 4YY

Acknowledgements

Cover: Mark Lyndersay, Lyndersay Digital, Trinidad
www.lyndersaydigital.com
Page make-up: OKS Prepress, India

Although we have made every effort to trace and contact all copyright holders before publication this has not been possible in all cases. If notified, the publisher will rectify any errors or omissions at the earliest opportunity.

Contents

Acknowledgements

Caribbean Examinations Council/Oxford University Press would like to acknowledge Lilieth Deacon for her assistance in preparing the content for this Self-Study Guide.

Introduction

Purpose

The **Caribbean Examinations Council** (**CXC®**), in collaboration with the Commonwealth of Learning (COL), has developed self-study guides for a number of **Caribbean Secondary Education Certificate** (**CSEC®**) and **Caribbean Advanced Proficiency Examination** (**CAPE®**) subjects. The main purpose of the guides is to provide both in school and out of school candidates with resource materials that should help them in preparing for **CXC** examinations. Each study guide is student centred and the language is student friendly.

This course is designed for persons over the age of 16 who wish to further their studies. The course is equally useful to persons who are pursuing part-time study and those enrolled full-time in an educational institution.

You may have completed five years of secondary education, or you may be a mature student with work experience. The course is based on the assumption that you already have a good grasp of the CAPE® Law Unit 1 syllabus or its equivalent.

Course Aims

The course aims to enable you to:

- promote knowledge and understanding of legal principles
- develop knowledge and understanding of selected areas of law in the Commonwealth Caribbean
- develop techniques of legal reasoning and the ability to analyse and solve legal problems, with reference to the recognised sources of law
- develop an appreciation of the role of law in society
- promote respect for the Rule of Law and legal institutions in society
- promote a critical awareness of the process of developing Caribbean jurisprudence
- encourage an awareness of the fundamental rights and freedoms enshrined in the constitutions of Commonwealth Caribbean states and the methods of their enforcement
- provide an awareness of the individual's right to proper State administration.

Course Structure

This course consists of five chapters, each of which addresses a specific module of the CAPE® Law Unit 1 syllabus. The syllabus module on which each chapter is based is always indicated at the beginning of the chapter because the sequence of the chapters does not mirror that of the law syllabus modules. The sequence of topics in this course is designed to facilitate study by leading you through each topic in a way that will enable you to build on previously learnt skills.

What Resources Will You Need?

Remember that these chapters will not be all that you need to complete the syllabus and prepare for your examination. You are expected to make use of the resources listed at the end of the course book as well as engage in other wide, general reading, which will improve your general knowledge, vocabulary and structural competence.

You will also need basic study equipment, such as paper, pens, pencils and highlighters for marking important parts of the text. A good dictionary and a thesaurus are also essential.

Managing Your Time

You should remember to put aside time each day for general reading in addition to your study time.

Chapter Structure

Each chapter is divided into seven sections to facilitate your study, as follows:

Introduction This places what you are about to study in the context of your everyday life and relates it to what you have done in previous chapters.

Content This lists the topics that are to be covered in the chapter.

Objectives These help you to identify the specific skills that you should have acquired by the end of the chapter. You should read these carefully to acquaint yourself with what you are meant to be learning during the chapter.

Activities Instructions are provided at the start of each activity. Read all instructions carefully before you attempt the activity. Some activities require you to think about something before you read any further. You should take the necessary time to do so. The thinking activity is designed to help you focus your thoughts to help you to complete the activities that follow.

Feedback Each activity has a feedback section that allows you to determine how you will have done in the activity. If you have not completed the activity successfully, you should re-read the preceding information carefully.

Examples These are meant to guide you to an understanding of the concept being taught. All examples should be read carefully before you attempt any activities that follow.

End test This comes at the end of each chapter and is designed to ensure that you have acquired those skills identified in the objectives. There is a feedback section following the end test, which allows you to measure the accuracy of your answers to the test so that you will know whether or not you have acquired the competencies. If there are questions in the end test that you have not answered satisfactorily, ensure that you return to the relevant section of the chapter and review those areas until you are satisfied that you have understood the concept.

Assignments

Course assignments are included in order to allow you to check your progress through the course. The assignments enable you to determine your areas of weakness and to check your understanding of the concepts.

Examinations

You must ensure that you have access to the version of the syllabus that outlines the structure of the examination for the year in which you intend to write it.

1 The concept of law

General objectives

On completion of this study guide, you should:

- understand the various meanings attached to the concept of law
- appreciate the interrelationship between law, morality, religion and ethics
- develop an understanding of the phrase 'sources of law'
- appreciate the interrelationship of the legal sources of law in the Caribbean.

Specific objectives

You should be able to:

- outline the various meanings attached to the concept of 'law'
- illustrate the interrelationships of law, morality and religion
- explain the phrase 'sources of law'.

Introduction

In this chapter, you are introduced to the 'varying ideas and thoughts about the subject of law'. It will expose you to the fundamentals and ethos of the subject. It takes you from the concepts of law to its sources and classification, as well as the operation of the judicial system.

When you have finished reading chapter 1, you will have seen how much the unique history of our Commonwealth Caribbean is integrally interwoven with our legal system. Thus, you will reflect on the influence of Roman-Dutch law in Guyana, the French influence on the St Lucia Civil Code and you will no doubt form your own views on the 'reception' or 'imposition' of the English system of law.

Content

- Definition of law
- Concepts, nature, origin, role and function of law
- Law, morals, religion and ethics
- Concepts of the phrase 'sources of law'

Definition of law

There are four popular definitions of law:

1 the legislative pronouncement of rules to guide behaviour
2 the total of those rules of conduct put in force by legislative authority or court decisions, or established by local customs
3 an institution which is essential to the social nature of man, without which he would be a very different creature; and
4 the enforceable body of rules that govern society.

All of these definitions are relevant to an understanding of 'law' and each definition can be used depending on the context in which the word is used. For example, let us examine definition four to get a clearer picture of the word 'law': 'the enforceable body of rules'. This statement indicates that some rules are enforceable and some are not. Let us consider, then, what is a rule.

Rules are normative. This means that rules set a standard of how things ought to be, rather than how they are. For example, 'no one should use profane language.' Rules may mandate action, they say something must or must not be done and there may be a penalty for disobedience if the rule becomes law and is therefore made enforceable. A good definition of a rule may be the following:

> 'a general norm mandating or guiding conduct or actions in a given type of situation.'

Activity 1.1

Now you should be ready to distinguish between those behaviours that are enforceable and, therefore, could be converted into laws, and those behaviours that are not enforceable and, as such, cannot be converted into laws. Listed below are some 'rules'. Complete by filling in the words 'enforceable' or 'unenforceable' in the space provided.

1 No one should steal. ________________
2 Everyone should love his or her neighbour. __________
3 No one should kill another human being. _________________
4 No one should park a vehicle in a manner that causes obstruction to traffic. _______________
5 No one should indulge in sexual activity before marriage. _____________________
6 Married women and men should not commit adultery. _________

Feedback

If you have identified the first, third and fourth rules as those that the law can enforce and the second, fifth and sixth as unenforceable, you are correct.

Concepts, nature, origin, role and function of law

Concepts of law

Concepts of law are essentially the theories of law. In order for you to understand the different concepts of law, you must first understand the different law theories, as propounded by legal philosophers. These different theories govern different peoples and societies alike. Concepts of law also extend to different cultural, racial and religious groupings. Examples include Islamic law and Judaic law. It is worthy to note that in Islam, the law becomes the religion and, thus, the religion becomes the law. Two of the most popular theories of law are natural law and positive law.

Natural law and positive law

Natural law

In Calvin Eversley's article on 'Law, Religion and Morality', at page 4 of the Guyana Law Review, he considers the definition of natural law, as posited by the legal philosopher Lloyd who says that 'natural law is believed to be a rational foundation for moral judgment'. Thus, according to Eversley, natural law can be seen as true law that emanates from a divine being.

According to many natural lawyers, natural law is directly connected to, or rather shaped by, those religious, moral or ethical considerations that are inherently part of that 'right reason in agreement with nature' as formulated by the early natural law philosopher, Cicero.

For the purposes of simplification, natural law is perceived to be that law which is shaped by a divine being and thus provides the guidelines for proper moral behaviour to be exhibited and practised by mankind.

Positive law

Within the theory of positive law is the belief that law has nothing to do with morals or religion but is shaped by 'certain specifically approved, or accepted procedures for law-making'. According to Eversley; 'Kelsen [a positivist] best epitomises this view in the formulation of his pure theory of law.'

Positive law is the law created by the sovereign and which must be obeyed even if and when it is unjust or repressive. Also, it is not acceptable for the citizenry to reject or refuse to obey an unjust law so long as it remains in force; rather it is for the sovereign itself or Parliament to change the unjust law.

Nature of law

According to Wollheim, 'The Nature of Law ... has long perplexed legal and political philosophers', the nature or essence of law may be found in the definition of law. The nature of law, therefore, may be characterised by its rules that seek to create and maintain order in society. In other words, the nature of law is to be found in its normative or rule-making content.

The law seeks to create and maintain the conduct desired of society. That is why the law lays down the procedure for doing things and sometimes attaches a penalty for non-performance of a particular act.

Activity 1.3

From the list below identify the item which best states the nature of law by placing a tick next to it:

1 The nature of law is characterised by the law's ability to impose sanctions.

2 The nature of law is characterised by the law's ability to lay down the procedure for doing things.

3 The nature of law is characterised by the law's rule-making content, which moulds the behaviour of society.

Feedback

If you have selected number 3 above as being the correct answer you are right, since this statement describes the nature of law in the broadest terms.

Activity 1.2

List two features of natural law and two features of positive law.

Feedback

A good answer should reflect your understanding of the fundamental distinction between natural law and positive law: that natural law theory springs from the belief in religious tenets, for example, the Ten Commandments which shape the morality of society and ultimately form the basis for the creation of the law; while positive law is law created by the sovereign or the State apparatus and must be obeyed despite the fact that it may be unjust.

The origin of law

The English perspective

Before the Norman Conquest in the 11th century England did not possess a unified legal system. Different areas of the country were governed by different systems of law, often adapted from those of the various invaders who had settled there. Thus, the law of England was fragmented and varied from place to place. The king had little control over the country as a whole, and there was no effective central government.

When William the Conqueror came to the English throne in 1066, he established a strong central government and began, among other things, to standardise the law. Eventually it was decreed that there would be one law common to all of England, hence the name 'common law'.

The Caribbean perspective

When the Europeans came to the West Indies they brought with them their laws, which they imposed upon the native population, then the slaves and eventually upon the indentured servants.

The laws that were known to the native Indians, the Africans and the indentured servants were displaced as the Europeans began to rule them under their transported legal system that was received into Caribbean territories. For instance, in Guyana, the Civil Law Act – Cap 6:01 allows for the reception of the English common law in 1917 and the retention of some areas of Roman-Dutch law.

Reception in the territories listed below is governed by:

- Antigua: The Supreme Court of Judicature Act, Cap 81
- The Bahamas: The Declaratory Act, 1799
- Barbados: The Supreme Court of Judicature Act, Cap 117, sections 31 and 37
- Jamaica: The Interpretation Act, Cap 165, section 37
- Trinidad and Tobago: The Supreme Court of Judicature Act, Cap 4:01, section 12.

Caribbean territories were ruled at different periods of the region's history by different European nations; for example, the Spanish, the French, the Dutch and the English. Guyana was ruled by the French and the Dutch, then lastly the English. Trinidad was ruled by the Spanish, then the English and St Lucia by the French, then the English. As a consequence, Guyana and St Lucia have inherited a hybrid legal system. Guyana has certain aspects of Roman-Dutch law that is practised alongside the English common law and St Lucia has retained certain aspects of the French civil code that is practised alongside the English common law.

Activity 1.4

In two short paragraphs, discuss events that led to the origin of Commonwealth Caribbean law.

Feedback

A good response to this question should be laid out chronologically. You should refer briefly to:

- the unification of English law after the Norman Conquest
- colonisation
- slavery; and
- reception in Guyana and the English-speaking Caribbean.

Role and function of law

The role and function of law is to bring cohesion to, and maintain order within, societies. William the Conqueror chose to introduce a single system of law into England because he sought to achieve unity and cohesion within the legal system of England, thereby improving it and rendering it more efficient. The more advanced and complex a society becomes the greater is the need for laws that will regulate human behaviour if peace and stability are to be maintained.

Activity 1.5

Identify any bit of legislation within your territory and comment on why you think it was created. An example of what you are required to do is set out below.

Example

Section 37 of the Coroners Act, Cap 4:03, Laws of Guyana, states:

> 'Where the body of any person is buried without any examination or without sufficient examination, a coroner about to hold an inquest or inquiry as to the cause of death of that person may order the body to be exhumed.'

The role and function of this piece of legislation is to confer upon the coroner the power to ensure that the bodies of persons who die are properly examined before burial, so that ultimately it would be difficult to conceal the cause of death of persons, especially those who may have died from unnatural causes, which may include the perpetration of a criminal act against the deceased.

The romantic or utopian view of the function of law is that it regulates human behaviour to achieve a well-ordered and cohesive society. However, the true function of the law has often been to regulate the activity of society at large in a manner that produces the effect most desirable for the maintenance of the prosperity and the continued protection of the ruling class, administration or government.

Professor Hart argues:

> '[that] ... the main function of law is simply to allow human beings to survive in a community ... Each member of society has, more or less, the same physical strength and intelligence, and both our powers of self-restraint and willingness to help others are limited. We therefore all face the danger of attack from the others and competition for such resources as are available ... The realisation that we are not safe in the world alone and can only be safe in a community if there are rules of self-restraint, leads to the development of such rules, protecting the property and person of others. It also leads to the idea that observance of the rules must be guaranteed by some kind of penalty directed at the rule breaker.'

Hart maintains that such rules are the minimum necessary content of law in any society.

For you to have a complete understanding of this area of your study you should read Commonwealth Caribbean Legal Systems by Rose-Marie Belle Antoine (1999) at page 12, in which she posits:

> '... mention is hardly ever made of the important immoral function which the law played in much of the history of the Commonwealth Caribbean.'

She continues:

> 'A discussion of the role and functions of law in West Indian society should, therefore, begin with an appraisal of the role and functions of the law and legal systems in instituting and upholding the systems of slavery and colonialism which existed ... throughout the region ... Law was thus an instrument of social control and public order in plantation society ... The slave laws were the most ubiquitous form of public control ... Their primary function was to maintain the slave system by guaranteeing the economic, social, and racial subordination of the Negroes.'

The history of the Caribbean islands reflects that slave laws ensured the security of the plantocracy by ensuring to the slave master an absolute authority over his slaves. A slave was considered a chattel. Thus the 1674 law of Jamaica described slaves as goods and chattels. Slaves were also referred to with reference to their collective weight, for example, 'a ton of slaves'.

Legally, a slave was barred from owning property and a Jamaican law of 1711 excluded slaves from owning almost anything at all, for example, livestock and important agricultural products such as sugar cane, coffee and cotton.

Activity 1.6

Assess the contribution of policies towards the shaping of the functions of law.

Feedback

You may wish to examine the policy behind legislation both historically and currently. For example, you could look at the policy behind slavery and the policy behind the creation of a bit of legislation of your territory.

Activity 1.7

Can society exist without laws?

Feedback

This type of question allows for many different approaches. You may wish to draw on the discussions above as well as the material contained in the suggested readings. A unique approach would be to examine the theory of a particular legal philosopher on the role and function of law and state whether you agree with the opinion of any legal philosopher of your choice.

Whatever areas of the law you choose to discuss, you should give detailed examples of the contribution of principles and policies behind them.

Law, morals, religion and ethics

The morality and ethics of a society are concerned with disapproval in one way or another of what is deemed to constitute unacceptable conduct. For instance, it is believed that the family is the 'cornerstone' from which the essential social values, such as honesty and truthfulness, are born.

Earlier in this chapter you were exposed to a definition of law. Now, let us consider the definitions of morals, religion and ethics. Before attempting to examine the relationship that exists between them and the law, as a student of law you may wish to note that there is no significant distinction between morals and ethics, thus the two concepts will be treated as possessing the same meaning.

Morals and ethics defined

Morals and ethics constitute 'that right reason', which exists within all men and which leads us to distinguish right from wrong and good from evil. Elliott and Quinn seek to define morals at page 517 of English Legal Systems. They state:

> 'morals are beliefs and values which are shared by a society or a section of a society...'

An individual who displays good ethics in his or her dealings with others is considered to be a morally upright person by the wider civil society. At this point you may be asking yourself 'What is morally upright behaviour?' It is posited here that morally upright behaviour is usually the socially acceptable manner in which one conducts oneself with respect to matters concerning:

- sexual relationships
- money transactions; and
- attitude towards one's spouse, family, friends and even strangers.

Note: Moral rules are also social rules, in that they all lay down how we should conduct ourselves in relation to others, but not all social rules are moral rules. For example, failure to take off one's hat when entering a room or sneezing without a handkerchief may be deemed unacceptable social behaviour, and as such would amount to a breach of a social rule, but they will have occasioned no breach of a moral rule.

Religion defined

Religion, according to the Oxford English Dictionary, at page 1788, is defined as:

> 'recognition on the part of man of some higher unseen power as having control of his destiny, and as being entitled to obedience, reverence and worship.'

We are now ready to examine the relationship between law, ethics and religion.

Law and morals (ethics)

Law and morals exist simultaneously to uphold the rules of proper social behaviour that is necessary for the achievement of social cohesion in every well-ordered society. While moral rules are not backed by the obvious sanctions that make some legal rules enforceable, they are often reinforced by pressure which in some cases may be as strong, if not stronger: for example, the disapproval of family and friends, loss of status and being shunned by the community are powerful deterrents against immoral conduct. For example, if a man has sex with his daughter he runs the risk of being ostracised by family, friends and the wider community.

Natural law theorists argue that law should reflect morality. Philosophers such as Thomas Aquinas see natural law as higher law that comes from God, the principles of which '... should be reflected in the laws societies make for themselves.'

Here are three examples of the relationship between law and morality. Examine them.

Example 1

A female was ostracised by the church and society if she indulged in sexual activity before marriage because under English law, the act of fornication is deemed to be morally wrong and the female would be held to be unchaste and unsuitable for marriage. This moral position was extended by the law to deny both a mother and her offspring any recognition at law if the child was born out of wedlock. The law in Guyana supported this moral position by the creation of the Bastardy Act. However, with the removal of the moral stigma as more and more children were born out of wedlock, the law followed suit in order to keep pace with changing morality and repealed the Bastardy Act.

Example 2

In the case of Shaw v. Director of Public Prosecutions [1962] AC 220, Shaw had published a ladies directory. Lord Diplock said:

> 'Shaw's act of publishing advertisements for prostitutes soliciting fornication tended to corrupt public morals. Therefore Shaw's agreement to do that act was a crime at common law.'

The Court of Appeal upheld a conviction against Shaw on the charge of 'conspiring to corrupt public morals'.

Example 3

In the case of R v. Knuller (Publishing, etc.) Ltd [1972] 3 WLR 143, the appellants were directors of a company that published a fortnightly magazine. On an inside page under a column headed 'Males', advertisements were inserted inviting readers to meet the advertisers for the purpose of homosexual practices.

The appellants were convicted on counts of conspiracy to corrupt public morals and conspiracy to outrage public decency. The House of Lords held that while the offence of 'conspiracy to outrage public decency' was unknown to the law, the appellants by their actions were nevertheless guilty of behaviour that could be deemed an offence known to English law, that is 'conspiracy to corrupt public morals'.

Law and religion

The religion of the European colonisers was and continues to be Christianity, which has influenced English law and helped to shape the morality of Caribbean people. This religious influence was so strong that religious rules were given statutory force and validity. For example, the religious rules 'Thou shalt not steal' and 'Thou shalt not kill' have been made law.

Activity 1.8

Look at the Summary Jurisdiction (Offences) Act and the Criminal Law (Offences) Act of your territory.

See if you can identify in these two Acts, laws that are based on the Ten Commandments.

This religious influence also finds expression in the symbolic wearing of the bib, or bands, by members of the legal profession. Guyana is the only Commonwealth Caribbean territory that has relinquished the use of the bib. The two rectangles of the bib symbolise the two tablets of stone upon which were written the Ten Commandments that God gave to Moses.

Influences of the religious rule that one should love one's neighbour as one loves oneself permeates the law of torts, which enforces society's conformity with the neighbour principle as laid down in the famous case of Donoghue v. Stevenson (1932) wherein one's neighbour at law is deemed to be anyone who is likely to be affected by one's actions.

The law's definition of marriage, for example, is based upon religious and moral principles: Lord Penzance formulated that which is considered the 'classic' definition of marriage in the case of Hyde v. Hyde (1866) LRP & D 130:

> 'I conceive of marriage, as understood in Christendom, to be the voluntary union for life of a single man and single woman to the exclusion of all others.'

In this area the law has continued to maintain its close relationship with religion and morality to defeat what is considered an unacceptable shift in morality: for example, the law of the Commonwealth Caribbean territories regarding marriage has not been changed to accommodate same sex marriages.

Activity 1.9

1. 'All laws are rules but all rules are not laws.' Discuss this statement.
2. 'Laws are necessary for the peace, stability, order and good governance of civil society.' Discuss this statement.
3. With close reference to the cases of Shaw v. DPP and Knuller v. DPP show how the law relates to morals and religion.

Feedback

1. A good answer plan should contain the following elements:
    - a the definition of a rule
    - b the definition of law
    - c the main distinction to be drawn between a rule and a law, for example, a rule is unenforceable while a law is enforceable
    - d at least one example of a social rule highlighting the characteristic of unenforceability and one example of a law, highlighting its enforceability.
2. A good answer to this question would attract a discussion of the role and function of law. You should first examine the role and function of law as explained by some European legal philosophers. For example, that the role and function of law relate to man's need to feel protected and to enjoy a sense of order.

    Next you should discuss the actual role and function of law as reflected in the history of Guyana and the rest of the Caribbean during the period of slavery. You should conclude with an analysis of the role and function of law in the Commonwealth Caribbean today.

    Your analysis should highlight the growing complexity of society and the need for the legislature to meet the challenges of shifts in moral attitudes; new developments in the area of crime, for example, computer fraud. Also, the need to lay down new procedures for doing things mandated by law.
3. Your answer to this question should address the attitude of the courts in these two cases with respect to morality. You should also examine the genesis of morality, for example, that English and hence Commonwealth Caribbean morality is founded upon Christian belief. Then give examples of morally reprehensible acts such as murder and theft, which are considered sins both in the eyes of God and man.

Concepts of the phrase sources of law

The Constitution

We have already established that there is a very close relationship between the law, morals and religion. In this section, we are going to examine the sources of law from the standpoint of how laws are documented and presented. We will examine five sources of law, namely, the Constitution, legislation, and interpretation of legislation by the courts, common law and equity, and precedent. First, we look at what comprises a constitution that is the premier source of law for all Caribbean Commonwealth countries. An important point to note is that England remains one of the few countries of the world that does not possess a written constitution.

Article 8 of the Guyana (1980) Constitution states:

> 'This Constitution is the supreme law of Guyana and if any law is inconsistent with it that other law shall, to the extent of the inconsistency be void.'

Like Guyana, in most of the Caribbean Commonwealth constitutions there is enshrined a supremacy clause. These include:

- the Jamaica Orders-in-Council Constitution (1962), section 2
- the Constitution of Barbados, section 1
- the Constitution of the Republic of Trinidad and Tobago, section 1.

The constitution of the territories above contains the establishment of and procedure to be adopted by the main organs of state. That is, the executive, the legislature and the judiciary, with their respective jurisdiction(s), function(s) and power(s); the establishment of service commissions; the establishment of the office, role and function of the Ombudsman. Finally, and very importantly, the fundamental rights section, which lays down the protection offered to every citizen in matters such as the right to work, the right to a fair hearing and the right to own property.

The Constitution is a source of law because it is often referred to by judges and lawyers who look to the Constitution for the continued protection of citizens' rights and the preservation of the rule of law. Some of the cases listed in this chapter help to illustrate this point. An example is the case of Maharaj v. The Attorney General of Trinidad and Tobago, which upheld the constitutional principle that a man must be told of the case being brought against him.

In a recent case which stirred much public interest in Jamaica, a judge dismissed a case which, after 38 trial dates over a period of 11 years the prosecution was not yet ready to proceed with the trial. On this 38th occasion, there were not enough persons from which to empanel a jury. The Prosecution expressed disappointment with the judge's decision. His Lordship, Campbell J spoke in an interview with a journalist and underscored that as a judge, he must safeguard the Constitution. His Lordship is quoted as saying:

"The Charter of Fundamental Rights and Freedoms (Constitutional Amendment) Act, 2011, by the Jamaican people, will be diminished and demeaned, if the courts contemplate for a moment the transference to the Executive, the responsibility for seeing that process of law is not abused...

The Constitution is the supreme law of the land and the courts are the guardians of the Constitution" The Sunday Gleaner, December 11, 2011.

The dismissal of the four men, accused of killing a policeman, did not mean that they were acquitted. The prosecution can put the matter back before the Court when their case is ready.

Activity 1.10

Explain the usefulness of the Constitution as a source of law.

Feedback

A good response to this question should contain the following:

- an understanding of the meaning of the term 'Constitution'
- the rights and principles that are protected by the Constitution
- the use the courts and lawyers make of the Constitution.

Legislation

Legislation is the second source of law for discussion. Legislation is defined as the process of making laws. There are two types of legislation, primary legislation and secondary legislation, which is also referred to as subsidiary legislation.

Primary legislation

Primary legislation is made by Parliament (statutes). It is the most important source of law. Examples of primary legislation are the Criminal Law (Procedure) Act of Guyana and the Gun Court Act 1974 of Jamaica.

Secondary or subsidiary legislation

Secondary legislation is made by a government authority or functionary that is given power by Parliament to make such legislation. An example of subsidiary or secondary legislation is contained in section 129 of the Constitution of Trinidad and Tobago, which authorises the Service Commissions to make regulations. Under the Trinidad and Tobago Constitution, some government functionaries are also given law-making power within defined boundaries.

For example, section 26 of the Hindu Marriage Act, Cap. 45:03 of Trinidad and Tobago provides that:

> The President may make such regulations as may be necessary for the proper carrying out of this Act and more especially prescribe:
>
> - the place at which shall be situated the offices of several District Registrars,
> - the forms of any certificate, declaration, register or other document required for the purposes of this Act.

Also, under the Motor Vehicle and Road Traffic Act of Guyana, Chapter 51:02, the minister is authorised to make certain regulations concerning:

- ID marks
- certificates of fitness
- licences
- seating capacity
- traffic signals
- conduct of drivers.

Activity 1.11

Explain what is meant by the terms primary legislation and secondary legislation.

Feedback

In your answer, you should explain the meanings of primary and secondary legislation and support your answer by reference to legislation as discussed above.

Interpretation of legislation by the courts

Another important source of law comes from the interpretation of legislation before the courts. You have seen how it is the legislature or Parliament that makes law, but it is left to the courts of law to apply it. In some situations, the meaning of a word or phrase in a piece of legislation before the court may pose a problem. To aid the courts' application of the law, rules of interpretation have been created.

Below are three of the many rules of statutory interpretation:

- literal rule
- golden rule
- mischief rule (the purposive rule).

The literal rule

This rule allows that the words and phrases in a statute should be given their ordinary and literal meaning, and once the ordinary meaning is clear the court should apply it even if to do so would result in injustice. Below is an example of a case in which the literal rule was applied.

Example 1: The literal rule applied

Baptiste v. Alleyne (1970) 16 WIR 437

The defendant was found outside a house with his hand through a window choking a female occupant. He was charged and convicted of the offence '... found ... in a building with intent ...'

A provision of section 29(d) of the then Larceny Ordinance allowed that for a person to be convicted of such an offence, there must be clear and unmistakable evidence that he had been, as the section says, 'found in' the building.

Mr Justice of Appeal, Michael De La Bastide, posited: 'he cannot in the Court's view be said to have been found in the building on a literal meaning or ordinary interpretation of the words of section 29(d) of the Larceny Ordinance.'

In this case the appeal was allowed, hence the conviction was quashed.

Example 2: The literal rule applied

R v. Ramsonahai and Duke [1961] 3 WIR 537

The appellants had conspired to and did plant two bottles of bush rum on one Mohamed Ali whom the police eventually found to have had the rum in his possession.

Charges were laid against the appellants. The indictment charged a conspiracy to prosecute Mohamed Ali, knowing him to be innocent of the summary conviction offence of being in unlawful possession of bush rum under section 330 of the Criminal Law Ordinance, Cap. 10 of British Guiana.

Counsel for the appellants argued that an offence under the section is not committed if the evidence discloses an intention merely to cause a public prosecution to be instituted against Mohamed Ali.

Counsel said, inter alia, 'The ordinary and primary meaning of the words "to prosecute" is to commence proceedings by laying an information.' Counsel further contended that if the legislature intended the meaning of the words 'to prosecute' to be extended to include 'cause to be prosecuted' then Parliament would have said so, as it had in many other enactments.

The golden rule

The second rule of statutory interpretation is the golden rule. This rule provides that if the literal and ordinary meanings of the words of the statute give rise to ambiguity and/or an absurd result which Parliament could not have intended, then the judge may substitute a reasonable meaning in light of the statute as a whole.

Example 3: The golden rule applied

Davis v. R [1962] 4 WIR 375

The defendant was convicted for the offence, which prohibited parking a vehicle '... elsewhere than in a place provided for that purpose and in a manner required by an authorised officer...' Chief Justice McGregor said:

> 'It seems clear that the intention of the Regulation was to create two offences, the one, parking otherwise than in a place provided by the Minister for that purpose; the other, parking otherwise than in a manner required by an authorised officer. To obtain this interpretation it is necessary to insert the words "otherwise than" between the word "and" and "in the manner ..."'

The dicta in this case provide an excellent example of the court's exercise of its power to reinterpret statute thus curing the absurdity that would result from a literal interpretation of a particular piece of legislation.

Mischief rule (the purposive rule)

The third rule of statutory interpretation is the mischief or purposive rule. This rule was laid down in Heydon's Case [1584] and provides that judges when deciding cases must consider three factors:

- What the law was before the statute was passed.
- What problem, or 'mischief', the statute was trying to remedy.
- What remedy Parliament was trying to provide.

The following cases will provide you with an insight into the operation of the mischief rule. Please note that later on the mischief rule became known as the purposive rule.

Example 4: The mischief rule applied

R v. George Green [1969] 14 WIR 204

The appellant was convicted on indictment of the offence of cultivating ganja contrary to section 7(c) of the Dangerous Drugs Act. At the trial the evidence did not disclose whether the plants which the appellant was found to be cultivating contained any pistilate plant known as cannabis sativa.

The court held that the term 'ganja' as defined by section 2 of the Act is referable only to the pistilate known as cannabis sativa and did not include any part of the staminate plant and therefore the offence of cultivating ganja contrary to section 7 of the law relates only to cultivating the pistilate plant known as cannabis sativa.

Shelly JA stated:

> I gather from the DPP's quotation from Hansard of March 31st 1942 that one of the reasons for introducing the Dangerous Drugs Law of 1942 was to follow international standards by conformity with legislation in other countries and colonies who were signatories to the International Convention on Dangerous drugs.

In this case, the court went behind the statute in order to discover the reason behind its creation.

> ### Activity 1.12
> Section 10 of the Transport and Harbours Act of Brobdingnag states:
>
> - If any ship is found moored within 1,000m of the Loponac Bridge the Captain of the said ship shall be liable.
> - Anyone found liable for breach of this section shall be fined 100,000 dollars.
>
> Ashrapi, though aware of this bit of legislation, brought his barge and moored it within 100m of the Loponac Bridge.
>
> The Brobdingnag Harbour Master seized Ashrapi's barge and fined him 100,000 dollars. Ashrapi wishes to contest the decision of the Harbour Master and has retained you as his lawyer.
>
> Advise Ashrapi.
>
> Hint: The section speaks of ships. Ashrapi's vessel is a barge.

Feedback

Your answer should identify the rules of interpretation and apply the one which best provides a remedy for Ashrapi. Your answer must contain reference to case law discussed in this chapter.

The common law and equity

The English experience

The fourth source of law for discussion is equity. Equity was originally inspired by ideas of fairness and natural justice. During medieval times, the common law was the only law practised in England. If a litigant wished to bring a claim before the court he could only do so by way of a writ. The number of writs available were limited and designed to fit specific claims. If the litigant could not find a writ into which his claim could fit, he was left without a remedy at law and his only alternative would be to petition the king.

The limitations and harshness of the common law were so severe that the petitions before the king grew in number. When he sat to hear petitions the king was advised by the Lord Chancellor who later became known as the king's conscience. The king eventually appointed the Lord Chancellor to hear all petitions and to deliberate upon them. Hence the creation of a separate division known as the Chancery Division for the hearing of matters, that were not entertained in the common law courts.

The Chancery Division headed by the Lord Chancellor dispensed justice based on principles of equity and offered new remedies that were never available at common law. Such remedies included the injunction and the order for specific performance. Certain rules of equity were also developed: for example, since the courts of Chancery never intended to interfere with the rules governing the common law, the principle 'equity follows the law' was created. This meant that if a party to an issue has acted in accordance with the law, equity would not interfere except in cases where the law was being used as an instrument of fraud. Here is an example: to hide the fact of something from the other party to an agreement and then await the expiration of the limitation period to claim that a particular act cannot be performed.

As time went on, with the change of each Lord Chancellor, the dispensation of justice in the court of Chancery contracted and expanded to suit the conscience of the Chancellor of the day. At one time the rules of equity were being applied so rigidly, that the courts of equity were accused of being as inflexible as the common law courts, which equity was designed to temper.

Eventually, the 12 maxims of equity were created in an effort to bring uniformity to the dispensation of justice in this branch of the law. Between the years 1873 and 1875 the Judicature Acts allowed that matters of common law and equity would now be heard in the same court. But more than this, the remedy known as 'damages', which was available only at common law, could be sought together with an equitable remedy, for example, an order for specific performance.

The reception of equity and common law into the Commonwealth Caribbean

When the English colonised the territories of the Commonwealth Caribbean they brought with them the common law and equity, which were received into these territories. This process was known as 'reception', which has been given statutory force by all of the Commonwealth Caribbean territories: for example, in Guyana, the Civil Law Act, Chapter 6:01 allows that except for the retention of certain portions of Roman–Dutch law, the common law of England, together with the principles of equity shall be the law of Guyana. Additionally, the High Court Act, Chapter 3:02 of Guyana allows that from the year 1917 (the year of reception) the laws of England shall be the laws of Guyana. In Trinidad and Tobago under section 12 of the Supreme Court of Judicature Act, Chapter 4:01, statutory force is given to the reception of English law and its attendant principles of equity.

Equity today, its relevance and importance to Commonwealth Caribbean States

As the area of equity continued to grow and develop, equity obtained the status of being a distinct branch of the law in its own right. New remedies were added to the ones originally created: for example 'rectification', 'restitution', the 'Anton Piller Order' and the 'Mareva Injunction', together with the development of the law of trusts and the principle of estoppel.

The remedy of rectification forces a party to a contract to rectify the terms of or a particular term of a contract in order to achieve fairness between the parties to the contract. The Anton Piller Order was created (when the case of the same name was heard) to preserve intellectual property material, for example, written, printed or recorded information inclusive of that found on CDs and on computer software. The Mareva Injunction was created to prevent the removal of assets (for example, money in a bank or an aircraft) from the jurisdiction of the court.

The creation of the law of trusts has proven to be invaluable to the protection of the rights of women and children in the Commonwealth Caribbean, wherein equity may deem a husband a trustee for a wife's interest in the matrimonial home.

In the area of injunctions the case of The Demerara Turf Club v. Phang (1968) LRG, laid down the principle of the assessment of the 'balance of convenience' between parties before the grant of injunctive relief. It was 12 years later in the locus classicus of American Cyanamid v. Ethicon that the same principle was developed and applied in England.

All of the Commonwealth Caribbean courts apply the principles of equity to the extent that these territories have built up and expanded upon their own jurisprudence in this area of the law. In the Trinidadian case of Coosals Quarry Ltd v. Teamwork (Trinidad) Ltd HCA 5011/85,

Sharma J suggested that where material favourable to the defendant is contained in voluminous material to be put before the court, the plaintiff when applying for injunctive relief ex parte, should mention all the said material in his affidavit.

It is evident therefore that equity today continues to command a position of great importance and relevance in the Commonwealth Caribbean.

Activity 1.13

'Equity was created to ease the harshness of the common law and it is still relevant today.' Discuss.

Feedback

A good answer to this question should include the following:

- The state of the common law before the creation of equity.
- The practice of equity in the early courts of Chancery.
- The remedies offered at equity.
- The reception of the common law and equity into the Commonwealth Caribbean.
- The development and application of the law of equity today in the territories of the Commonwealth Caribbean.

Your answer should include reference to the cases discussed in this section of the chapter.

Precedent

The fifth source of law to be discussed is precedent. The principle of precedent is that decisions taken at a higher court are to be followed by a lower court. In some cases the precedent is merely persuasive; in others, it is binding, meaning that the lower court is under an obligation to follow the decision of the higher court. But the lower court is bound to follow the decision of the higher court only if the decision in the case coming from the higher court turns upon similar facts and principles as those contained in the matter to be decided in the lower court.

In those territories of the Commonwealth Caribbean where the Privy Council is the final court of appeal, the decisions of the Privy Council are binding upon the Court of Appeal and the High Courts of those jurisdictions. However, in Guyana, appeals to the Privy Council were abolished in 1967 so that decisions from that court are of persuasive value in Guyana and the courts in this territory are not bound to follow the decisions of the Privy Council.

It is important for you to bear in mind when dealing with the doctrine of precedents in the Commonwealth Caribbean that a High Court is not obliged to follow the previous decision of another High Court, but may do so based on the principle of stare decisis – meaning, let the decision stand – and the said court will only depart from this concept for good reasons. It must, however, follow the decisions of courts above, that is, the Court of Appeal and the Privy Council. The decisions from all other jurisdictions are merely persuasive and the judges are free to reject the submissions posited by counsel at any time he wishes to do so.

Example 1: Precedents applied

Precedents are found in many law reports and are often referred to as case law. For example, in the case of The State v. Sharma and Williams 25 WIR 166, the Court of Appeal of Guyana referred to and applied the interpretation it placed on the phrase 'to prosecute', in the earlier case of R v. Ramsonahai and Duke [1961] 3 WIR 535.

Example 2: Precedents applied

Vierra v. Winchester [1966] 10 WIR 400

It was argued in the Court of Appeal of Trinidad and Tobago that its previous decision in the case of Camp v. Harris was wrong. Justice of Appeal McShine dissented thus:

> 'before this court could say that its own decision was wrong, it was bound by a principle and it is this: the Court of Appeal is bound by its own decisions unless it can be shown that such was given per incuriam [in error].'

Having examined the arguments and facts, the court held that it was bound by the decision in Camp v. Harris.

A Court of Appeal is bound by its own decisions. Example 2 illustrates this point.

Terms associated with the use of precedent

In order to fully appreciate the principles of precedent, you need to become familiar with the following terms:

Ratio decidendi

This term means 'the reasoning upon which the case turns' or the principle/s of law upon which the court arrived at its decision. It is really the ratio of a previous case, which the lower court must examine before deciding whether it will follow the decision of the higher court.

Obiter dictum

This term means 'things said by the way': something said by a judge that was not essential to the decision of the case. It does not form part of the ratio decidendi and, therefore, creates no binding precedent. However, it sometimes happens that obiter dictum may become persuasive authority in a later case.

Stare decisis

This is the Latin term expressing the principle 'let the decision stand': that it is necessary to abide by precedents when the same points arise again in litigation.

Distinguishing a case

This term means that a previous case is distinguished when the reasoning upon which it turns and its facts or circumstances are different from those in the case now being tried in court.

Overruling a Case

This term means the setting aside of the decision of an earlier case. This is usually because, according to the doctrine of precedent, a court can only overrule the decision of a lower court.

Activity 1.14

Explain the meanings of the following terms:

1. ratio decidendi
2. obiter dictum
3. judicial precedent
4. stare decisis; and
5. distinguishing a case.

Feedback

Your answer should include clear meanings of each of the terms and your explanation should reflect that you understand the significance of each term. Please note that your explanation of the meaning and significance of judicial precedent should contain reference to the cases discussed in this section of the chapter.

Suggested further reading

Elliott and Quinn, English Legal Systems, 3rd ed., Longman, 2000.

Belle Antoine, Rose-Marie, Commonwealth Caribbean Law and Legal Systems, London: Cavendish, 1999, pages 67–82, 121–32, 167–93, 195–8.

Eversley, Calvin A., 'Law, religion and morality' (1999) in The Guyana Law Review, No. 1, Vol. 1.

End Test

Answer all questions. **Time: 3 hours**

1 Discuss two legal sources of law and comment on their importance to two of the following: lawyers, judges or citizens.

2 Using examples, explain the meanings of primary legislation and secondary legislation.

3 'Sometimes the court must go beyond the literal meaning of the words in a section in order to interpret sensibly the piece of legislation before it.' Discuss this statement.

4 'Equity was and in many ways still is the common law's safety valve': Lord Denham. Does this statement accurately describe the role of equity both in the past and the present?

5 Using case law, outline the role and function of judicial precedent.

6 Explain the concepts of 'stare decisis' and 'ratio decidendi'.

End Test Feedback

1 A good answer should first identify any two of the three legal sources of law discussed in this lesson. Secondly, your answer should reflect that these sources of law are often helpful in cases brought before the courts.

Also, in order to support the point that these sources of law are helpful, you should mention, for example, that both judges and citizens alike depend upon these sources of law: judges depend upon them for guidance when dispensing justice. For example, a judge's duty is not to allow any government organisation or official to act in a manner that infringes the rights of citizens. Citizens depend heavily upon these sources of law for the protection of their rights as citizens.

2 A good answer to question 2 should contain one example of primary legislation and one example of secondary legislation. The examples may be taken from those provided in this chapter or from the legislation of your territory. Next, you should explain why each falls into that category. To do this you should state whether it is a piece of legislation created directly by Parliament or whether it has been created by a government functionary or organisation vested with the power to create laws.

3 A good answer to question 3 should identify and discuss the three rules of interpretation discussed in this chapter. Your discussion should include the situations that give rise to the need for the application of these rules by the courts – for example, the literal rule is applied when the plain and ordinary meanings of the words of the statute are clear. The golden rule is applied when the plain and ordinary meanings of the words of the statute, if applied, would lead to ambiguity or confusion. The mischief rule or the purposive rule is applied when the court attempts to discover the intention of Parliament or the purpose for the creation of the section or the mischief that Parliament intends to cure. Finally, you should show, for example, that the application of the literal rule does not always solve the problem of interpretation before the court. Therefore, it is necessary at times that the court apply the golden rule or the mischief/purposive rule. Your answer should be supported by case law referred to in this chapter on the subject of the interpretation of statues/legislation by the courts.

4 Your answer to question 4 should adhere to the following format: you should begin with a discussion of the rigidity and unfairness of the common law before the creation of equity. For example, the existence of the writ system, namely its severe limitations and inflexibility and the availability of only one remedy at common law. This would provide the background against which the need for equity ('the common law's safety valve') arose. You should next be able to display knowledge of the fact that the common law was practised in the courts of King's Bench or Queen's Bench, and that equity's jurisdiction was that of the Chancery Division.

It would be good at this juncture to define equity (which means 'fairness').

You should then go on to identify and discuss the new remedies made available at equity – for example, those of the injunction, and specific performance, which could be obtained only at the discretion of the Lord Chancellor (the head of the Courts of Chancery). You should also mention that the discretion of each successive chancellor varied according to his individual conscience, causing much widening and contracting of the application of the principles of equity.

Eventually this led to the very mischief that equity sought to cure, in that equity itself had grown too rigid.

The fusion of the separate jurisdictions of the courts of King's Bench/Queen's Bench and the Courts of Chancery by virtue of the Judicature Acts, which made it now possible for remedies at common law and remedies at equity to be granted in one action under one roof.

The 12 principles of equity were then created in an attempt to achieve some measure of uniformity. You should be able to identify at least 3 of these 12 maxims and show through reference to case law how they operated.

You should discuss with reference to case law the introduction of the principles of the balance of convenience, and the duty of full disclosure.

Reference should be made to the later addition of new remedies – those of rectification, recession and new forms of injunctive relief, for example, the Mareva Injunction and the Anton Piller Order.

If the above answer plan is followed you will have succeeded in setting out chronologically the reasons giving rise to the creation of equity, the role and function of early equity and the relevance and importance of equity today.

Include the reception of the law of equity together with the common law in the Commonwealth Caribbean States, for example, in Guyana, by virtue of the Civil Law Act, Chapter 6:01 the common law and equity were received into this jurisdiction.

The common law and equity are still applied in all Commonwealth Caribbean territories. And much case law has developed through the application of the principles of equity. A good example of this is the case of Demerara Turf Club v. Phang, which applied the principle of the balance of convenience 12 years before the same principle was applied in England in the locus classicus case of American Cyanamid.

5 Your answer should include the definition of judicial precedent; a discussion of the hierarchy of the courts in your jurisdiction; and how judicial precedent operates. Your answer should be supported by reference to case law.

6 You should simply define and discuss the terms 'ratio decidendi' and 'stare decisis' and give examples of their application by referring to case law.

2 The Commonwealth Caribbean court system: nature and structure

General objectives

On completion of this chapter, you should:

- understand the importance of classifying laws
- develop awareness of the workings of the court system
- appreciate the issues involved in establishing the Caribbean Court of Justice
- develop the ability critically to analyse alternative ways of settling disputes.

Specific objectives

You should be able to:

- identify the bases on which the law is classified
- describe the structure of the court system in the Commonwealth Caribbean
- distinguish among the jurisdiction of courts in the Commonwealth Caribbean
- explain the reasons advanced for the establishment of the Caribbean Court of Justice
- outline the main provisions of the proposed Caribbean Court of Justice
- evaluate alternative ways of settling disputes in Commonwealth Caribbean territories.

Introduction

In this chapter, you will investigate the nature and structure of the courts in Commonwealth Caribbean territories. Firstly, you will develop an appreciation of the importance attached to classifying law and identifying the bases upon which different laws are classified. Secondly, you will examine the different courts and jurisdictions and note their status and rank within the hierarchical structure of the court system. Thirdly, this chapter examines the issues involved in the attempts to establish the Caribbean Court of Justice (CCJ) to replace the Privy Council as the court of last resort for Commonwealth Caribbean territories. Finally, this chapter looks at alternative ways of handling disputes, or alternative dispute resolution strategies (ADR) through arbitration, and mediation.

On completion of chapter 2, you will be able to identify the differences between public and private law and have a working knowledge of the hierarchical structure of the court system. This chapter will help you to become aware of the structure of the court system and the names of the various courts that have jurisdiction over specific matters. You should also develop awareness of the main issues surrounding the proposed Caribbean Court of Justice and you should appreciate evolving strategies being used to settle disputes.

Content

- Classifications of law
- Nature and structure of the court system
- Jurisdiction of courts in the Commonwealth Caribbean
- The Caribbean Court of Justice
- Alternative dispute resolution (ADR)

Classification of law

There are three main ways by which Commonwealth Caribbean law is classified. These are:

1. by subject matter, for example, tort, contract and real property
2. by function, for example, substantive, procedural, civil and criminal
3. by concept, for example, private law and public law.

Laws can be further classified using different approaches. Let us take private law and public law as headings. This could result in a form of classification as shown in the table below.

Private law	Public law
The law of torts	Constitutional law
The law of contracts	Administrative law
The law of real property	Criminal law

The importance of classification

You may at this point be wondering why we need to classify the law. Let us look at the scenario opposite in the example.

Example

You are struck down on the road by a motor car driven by a drunk driver. The matter is reported to the police who bring criminal proceedings against the driver of the car for negligent driving. But what about your medical bills and loss of income? How are you to be compensated? The answer is that you can seek remedy in tort against the negligent driver and the owner of the vehicle if the driver was not the owner, and you can take civil law action within the realm of private law.

One main reason for the classification of law is that classification brings a uniform set of research, precedent, experiences and procedures to bear on a case. It gives attorneys the ability to know exactly where to conduct the research that will contain a solution to specific problems. If an attorney is convinced that the law governing your problem will be found within the law of torts, the attorney will research that area of the law. The research will be facilitated since all of the books containing material on the law of torts will be found in the same place in the law library. It is for this reason that available library material is classified and catalogued.

Another reason for the classification of law is that it makes available a variety of options to clients and attorneys in their attempts to seek redress. In the scenario described the police will prosecute the driver for negligence under public law, but it is up to the injured party to seek redress under private law. Private law is that area of the law that is concerned primarily with litigation and procedures and which does not attract punishment of any of the parties by the imposition of a term of imprisonment. Within the field of private law a litigant may seek damages; an injunction; costs against the other party; compensation; and any of the remedies available at equity.

The classification of the law also helps us to know the remedies available under the law. For example, under the law of torts, the remedy most usually sought is damages and sometimes an injunction may also be applied for and obtained by the plaintiff.

Activity 2.1

Write two paragraphs explaining, in your own words, why you think it is a good idea to classify the law.

Feedback

A good answer must contain the following elements:

- the meaning of classification of law
- the importance of knowing where to find the law under which a particular problem will fall for the purpose of problem-solving and research by both lawyers and students
- the importance of knowing the remedies available under a particular area of the law.

Activity 2.2

Anita bought a car from an unscrupulous car dealer. After only four months of having driven it, the car breaks down. The dealer refuses to repair it or to refund any part of the purchase price, which Anita had paid in full.

In anger Anita cuffed the car dealer, knocking out two of his front teeth. The car dealer reports the matter to the police who have laid a charge against Anita. Anita wishes to retain you as her attorney and she would also like to obtain relief with respect to the car.

Explain how knowledge of the classification of law will be of advantage to you in providing legal services to Anita.

Feedback

A good response would show that you are aware of the various heads under which the law is classified and where pertinent research material may be found. You must show that both substantive and procedural laws are to be applied. You must also be able to recognise that Anita's act against the dealer falls within the area of public law or, more precisely, criminal law, since it constitutes a criminal act. In addition, you should show that the actions of the dealer must be examined under private or civil law or, more specifically, the law of contract.

You should explain that knowledge of the classification of the law is vital to finding the law necessary to inform the research, which is an essential prerequisite to giving legal advice or taking legal action on behalf of a client.

Nature and structure of the court system

Introduction

This section focuses on the structure and operation of the courts in Commonwealth Caribbean territories. This section also discusses the views of proponents and opponents of the establishment of the Caribbean Court of Justice (CCJ). Finally, this section examines alternative systems of dealing with matters before the courts, known as 'alternative dispute resolution' (ADR) that uses arbitration, conciliation and mediation to resolve some issues.

Criminal and civil courts

Courts in the Commonwealth Caribbean have adopted the hierarchical structure of courts in England. As in England, and lying at the apex of the hierarchy of courts, is the Judicial Committee of the Privy Council, based in England. This court is the final Court of Appeal for all the Commonwealth territories, except the Republic of Guyana. You should bear in mind that this court of last resort may be replaced by the Caribbean Court of Justice (CCJ).

The highest locally-based court in the Commonwealth Caribbean is the Supreme Court of the High Court. This court consists of a Court of Appeal, a High Court and a Full Court of the High Court. The territories, Barbados, Jamaica, Guyana and Trinidad and Tobago, have their own Supreme Court. In the Organization of the Eastern Caribbean States (OECS), however, although each territory has its own High Court, there is only one Court of Appeal that serves them all. This court is called the Eastern Caribbean Supreme Court.

Below is a list of the various courts that operate in Commonwealth Caribbean territories. The list is arranged in hierarchical order according to function and the power to exercise authority over other courts. The list also includes a column that briefly explains the jurisdiction of the different courts.

Rank order	Name of court	Jurisdiction
1	The Judicial Committee of the Privy Council	The court of last resort for some Commonwealth Caribbean territories, except Guyana, Barbados and Belize
2	Court of Appeal	With the Caribbean Court of Justice, this is the highest ranking locally-based court. They can send a case back to the High Court, for a rehearing
3	The High Court of the Supreme Court	Hands down decisions based on the common law
4	The Full Court of the High Court	The court of appeal for decisions from the magistrates' court
5	Family court	A court vested with the power and authority to hear and determine all matters pertaining to the family with the exception of divorce
6	Juvenile court	A court vested with the power and authority to hear and determine all matters pertaining to juveniles
7	Magistrates' court	Court established to deal with petty crime. Decisions are not reported and cannot produce binding or persuasive precedents
8	Industrial courts	Court established to deal with industrial relations matters, only in Trinidad.

In at least one jurisdiction, Jamaica, there is a Court of Petty Sessions, which is presided over by a panel of justices of the Peace.

Jurisdiction of courts in the Commonwealth Caribbean

Let us now examine the real power that each court has over other courts within the system. This will help you to understand the relative importance of the judgments handed down by these courts and whether you can bypass their judgments and seek redress in other courts.

The Judicial Committee of the Privy Council

Though the Judicial Committee of the Privy Council has the power to hear matters of a criminal and civil nature, in civil matters, the Privy Council will limit its power to hearing matters concerning property above a certain value, and in criminal matters the Privy Council has to be satisfied that there is some serious miscarriage of justice. There is, however, an unfettered right to appeal to the Privy Council in any case that raises a constitutional or a fundamental right issue.

Court of Appeal

The decisions of the Court of Appeal can be overturned by the Judicial Committee of the Privy Council. The Court of Appeal can hand down separate and independent judgments in civil and criminal matters without having to ensure that one judgment has any bearing on the other.

The Court of Appeal has the authority to send back a case to the High Court for rehearing. In addition, the Court of Appeal can impose a harsher or lighter sentence. It can dismiss appeals to the Full Court of the High Court and can also quash a decision of the High Court of the Supreme Court acting in its jurisdiction as a court of first instance.

The High Court of the Supreme Court

The High Court of the Supreme Court is vested with power to handle matters of common law, including the following:

- the hearing of allegations of breach of a fundamental right
- the hearing of allegations of an Act of Parliament being inconsistent with the Constitution other than the fundamental rights provision
- supervise any statutory functionary or public body to ensure they keep within the ambit of the powers vested in them
- to make determination under certain statutes, for example, under the Companies Act, to wind up a company, or under the Partnership Act, to dissolve a partnership.

The Full Court of the High Court

The Full Court of the High Court is also a court of inherent jurisdiction. This means that it is empowered at common law to make decisions based on case law as well as statute. The Full Court of the High Court is also the court of appeal for decisions from the magistrates' court. Note that in Guyana, since there is no recourse to appeals to the Privy Council, certain issues that arise at Appeal Court level are sent to be heard by the Full Court.

Family court

Not all Caribbean territories possess in their hierarchy a family court. This type of court is found in Jamaica, where it was established by the passing of the Judicature (Family Court) Act 1995, in Belize, as established by the Family Court Act 1988, Cap. 83A – 1990 Rev, in St Vincent, as established by the Family Court Act 1992, and in Trinidad and Tobago.

Juvenile court

The establishment of juvenile courts in the Commonwealth Caribbean was aimed at reforming existing law to bring about an improvement in the welfare of juveniles within the court system. As an example, in Guyana the law is classified under the Juvenile Offenders Act of Guyana, Cap. 10:03. In section 17, the law describes a juvenile as one who is apparently under the age of 17, and who may be found 'begging or receiving alms, wandering ... or having no parent or guardian, or is found destitute..., or frequents the company of any reputed ... thief, or reputed prostitute.'

Magistrates' court

The magistrates' court handles matters of a summary, hybrid and indictable nature. The criminal jurisdiction of the magistrates' court deals with assault, theft, embezzlement of money and damage to property and crops. On the other hand, the civil jurisdiction deals with family matters, for example, orders of separation, orders for maintenance of spouse or child or children under the Domestic Violence Act, No. 18 of 1996 (Guyana), rectification of errors on birth certificates and breaches of contract.

Industrial court

Only Trinidad and Tobago has an Industrial Court. Other territories such as Jamaica, Dominica and Belize have separate quasi-judicial bodies.

These institutions are commonly termed industrial courts or industrial tribunals. These courts may be separate quasi-judicial bodies as in Jamaica, Dominica and Belize, or they may be a subsidiary under the Ministry of Labour.

The jurisdiction of such a court is to determine the majority union in any firm or industry, to register agreements made between union and employer and to settle industrial disputes. The Industrial Stabilisation Act of 1965, of Trinidad and Tobago, first established the Industrial Court of Trinidad and Tobago. It was replaced and repealed by the Industrial Relations Act of 1980.

The written constitution of each Commonwealth Caribbean state makes provision for the establishment of other tribunals, such as the Service Commissions, Teaching Service Commissions, the Public Service Commissions and the Judicial Service Commissions. These tribunals were created to deal with, inter alia, the discipline of the respective categories of public servants under their control. In Trinidad and Tobago, there is the National Insurance Appeals Tribunal to resolve and adjudicate disputed claims for such insurance.

You may at this point wish to refer to the National Insurance Act, Cap. 32:01, section 62 of the Laws of Trinidad and Tobago, and the Labour Relations and Industrial Disputes Act (Jamaica).

The Caribbean Court of Justice

The agreement to establish the CCJ was made at the 6th Heads of Government Conference of Caribbean Commonwealth leaders, held in Jamaica in 1970. At the time of writing, the CCJ is not yet the final court for all Commonwealth Caribbean jurisdictions.

It is proposed that the CCJ will possess two jurisdictions:

1 an appellate jurisdiction; and
2 an original jurisdiction.

The appellate jurisdiction of the CCJ, when established, will hear appeals, both civil and criminal, from the domestic courts of all Commonwealth Caribbean territories. For example, imagine that A and B are Jamaicans who were parties to a contract, which they had entered into with one another. B breaks the contract, so A takes B to the Civil Court of the High Court and B wins. A not being satisfied with the decision of the High Court, appeals to the Jamaica Court of Appeal, which grants a decision in favour of A. If B is now dissatisfied with the decision of the Court of Appeal, he could, after he has applied for leave to appeal to the CCJ and such leave has been granted him by the Court of Appeal, appeal to the CCJ for relief.

Example

In criminal cases, if A kills B, the State takes A to court (the magistrates' court, since all criminal matters begin there). A is then bound over for trial in the High Court which finds him guilty at the end of the trial. A is dissatisfied with this decision and appeals to the Court of Appeal, which reaffirms the decision of the High Court. A can now apply to the Court of Appeal to allow him to appeal further to the CCJ.

Note: While in civil cases either party can appeal the decision of the court the same is not true for criminal cases. In England the right of appeal in criminal cases is open to the defendant as well as the prosecution. However, this is not so for the Commonwealth Caribbean territories. Here, the prosecution has no right of appeal. The defendant could, on the other hand, appeal all the way up to the CCJ if he so desires.

The original jurisdiction of the CCJ will hear:

- matters arising out of issues between Commonwealth Caribbean States
- matters establishing the rights of private individuals under certain international treaties
- matters arising out of trade disputes.

Example

Imagine that Barbados, Trinidad and Dominica have entered into an agreement concerning the use of one another's fishing waters. Eventually Barbados accuses Dominica of over-fishing in the waters of Barbados and, therefore, seeks to end the agreement, not only with Dominica but also with Trinidad. Trinidad and Dominica could, if they wish, approach the CCJ to have the conflict aired and resolved.

Arguments for and against the establishment of the CCJ

Some persons believe that the Commonwealth Caribbean is not yet ready for the establishment of the CCJ. These persons are popularly known as opponents of the establishment of the CCJ. However, there exists also the widespread sentiment that the establishment of the CCJ is something long overdue. Those persons who share this view are known as proponents for the establishment of the CCJ.

Example

Imagine another situation: there is a clause in the Treaty of Chaguaramas (signed in 1973, establishing the community later known as CARICOM) or a clause in some agreement entered into between States. Each of the parties to the treaty or the agreement interprets the clause differently and this creates a problem. Any of the States affected may apply to the CCJ to have any question on the interpretation of the clause answered.

Perceived disadvantages of establishing the CCJ

Opponents of the establishment of the CCJ argue that:

- the Privy Council is properly and satisfactorily functioning as the final court of appeal for Commonwealth Caribbean territories
- there may not be available in the Commonwealth Caribbean enough judges of the level of erudition and skill to enable them to function effectively at the level of the CCJ
- the decisions therefore of those judges appointed to the CCJ may be of a poor quality

- adequate and sustainable funding for the running and maintenance of the CCJ may not be forthcoming from member States
- the judges of the CCJ may be vulnerable to political manipulation from member States.

Perceived advantages of establishing the CCJ

Proponents for the establishment of the CCJ make the points listed below:

- Since the Law Lords of the Privy Council are both geographically and culturally removed from the Commonwealth Caribbean experience, they are not fully equipped with the knowledge and level of understanding required to make decisions, which reflect sensitivity for Caribbean people.
- The establishment of the CCJ will foster a greater sense of security and stability in the region: acting in its original jurisdiction, the CCJ will be the only court responsible for the interpretation and application of the Treaty of Chaguaramas This will eliminate the possibility of conflicting decisions coming from other international courts. The CCJ acting in its original jurisdiction will also be responsible for hearing and deciding on issues arising between States after the establishment of the Caribbean Single Market Economy (CSME) (which will facilitate the free movement of goods services and skills within the Commonwealth Caribbean under a single currency). This will help member States and foreign investors alike to feel secure in the knowledge that there is one highly respected court for ensuring fairness, proper observation of rules by member States and predictable decisions.
- There are enough members of the legal profession possessing the requisite degree of skill and integrity to occupy positions within the CCJ.
- Though a decision handed down by the CCJ acting in its original jurisdiction may not be enforceable, it is believed that sanctions and pressures brought to bear on a disobedient State (party) to a decision of the CCJ will be enough to ensure compliance.

Alternative dispute resolution (ADR)

Definition

Alternative dispute resolution, more familiarly called ADR, usually refers to mechanisms that are used to settle disputes instead of resort to litigation. Embodied within the doctrine of ADR are different alternative mechanisms, the most popular of which are arbitration, mediation, conciliation and negotiation.

Note: For the purpose of the Caribbean Advanced Proficiency Examination (CAPE), you are required to pay special attention to mediation and arbitration.

Arbitration

Arbitration is a process by which a neutral third party hears the testimony of both parties to the dispute in a relatively informal setting. Unlike mediation, arbitration proceedings contain some elements of proceedings conducted in a court of law.

In arbitration proceedings both parties must agree to come to the bargaining table to commence arbitration. It is important for you to be able to draw the distinction that, while in a court of law, the litigants do not have a choice in deciding who the adjudicator is, with respect to arbitration the parties to the dispute must decide and agree on the selection of an arbitrator.

After hearing and weighing the testimony, the arbitrator makes a decision that can be deemed binding on all parties to the arbitration and an order of the High Court may be obtained in order to secure the enforcement of the decision of the arbitrator.

The process of arbitration also allows all parties involved, including the arbitrator, to refer to statute and case law in support of their respective arguments. The arbitrator is also free to apply general community standards of fairness to assist him in arriving at a decision. In arbitration, the rules of evidence are less strictly applied and the arbitrator sits as the judge of both fact and law.

The following are some advantages of arbitration:

- the decision of the arbitrator may be enforced
- arbitration proceedings are less costly and less time-consuming
- the informal setting promotes relaxation of tensions between disputants.

Mediation

Like arbitration, mediation also employs the services of a third party, referred to as the mediator, who most often acts as a shuttle between the two parties, communicating the position of the disputants to one another as they try to reconcile their differences towards the achievement of a settlement. The mediator acts as both judge and jury, holding separate meetings or caucuses at which further clarification may be obtained as regards the position of the respective parties with a view towards suggesting possible advances by which agreement may be reached. These caucuses are conducted in private and the findings are not revealed to the other side unless each party approves.

The following are some advantages of mediation:

- it is time- and cost-effective
- confidentiality is maintained
- fairness and flexibility are promoted
- it has shown reliability in terms of compliance with the final decision. In some jurisdictions mediation is now mandatory in some civil proceedings.

Activity 2.3

Mr John Muir entered into a contract with B.V. Enterprises to construct a bridge for the company. Mr Muir fails to complete the bridge on time so the company refuses to pay him the remainder of the money owed to him under the terms of the contract. Mr Muir would like to have his problem solved but is afraid of courts.

Advise Mr Muir of all the options of dispute resolution available to him and explain to him why you have chosen either mediation or arbitration to handle this matter.

Feedback

A good response to this question should first state that there are different methods of dispute resolution including the traditional court system to which parties can resort for help. There is also the office of the Ombudsman and there are those methods of resolution of disputes known as ADR.

You should then state that since Mr Muir is afraid of courts and since assistance from the Ombudsman is limited to problems occurring between individuals and State entities, the alternative open to Mr Muir would be one of the processes available under ADR.

Note: This question requires that you select only one of the ADR methods available for your answer. You may wish to choose either mediation or arbitration. Finally, you should discuss the advantages of the ADR process that you have chosen.

Suggested further reading

Rose-Marie Belle Antoine, Commonwealth Caribbean Law and Legal Systems, 1999

Peter Britton, Alternative Dispute Resolution, 1999, Guy LR, Vol. 1

Duke Pollard, The Caribbean Court of Justice, 2000, Guy LR, Vol. 2

End Test

Answer 5 questions: all of Questions 1 to 3, either Question 4 or 5, and Question 6. **Time: 3 hours**

1 a List the main divisions into which law may be classified.

b Explain why it is important to be accurate when classifying law.

2 Read the story below and answer the question that follows.

John and Myra were driving out one night in John's car when they were stopped by two policemen in uniform. The officers claimed that John had exceeded the speed limit, ordered John and Myra out of the car, forced them into the police car and said that they would take them to the police station.

On the way to the police station, the policemen stopped the car, dragged John and Myra into the bushes, and beat John and raped Myra. The police officers then ran back to their car and drove off leaving John and Myra by the side of the road. When John went back to his car he found that it had been vandalised.

Using your knowledge of the classification of law, advise John and Myra with respect to the areas of the law under which their claims may be brought and what are the remedies available under each.

3 State briefly what is meant by:

a the appellate jurisdiction of the CCJ; and

b the original jurisdiction of the CCJ.

4 'A Caribbean Court of Justice is not important for the development of the Commonwealth Caribbean.' Do you agree with this statement? Give reasons for your answer.

5 'Without the establishment of the CCJ, the Commonwealth Caribbean will not achieve true unity and prosperity and the idea of a single market economy will remain just a dream.' Discuss.

6 'The process known as ADR is ineffective because it achieves nothing beneficial for the parties.' Discuss.

End Test Feedback

1 An answer to part a requires that you list the areas of classification and outline briefly the content of each. For example, you should point out that the criminal law is an area of public law. It concerns those provisions and procedures that contain the rules governing the State's attitude towards the criminal offender and the types of punishment that are attached to the various crimes.

An answer to part b of this question would require that you explain that lawyers and students alike would be unable to find anything on a particular area of the law in a law library. In addition, you should explain that judges and lawyers would be unable to find easy access to the writings on the various principles of law and the remedies to be attached to the issues that are being researched.

2 You should display knowledge of what is meant by the term 'classification of law'. This would set out the categories listed in the illustration. Next you should select from said list those categories of law that would apply to the problem at hand; for example, the criminal law and administrative law. You should support your selection by explaining why you chose those categories, for example, that the police officers abused their power while they were on duty and that the acts of assault and rape constitute a criminal offence.

Finally you should identify the types of remedies available to John and Myra: for example, compensation/damages under administrative law for the loss and injury suffered and a term of imprisonment for the acts of assault committed against John and rape committed against Myra.

3 A good response to this question should show that:

a when the CCJ is sitting in its appellate jurisdiction it is sitting to hear appeals from decisions of the lower domestic courts of member States. In other words the matter being brought before the CCJ on appeal is not a matter that is being heard for the first time since it was heard before in the lower courts.

b when the CCJ is sitting to hear matters in its original jurisdiction, the said matter is being heard for the first time in a court of law.

4 A good response to this question should include: a statement saying whether you agree or disagree with the statement. If you disagree you should then draw from the pool of disadvantages listed above, as well as any others you have discovered in your readings of pages 227–49 of Rose-Marie Belle Antoine's Commonwealth Caribbean Law and Legal Systems.

If on the other hand you happen to agree with the statement then you should first say so, then go on to draw from the pool of advantages listed above as well as any other advantages you have found in your readings.

5 A good response to this question would focus on the positive aspects of the idea behind the implementation of the CCJ. For example, you could mention that the time is ripe for (a) the replacement of the Privy Council with the CCJ as the court of last resort for Commonwealth Caribbean States and (b) the establishment of a court of original jurisdiction for dealing with the interpretation of the Treaty of Chaguaramas and other issues arising among States, trading entities or private individuals.

Next, you should discuss the idea behind the proposed establishment of the CSME. For example, it is hoped that the CSME will cater for the free movement of goods, services and skills across the Commonwealth Caribbean under a single currency.

Having done so, you may now wish to comment on the importance of and the need within the Commonwealth Caribbean for these two institutions. You may add that while Europe has already brought the European Court and common market into being, the Commonwealth Caribbean's movement towards achieving same still remains a dream.

You may then wish to conclude your answer by showing the symbiotic relationship between the two institutions. In other words, how the establishment of one will lend support to the other. The CCJ, which will be comprised at all levels by staff from all member States, will be testimony of the free movement of skills under the CSME whose smooth functioning will be supported by the CCJ as legal watchdog and supervisor.

6 An answer to this question requires that you discuss all of the advantages of at least two of the ADR processes.

3 The Commonwealth Caribbean court system: personnel and procedures

General objectives

On completion of this chapter, you should:

- develop an appreciation of the role and function of members of the legal profession
- appreciate the arrangements for legal aid in Commonwealth Caribbean countries
- understand procedures for law revision and law reform in Commonwealth Caribbean countries.

Specific objectives

You should be able to:

- explain the role and function of named members of the legal profession
- evaluate the effectiveness of the jury system in carrying out its function
- outline the provisions for legal aid in Commonwealth Caribbean countries
- describe procedures for law revision and law reform in Commonwealth Caribbean countries.

Introduction

In chapter 2, we investigated the nature and structure of the courts in Commonwealth Caribbean territories. We recognised the importance of classifying law and identified the bases upon which different laws are classified. Next, we examined the different courts and jurisdictions and explained their status and rank within the hierarchical structure of the court system. Finally, we discussed the issues involved in the attempts to establish the Caribbean Court of Justice (CCJ) and evaluated alternative ways of handling disputes by focusing on alternative dispute resolution strategies (ADR) through arbitration, conciliation and mediation.

In chapter 3, we will continue to examine the court system but this time from the standpoint of the people who walk the corridors of the courts. We will study the role of members of the legal profession, including the role of attorneys, judges and the Ombudsman. Next, we will investigate some of the main procedures used in the courts, such as the jury system, the provisions for legal aid and for revision and reform of the laws.

On completion of this chapter, you will be able to identify the different roles performed by members of the legal profession. This chapter will also help you to become aware of some of the main procedures used in the courts, including the selection of jurors and the handling of issues related to legal aid, law review and law reform.

Content

- The legal profession
- The role of the Ombudsman
- The jury system
- Legal aid
- Law reform and law revision

The legal profession

Members and training

The legal system is manned by the officials listed below:

- Attorney General
- Director of Public Prosecutions (DPP)
- Deputy DPP
- State lawyers
- Chancellor
- President of the Court
- Appellate judges
- Chief Justice
- Puisne judges
- Chief Magistrate and magistrates

- Court marshalls
- Bailiffs
- Registrars
- Clerks
- Orderlies
- Police prosecutors
- Mediators

Functions of members

The Attorney General is in charge of all civil litigation begun by the State or brought against the State.

The Director of Public Prosecutions (DPP) is in charge of all criminal matters begun by the State or brought against the State.

The Deputy DPP and all State prosecutors assist the DPP with his or her work in the DPP's Chambers. They appear in court to conduct cases on behalf of the State.

The Attorney General is also assisted by a team of lawyers who work with him or her in the Attorney General's Chambers. The Attorney General and the team of lawyers represent the State in all civil matters.

The Chancellor of the Judiciary is in charge of the entire judiciary. He or she presides over the Court of Appeal and sits there to hear appeals together with the other Appeal Court judges.

The Registrar of the Supreme Court Registry is a qualified attorney-at-law and possesses the status of a puisne judge.

Activity 3.1

Ensure you know how the courts are administered in your country.

In Trinidad and Tobago the High Court is run on an everyday basis by the President of the Court. However, in Guyana this function is performed by the Chief Justice. The difference between the two offices is limited to name only since they both wield the same degree of power and perform the same functions. Further, they both preside over the High Court of the Supreme Court and the Full Court of the High Court and are responsible for the distribution of cases to the various judges.

The Chief Magistrate is directly in charge of all magistrates' courts and hears matters of both a civil and criminal nature. The Chief Magistrate is also directly responsible for the distribution to all other magistrates of cases that come before her or him.

Marshalls are peace officers of all courts above the level of the magistrates' court. Orderlies and bailiffs are peace officers of the magistrates' court.

Training

The legal profession in the Commonwealth Caribbean mirrored the English system in a way similar to its law and jurisprudence. At one time, there existed a division in the profession caused by the failure of the authorities to recognise trained solicitors and barristers as equally entitled to be admitted to one of the Inns of Court in the UK, upon passing their respective examinations.

This is no longer the situation in the Caribbean, and there is now fusion of the profession. This means that now a prospective law student is trained as both barrister and solicitor and is referred to as an attorney-at-law. The education of an attorney-at-law based on a unified profession and a combination of academic and professional training.

In the Caribbean, one is now required to undertake a three-year course at the Faculty of Law, University of the West Indies, or in the case of Guyanese students, three years must be spent at the Faculty of Law, University of Guyana. The law programme is mainly conducted at four centres across the region, namely, the three campuses of the University of the West Indies (Mona in Jamaica, Cave Hill in Barbados and the St Augustine Campus in Trinidad and Tobago), and at the Turkeyene Campus of the University of Guyana or at the College of the Bahamas in Nassau. Increasingly, persons are acquiring their law degrees from overseas universities. In addition, the University of Technology in Jamaica has been offering a law degree programme in recent years.

After a full completion of the LL.B. degree, the undergraduate law student may proceed to either the Norman Manley Law School in Jamaica, or the Hugh Wooding Law School in Trinidad and Tobago, or where the student will read for professional training. This training covers the procedural aspects of the law course, and after a completion of the two-year course, the law graduate is awarded with the Council of Legal Education, Legal Education Certificate (LEC).

In 2000, the Caribbean Examinations Council introduced a syllabus for Law at the Caribbean Advanced Proficiency Examination level. Prospective law students who wish to pursue a career in Commonwealth Caribbean law may commence studying law from this level. The syllabus is designed for students who wish to embark on further study and training for entry into the legal profession, as well as for persons who wish to learn about the law in a practical way, as part of their experience, without becoming lawyers.

The role of lawyers

In order to facilitate your understanding of the separate function of each officer of the court, we will divide the role of lawyers between two major functions, namely:

- role of the prosecution counsel; and
- role of the defendant counsel.

Role of prosecution counsel

In his book, On Criminal Procedure (5th edition), John Sprack states that counsel appearing on behalf of the prosecution are not in court to win the case at all costs. Sprack is of the view, however, that counsel should do their best to present the evidence properly and persuasively, and in addition counsel should cross-examine defence witnesses with all the necessary vigour and guile to the best of their ability. As Justice Avory in R v. Banks [1916] 2 KB 621 expounded:

> 'prosecuting counsel ought not to struggle for the verdict against the prisoner, but they ought to bear themselves rather in the character of the ministers of justice assisting in the administrating of justice.'

Sprack continues:

> 'Should the defence suggest a plea of guilty to a lesser offence or guilty on some but not all counts of the charge, then prosecuting counsel does not consider only whether the evidence, as available, might secure a conviction on all counts as charged, but whether the proposed pleas represents a fair way of dealing with the case. If they do and subject to any comments by the judge, he should accept the pleas, even though that means giving up the chance of "extra" convictions. Again, if the prosecution knows that one of its witnesses has had previous convictions, there is a duty to reveal to the defence

the nature and occasion of those convictions although by doing so the defence is presented with a useful line of cross-examination.'

R v. Paraskwa (1983) 7 Cr. App R

In this case the Court of Appeal quashed Paraskwa's conviction for assault occasioning actual bodily harm because the case against him turned upon whether the victim of the alleged offences was telling the truth or deliberately lying, and the prosecution failed to disclose that victim had been convicted in 1975 of an offence of dishonesty.

Important consideration

Please note that having been informed that a prosecution witness is not of good character, the defence may sometimes choose not to cross-examine him. In such a case, the prosecuting counsel might himself reveal his witness's character to the jury, but he is under no duty to do so. The principle is that the prosecution should be scrupulously fair to the accused but need not be quixotically generous.

Role of defence counsel

It is the task of the advocate for the defendant to use all means at his or her disposal to secure an acquittal for his or her client. For instance, if the advocate notices a flaw in the prosecution's case, he or she may object to oppose the issue but need not draw his or her opponent or the court's attention to the matter before the last possible moment.

It is important for you to note that, if a procedural irregularity occurs before the decision or judgment of the court, it is the task of counsel to inform the court as soon as possible.

R v. McFadden and Cunningham (1976) 62 Cr. App R 187

The Chairman of the Bar said:

> 'defence counsel's duty is to present to the court, fearlessly and without regard to his personal interests, the defence of the accused. His personal opinion of truth or falsity of the defence, or of the character of the accused, or of the nature of the charge should all be left out of the account – that is a cardinal rule of the Bar, and it would be a grave matter in any free society were it were not.'

Activity 3.2

Jenel has just completed her CXC examinations and is bent on becoming an attorney-at-law in a named Caribbean jurisdiction.

Advise her on the training facilities that are available in the Caribbean.

Feedback

In your answer to Activity 3.2, you should mention:

- the fusion of the profession
- centres of study
- where the centres are located
- the duration of study, and
- qualification attained after studying.

Discipline of lawyers

Discipline of members of the legal profession is carried out by an organisation in each State. Invariably, the organisation lays down a code of conduct, breach of which renders the errant member liable to varying sanctions, including being debarred from practising their profession.

Example of indiscipline: Forde v. The Law Society 40 WIR 36

A solicitor received funds by cheque for a particular transaction, deposited it to his account and thereafter issued to the complainant in respect of the said transaction a cheque for an amount that should have come from the same fund, but the cheque was dishonoured. The Disciplinary Committee, after an inquiry, found a case of professional misconduct, and referred the case to the High Court. The High Court found Forde's misconduct to be gross and struck him off the Roll of Attorneys.

Another example of indiscipline

Emanating from the jurisdiction of Barbados was the case of Re Niles (1993) 47 WIR 38. In this case the client gave the attorney money to purchase a piece of land. The attorney never completed the transaction and failed to turn over the funds to another attorney whom the client retained to complete the transaction. The Disciplinary Committee investigated and found professional misconduct. The committee referred the matter to the High Court and this court found Niles guilty and thus he was removed from the Roll of Attorneys.

Rules of conduct

Embodied within the issue of discipline are the rules of conduct that must guide lawyers as to their professional behaviour. Examples of these are:

- never introduce yourself to the Bar
- always address judges as Madam, Sir, Your Honour
- address magistrates as Your Worship
- never put your briefcase on the Bar Table
- never stand when another lawyer is standing
- never represent to your client that he or she has a good case when he or she does not
- always acquaint yourself with the law as it pertains to your client's case
- the attorney-at-law must respect the principle of lawyer–client confidentiality.

Role of the Ombudsman

Unlike most aspects of Commonwealth Caribbean law and jurisprudence, the concept of the Ombudsman was not derived from England but from Scandinavia. Guyana was the first territory in the Commonwealth Caribbean to adopt the concept of the Ombudsman.

In their search for a legal system that affords access to justice for an aggrieved individual, Caribbean Commonwealth jurisdictions have transported the concept of the Ombudsman, an office which allows for the application of law as well as morality to flourish in a system of justice designed to complement the adversarial approach.

The Ombudsman is a relatively new institution in the Commonwealth Caribbean. In some cases the office is established by the Constitution, as is the case for Guyana and Trinidad and Tobago. In other territories, such as Barbados and Jamaica, the office is created by Acts of Parliament. For example, in Guyana, the source of the Ombudsman's power is derived from Article 191(1) of the Guyana Constitution and the Ombudsman Act, Cap. 19:04. On the other hand, it is derived in Jamaica from section 21(5) of the Jamaican Ombudsman Act.

The Ombudsman in Guyana

In Guyana, the original purpose for creating the office of the Ombudsman was to deal with the problem of racial upheaval existing within that jurisdiction. In Jamaica, the need was centred around the political arena. According to the Annual Report of the Guyanese Ombudsman (S.Y. Mohammed), the office is committed and dedicated to doing the following:

- investigate and resolve complaints against injustice done to members of the public, by a government department and other authority
- provide informal, dependable and freely accessible service to members of the public
- treat members of the public with courtesy, compassion, honesty and respect their privacy
- educate members of the public about the services of the office of the Ombudsman
- be ethical, transparent and accountable
- offer guidance to members of the public whose complaints are outside the jurisdiction of the office of the Ombudsman; and
- ensure that members of the public are treated alike and there is no discrimination on the grounds of race, place of origin, political opinion, creed or sex. (page 3 of the report)

In Guyana and Jamaica there has been rapid expansion of government departments. This has unavoidably resulted in the alienation of the State from the individual. As a result the operation and control of government bodies began to adversely affect some members of society while the problem of exercising effective control over officialdom became increasingly important but at the same time more intractable.

According to Rose-Marie Belle Antoine, at page 126 of Commonwealth Caribbean Law and Legal Systems:

> 'The role of the Ombudsman emerges as a protector of the citizens against the inherent abuses of the machinery of such complex and powerful administration.'

The Ombudsman's office, according to the same author at page 126:

> '... is an additional weapon in the battle for the protection of citizen's rights and future protection against the administrative error, inefficiency and abuse of power.'

With respect to the jurisdiction of Guyana, the Ombudsman may investigate any action as aforesaid in any of the circumstances listed under subsections 2(a), (b) and (c) of Article 192 of the Guyana (1980) Constitution with Amendments, all of which predicate upon the theme of injustice.

The Political Ombudsman

In Jamaica, the office of the Political Ombudsman appears to have emerged from the high incidence of alleged political violence in that jurisdiction: the creation of the office, therefore, is an attempt on the part of the leading parties to have a conciliator to help reduce any political terror and conflict.

The Public Utilities Ombudsman

The Public Utilities Ombudsman, replaced for the most part by the Office of Utilities Regulation, has the power to intervene in disputes relating to the following government agencies in Jamaica:

- National Water Commission
- Jamaica Railroad Corporation
- Post and Telegraph Department
- Jamaica Public Service Commission.

Complaints that are received by the Public Utilities Ombudsman include:

- excessive billing
- incorrect billing
- defective meters
- disconnections
- unavailability of services
- inadequate street lighting
- illegal telephone calls
- estimated billing; and
- lost luggage.

The Parliamentary Ombudsman

The Parliamentary Ombudsman deals with matters relating to governmental agencies in general and some statutory agencies. Many successes have been recorded, for example, the Parliamentary Ombudsman has helped change laws through advocacy and has identified serious flaws in policy and in practice.

The Ombudsman for Contracts

The Ombudsman for Contracts deals with civil disputes between parties and determines the liability that attaches to any of the parties to a dispute. In other words this office deals with breaches of the terms of a contract.

As discussed above, the jurisdiction of Jamaica contrasts somewhat with that of Guyana in that in Jamaica there are more Ombudsmen to deal with different areas of administration by public authorities. In Guyana the existence of only one Ombudsman puts a tremendous strain on the service due to a voluminous workload and inadequate resources.

The functions of the Ombudsman

You are advised to examine Article 194 of the Guyana Constitution, which outlines the functions of the Ombudsman. (As you examine this Article, look in the Constitution of your State to see if there is a specific section that is devoted to the functions of the Ombudsman in your jurisdiction.) Article 194 states:

'[1] after conducting an investigation under this subtitle the Ombudsman ... shall inform the ... authority concerned ... of the sustained injury, [and] he shall inform that department or authority of the reasons for that opinion and may make such recommendation for action by that department or authority as he thinks fit.

[2] after conducting an investigation [whether at the] request [of a private citizen or a Minister or Parliament, etc.] ... The Ombudsman shall___

a if he is of the opinion that the complainant or, [the officer requesting same] has sustained injustice in consequences of a fault in the administration, inform the person or the body of persons who made the complaint or request that he is of that opinion and the nature of the injustice that he considers has been sustained.

b if he is of the opinion that the complainant or ... the person or body of persons specified in the request has not sustained injustice, inform the person or body of persons who made the complaint or request that he is of the opinion at the reason therefore.

[3] Where the Ombudsman has made a recommendation under paragraph (1) and within a reasonable time thereafter no action has been taken which appears to the Ombudsman adequately to remedy the injustice, he may lay before the Assembly a special report on the case.

[4] The Ombudsman shall annually lay before the Assembly a general report on performance of his functions under this subtitle.'

More importantly, the Ombudsman may also investigate a complaint of a contravention of any of the fundamental rights and freedoms guaranteed by the Constitution. (See Article 192(3)(ii) of the Guyana Constitution.) The authorities are certain statutory bodies that carry out certain essential public services on behalf of the State. The schedule of the Guyana Ombudsman Act, Cap. 19:04, lends itself to giving examples of some public services. They are as follows:

- the Central Board of Health
- Sea Defence Board
- Drainage and Irrigation Board
- Guyana Rice Development Board
- Central Planning and Housing Authority
- Guyana Power and Light Company; and
- National Insurance Board.

Note: The Ombudsman is not allowed to investigate the Defence and Police Forces in the jurisdiction of Guyana.

Activity 3.3

Check your local legislation to see whether the Ombudsman in your jurisdiction possesses the same powers as the Ombudsman in Guyana.

The Ombudsman may in his discretion refuse to investigate a complaint that is frivolous or vexatious or where the complainant had knowledge of the complaint more than 12 months before it was received by the Ombudsman.

With respect to Jamaica the Ombudsman may investigate extensively into various matters, for instance, where there is a breach of fundamental rights. A more problematic situation is the provision that does not prevent the Jamaican Ombudsman from conducting his investigation in respect of any matter by reason only that it is to the complainant to apply to the court for redress under section 25(1) of the Jamaican Constitution.

The section states:

> 'Subject to provisions of subsection 4 of this section if any person alleges that any of the provisions of sections 14 to 24 (inclusive) of this Constitution has been, is being or is likely to be contravened in relation to him, then, without prejudice to any other action with respect to the same matter which is lawfully available, that person may apply to the Supreme Court for redress.'

Section 21(5) of the Jamaican Ombudsman Act 1978 allows the Ombudsman to recommend that an enactment, rule or regulation which causes or may cause injustice should be altered. This provision seems to encourage investigation into the substantive merits of legislative and executive actions and improvement of statute. Rose Marie-Belle Antoine states, at page 308:

> 'Further, the existence of written constitutions in the Commonwealth Caribbean, such constitutions being the supreme law against which all other laws are measured means in effect that any statute may be challenged as being ultra vires this constitution, thus giving locus standi to any citizen, and [allowing] the Ombudsman to embark upon such inquiry.'

Activity 3.4

Sharon and Gary are neighbours. Gary is in constant dispute with Sharon because she is trying to take over his land. Gary wishes to have the matter brought to court but the cost of litigation is too expensive.

Can the Ombudsman be of assistance to Gary? Give reasons for your answer.

Feedback

Your answer should include a description of the role and function of the Ombudsman. The matters into which he may legitimately inquire should be discussed with reference to your jurisdiction, or any jurisdiction of your choice.

The jury system

The jury system of the Commonwealth Caribbean territories, like that of England whence it was received, is founded on the old belief that a man must be tried by his peers consisting of 12 reasonable men (and women these days) who are called jurors. Following arraignment and a plea of not guilty the accused is put in charge of the panel of jurors. The relevant Jury/Juries Act of your jurisdiction provides for the selection of jurors:

- Anguilla – Cap. 38, Jury Act, sections 26, 27, 38 and 35
- Antigua – Cap. 41, Jury Act, sections 26, 27, 28 and 35
- Bahamas – Cap. 41, Juries Act, sections 19, 20, 21 and 25
- Barbados – Cap. 115B, Juries Act, sections 24, 28 and 38–40
- Belize – Juries Act
- Dominica – Cap. 5:70, Juries Act, sections 21, 22, 23 and 30
- Grenada – Cap. 151, Jury Act as amended by Act 10 of 1977, Act 13 of 1985 and Act 13 of 1986
- Guyana – Cap. 10:01, Criminal Law (Procedure) Act, sections 17–47 and 155–158
- Jamaica – Jury Act
- St Kitts/Nevis – Cap. 38, Jury Act, sections 26, 27, 35 and 38
- St Lucia – Code 78 et Seg., sections 809, 817, 821 and 970–7
- St Vincent – Cap 21, Jury Act, sections 13, 14 and 16
- Trinidad and Tobago – Cap. 6:53, Jury Act, sections 23 and 28

Rose-Marie Belle Antoine posits in her work, at page 217:

> 'the jury system of trial is an essential element of the democratic process. It attempts to secure fairness in the justice system.'

In the Commonwealth Caribbean the jury is used in both civil (for example, in actions for libel) and criminal matters. However, in the jurisdiction of Guyana, the jury system is used only in criminal matters at the commencement of the Criminal Assizes in the High Court. The modern jury is composed of a minimum of 12 jurors, in State offences, for example, murder and treason, while in some criminal matters it may be 9. Belle Antoine captures the purpose of jury trials in a nutshell when she says: '[The purpose of the jury] is to be the sole judges of the facts as opposed to law.'

Challenges to the jury

Challenges to the jury fall into the following two categories:

- challenge for cause, and

peremptory challenge.

> **Activity 3.5**
> Check to see if your local legislation makes provision to challenge a jury.

With respect to a peremptory challenge, a reason is not necessary but a good reason, such as suspicion of bias, must be advanced before one may challenge or question a juror for cause. A limited number of peremptory challenges are allowed for each matter. 'Peremptory' means that jurors may be challenged without any reason given by the party making the challenge. What then is a challenge for cause? This arises where counsel for the prosecution or defence perceive or know of any bias or other reason which could possibly influence a juror to take sides in the matter. For example, if one of the juror is a mechanic or loss adjustor, the defence attorney may not want to utilise the services of this juror in a trial of his client in a motor vehicle accident. Another example could be where a juror is a known homosexual, the defence Attorney would not want to utilise the services of this juror in a trial of his client for some homosexual offence.

Discharging a member of the panel of jurors

It is important to note that the discretion given to a judge, to decide whether prejudice that has occurred is sufficient to discharge a juror, is wide. In many cases a judge may decide that although an irregularity has occurred, it is not serious enough to warrant a discharge.

A jury member may be discharged for any of the following reasons:

- drunkenness
- illness
- lateness
- accepting bribes.

> **Activity 3.6**
> Check your Jury Act and write notes on:
> a persons excluded from jury duty
> b qualifications to serve as a juror

Discharge of the entire panel of jurors

The trial judge may discharge the whole jury panel under any one or a combination of the following circumstances:

- if inadmissible or prejudicial evidence is accidentally given
- if a juror is seen speaking to a relative of the other side and that juror has had enough opportunity to corrupt the whole panel.

Legal aid

The term legal aid usually refers to the legal help given to citizens who suffer financially and are not able to retain an attorney in private practice. Let us examine legal aid practices in the jurisdictions of Guyana and Trinidad and Tobago.

Legal aid in Guyana

The legal aid organisation in Guyana comprises a board of directors, a managing attorney, together with legal practitioners and their supporting staff. The legal aid organisation in Guyana is known as the Legal Aid Clinic and is partly funded by contributions made by private persons and organisations. At present the work of legal aid in Guyana is overwhelming since the clinic suffers from insufficient staff and other resources. There is also a move afoot to expand the ambit of legal aid in Guyana, that is, to have it extended to all courts in Guyana irrespective of the location and also to help more persons in the area of criminal law, where there is a great need for such assistance.

Prospective clients are interviewed by members of the support staff who decide whether the case will be taken or whether the person(s) satisfies the case to be legally aided. If the applicant for legal aid is admitted by the clinic then the applicant is required (where he or she can afford) to pay up to 75 per cent of the retainer charged by private practitioner plus consultation fees. The clinic then assigns one of its attorneys-at-law to the case.

Counsel appears in summary, hybrid, indictable and appeal court matters in both criminal and the civil jurisdictions of the court, as well as the land court. The Legal Aid Clinic in Guyana is financed by private international donor agencies and in part by the Guyana government, which disburses sums through the Ministry of Finance to pay expenses, for example, rent for office space and electricity.

The object of the clinic since its incorporation in 1994 as a charitable institution has been to enable persons with little or no means to bring or defend actions. Two parallel problems arise in legal aid, the question of whether the applicant is absolutely incapable of financing his claim or defence and the question whether the projected litigation is justifiable, in view of the expense to the public. If it is ever discovered that a client of the clinic has failed to make full and fair disclosure to the clinic that his or her financial situation has improved since the date of the interview, the clinic reserves the right to reassess the client for increased contribution or to refuse to continue to act on his or her behalf in the matter. The Law Schools have their own Legal Aid clinics. These are utilised as part of the training administered to Attorneys and which allows for the practical, hands on experience in dealing with clients.

Check on facilities for Legal Aid in your country. In addition to the Legal Aid clinics that are located at all Law Schools, there are two independent Legal Aid clinics in Jamaica, one in Kingston, the other in Montego Bay.

The means test

Detailed rules for assessment are laid down. The assessment of the wage earner's income is based on his or her wages for the preceding 12 months, less reasonable expense connected with his employment. From this is deducted full income tax for a year and any reasonable rent payable. Allowances are made for maintenance of children and a spouse.

Reasonable grounds

Assuming that the applicant is entitled to some legal aid the applicant must show that he or she has reasonable grounds for taking, defending or being a party to proceedings, that is to say, the applicant must be able to establish some prima facie case or defence. The decision as to whether he has done so is for the attorney-at-law to whom he or she has been assigned. As a part of its policy the clinic does not represent opposing sides in the same matter. The full financial burden of all orders of court at all levels is borne by the client.

Civil and criminal cases

A legal aid order may be made by a magistrates' court in summary cases, in appeals from the magistrates' court to the Full Court of the High Court may order that a defendant seek the assistance of legal aid. A judge of the Supreme Court of the High Court may also make such an order where a person appears before it for trial or sentence, or is committed to it for trial. The court must be satisfied that the interest of justice would be served by such an order, and in murder cases aid must be given.

The defendant or the litigant whether in person or represented by someone else must approach the clinic and submit to a means test, which takes the form of an interview. Until 1 December 2000, the clinic did not offer assistance for criminal matters or for geographical districts outside of Georgetown.

Legal aid in Trinidad and Tobago

While legal aid in Guyana is conducted and run by fully qualified legal practitioners who research cases and present them in court, the system of legal aid in Trinidad and Tobago is structured somewhat differently. The legal aid clinic in Trinidad and Tobago is annexed to the Law School and provides an integral part of the training to be undergone by students of the institution. Like Guyana, the legal aid clinic in Trinidad and Tobago is headed by a board of directors, one of whom is the head of the clinic.

The legal aid clinic in Trinidad does much work in the areas of criminal law and clients are represented through legal aid in all courts in Trinidad. Students of the Law School in Trinidad are assigned some of the cases and assist in matters of:

- interviewing prospective clients
- research of cases, and
- civil and criminal procedure.

Note 1: Fully trained attorneys-at-law represent clients in court. All of the work of the students is closely supervised by the attorneys-at-law to whom each student is assigned.

Note 2: Recipients of legal aid do not always seek the services of the clinic. There are many lawyers, both in Guyana and Trinidad and Tobago and in the wider Caribbean in private practice, who offer their services to persons who may come to them for help without being able to pay for it. This is referred to as pro bono.

Note 3: Some territories have enacted legislation to provide for legal aid, invariably establishing an institution to administer the system. Trinidad and Tobago has statutory provision establishing the clinic, under the Legal Aid and Advice Act, Cap. 7.

Activity 3.7

Read the scenario and answer the question that follows.

James has a dispute with his neighbour John. John erected a fence on James's land, claiming that the land is his. James wants to sue John to recover his property but cannot afford the expense.

Examine the provisions available, in a jurisdiction of your choice, which may assist James to access legal aid.

Feedback

In order to give a good answer, you should include the following elements in your discussion:

- the provision that obtains in your jurisdiction or in a jurisdiction of your choice, for the grant of legal aid
- method of assessment of means
- restrictions on the grant of aid.

Law reform and law revision

You already know that essential to the understanding of each new area of law is a definition of that area or concept. One definition of law reform is 'the making of fundamental changes in the law'. These changes may be made with respect to both statute and case law to reflect changing social values or new ways of doing things as a result of the development of science and technology. Therefore, when we speak of reform we refer to change with respect to improvement.

Today, it is the view of many Caribbean jurists that we live in a 'global village' and there is a strong need for Commonwealth Caribbean States to develop a jurisprudence to meet its particular values and other requirements. This is so, especially in the light of the colonial background of much of Commonwealth Caribbean law today, thus making law reform and law revision a very important aspect of the Commonwealth Caribbean legal system.

Nearly all Commonwealth Caribbean territories have enacted legislation dealing with law reform and revision. Some have established a permanent Commission for Law Reform on an ongoing basis. Examples of territories that have enacted legislation are:

- Guyana – Law Reform (Miscellaneous) Provisions Act, Cap. 6:02, as amended by Law Reform (Miscellaneous Act) No. 14 of 1988
- Grenada – Law Reform Act, Cap. 167
- Barbados – Law Reform (Miscellaneous Provisions) Act, Cap. 205
- Dominica – Law Reform (Miscellaneous Provisions) Act, Cap. 7:99

Activity 3.8

These Acts do not provide the full scope and limitations of law reform and revision. If you are a student from a territory other than any of those listed above, check your statute books to see if there is a Law Reform Act in your territory and write down its reference as indicated above.

In their text, English Legal Systems, Elliott and Quinn state:

> 'An effective legal system cannot stand still. Both procedures and the law must adapt to social change if they are to retain the respect of at least most of society, without which they cannot survive.' (page 84)

Judicial change

A good example of reformation in the Commonwealth Caribbean has been the repeal of the Bastardy Act. In Guyana, Act 12 of 1983, the Children Born Out Of Wedlock (Removal of Discrimination) Act repealed the Bastardy Act, wherein it is stated:

> 'the distinction which was previously made between children born out of wedlock and children born within wedlock is renewed, and attaches equal status to both.'

In addition, the Equal Rights Act (1990) Act 19, provides equal rights for women in relation to men. It is also of fundamental importance for you to remember that case law has the power to bring about reform. One recent example is the case of R v. R. In this landmark case, the House of Lords declared that a husband who has sexual intercourse with his wife without her consent may be guilty of rape. Before this decision, the law on rape within marriage was based on an assertion posited by an 18th-century jurist, Sir Matthew Hale, who said:

> 'by marrying a man, a woman consents to sexual intercourse with him, and may not retract consent.'

For further enlightment on this area of law you may wish to see the New Zealand case of Kaitamaki v. R [1985] AC 147. In light of the view posited by Hale, Lord Keith stated:

> 'The modern view of husband and wife as equal partners meant that a wife could no longer be considered to have given irrevocable consent to sex with her husband; the common law was capable of evolving to reflect such changes in society and it was the duty of the court to help it do so.'

Reform by Parliament

You will have already seen how it is the Parliament or legislature of any country that makes a law, so for a law to be changed to suit the needs of society, Parliament has a role to play. Reform by Parliament is done in four ways, as listed below:

1. choosing to repeal laws and/or obsolete laws
2. creation of new law(s) or adaptation of existing provisions to meet new needs
3. consolidation where new statutes are created when old ones are repealed
4. codification, whereby a particular area of law has developed over time to produce a large body of case law and statute, and a new statute may be created to combine all the rules (both substantive and procedural) in one place.

Note: Apart from the above, there are other forms of reformation; a good example is amendments made to various Acts and even the Constitution.

Activity 3.9

Check your statute books and the Constitution of your State or any State of your choice and identify sections and Articles that have been subject to reform.

Pressure sources

For a change to be made to a country's laws certain pressure sources must be at work. These sources may have an influence during the consultation stage of legislation. In the Caribbean changes may be brought about by pressure groups, political parties, public opinions and media pressure:

Pressure groups

These are members of society concerned with a particular area of law that they wish to have changed or amended. They may employ various tactics in executing their intention, for example, they may:

- lobby against Members of Parliament
- gain public support
- organise petitions; and
- exercise their right to protest.

An example of a pressure group in Guyana is the Mothers in Black, who wish to see a change made to the traffic laws of the country. This group was created in a bid to reduce the high incidence of road accidents.

Political parties

Elliott and Quinn state in English Legal Systems:

> 'some of the most high-profile legislation is that passed in order to implement the Government party's election manifesto, or its general ideology.'

Problems with law reform

It would be wise at this point to quote the adage, 'where there exists something good, something bad always follows'. In other words, even though law reform may be an ideal source of improvement to the laws of a particular jurisdiction there are certain drawbacks such as:

- lack of power
- political difficulties
- lack of ministerial involvement; and
- the influence of the legal profession.

Suggested further reading

Belle Antoine, Rose-Marie, Commonwealth Caribbean Law and Legal Systems, London, Cavendish, 1999, pages 217–26

Fiadjoe, Albert, Commonwealth Caribbean Public Law, London, Cavendish, 1999

End Test

Answer the following questions.

1 Give an outline of the functions of the following officers of the court:

   a the Chancellor of the Judiciary

   b the Chief Magistrate

c the Attorney General

d the Chief Justice; and

e the Marshal of the Supreme Court.

2 Jenel is a qualified as an attorney-at-law. Anthony, one of Jenel's many clients, gives her some money to execute a particular transaction on his behalf. However, Jenel converts the money to her own use.

Advise Jenel about the disciplinary measures that may be taken against her.

3 Jenel is the defence attorney in a matter. Midway through the trial, Jenel's client admits that he was indeed guilty of the commission of the act as charged.

Advise Jenel on the course of action which she may wish to take at this stage.

4 Critically evaluate the role of law reform bodies.

5 'If law reform was not created, then the old law would be a constant threat to society.' Discuss.

End Test Feedback

1 The answers to question 1 require you to recall and set down what was said about the members of the court system.

2 In your answer to 2 you should mention:

- whether she was in breach of the code of conduct
- what is the likely punishment she may receive
- where and by whom her matter will be heard, and the use of case law to give completion to your answer.

3 A good response to question 3 would require that you discuss Jenel's role and duty as defence counsel. For example, that defence counsel owes a duty to his client and none other. However, while every defendant or accused is entitled to a fair trial, Jenel as defence counsel may exercise her right not to proceed with the defence in these new circumstances.

If the trial is at a critical stage the judge has the right to refuse to accept Jenel's request to be excused from the case if the judge believes that great injustice would be done to the accused or defendant. If the judge accepts the request to be excused Jenel may request time within which to assist her client to secure the services of another lawyer. It is important to note that Jenel is not entitled to disclose to the judge her reason for declining to continue to act as defence counsel in the matter.

4 This question can apply not only to the official bodies such as the Law Reform Commission, but also to the informal ones such as pressure groups, and you need to discuss both types. It may be a good idea to divide your answer into official and unofficial law reform bodies, taking each in turn. You can describe how they operate and assess their effectiveness, pointing out any problems in the way they work. You are cautioned that what is needed is a critical account. In your conclusion you may wish to sum up the effect of these multiple bodies, saying whether, taken together, you feel they do adequate jobs in reforming the law in your territory.

5 A good response to this question requires that you first define what is meant by law reform. Next you should identify the main types of law: for example, statute, the common law and equity. Then, using at least one example in support of each, show how law reform has taken place to bring about changes and improvements in the law.

For example, as was stated above, statutory enactments and repeals have served to improve the lives of all Commonwealth Caribbean peoples. You were given examples taken from the Bastardy Act. With respect to the common law, please see the case referred to in the relevant section.

4 Principles of public law

General objectives

On completion of this chapter, you should:

- develop an understanding of the concept of public law
- develop the ability to apply legal principles of public law to situations of fact.

Specific objectives

You should be able to:

- identify the distinguishing features of the constitutions of Commonwealth Caribbean States
- outline the general principles of administrative law
- explain the major concepts of public law
- evaluate issues related to public law using legal principles.

Introduction

In chapter 3, we examined the court system from the standpoint of the people who carry out the day-to-day activities associated with the courts. We studied the role of members of the legal profession, including attorneys, judges and the Ombudsman. We investigated some of the main procedures used in the courts, such as the jury system, the provisions for legal aid, and for revision and reform of the law.

In chapter 4, we turn our attention to the principles of public law, which refers to two areas of law, namely, administrative and constitutional law. On completion of chapter 4, you will be able to identify the main characteristics of the constitutions of Commonwealth Caribbean States including provisions for the separation of powers aimed at guaranteeing the independence of the judiciary. You will be introduced to procedures for judicial review and to concepts such as the ultra vires doctrine and locus standi.

Content

- The constitutions of Commonwealth Caribbean Territories
  - organs of State
  - separation of powers
  - Rule of Law
  - supremacy of the constitution
- locus standi
- the ultra vires doctrine
- judicial review.

Commonwealth Caribbean constitutions

Organs of State

Later in this chapter, when we look at the separation of powers doctrine, we shall discuss the relationship between the three organs of the State, namely, the legislative, the executive and the judicial.

For now, you should examine the constitution of your own State and become familiar with the provisions relating to the three named organs. The constitution of reference in this section is that of Jamaica.

Parliament – the legislative organ

Section 34 of the Constitution of Jamaica establishes a Parliament for Jamaica. The Parliament is bi-cameral in nature; that is, having two chambers, namely an Upper House or Senate (section 35) and a Lower House or House of Representatives (section 36). The Senate comprises 21 members, 13 appointed by the Prime Minister and 8 appointed by the Leader of the Opposition.

In 1983 these provisions were tested when the People's National Party (PNP) did not contest 'snap elections' called by the Jamaica Labour Party (JLP) led government at the time. It meant that all 60 parliamentary seats were held by the JLP. The Prime Minister appointed eight 'independent' senators and the system worked well.

Eligibility to vote in parliamentary elections or to become a member of either House is restricted to citizens of Jamaica and citizens of the Commonwealth who have been resident on the island for at least 12 months at the date of registration. They must have attained at least the age of 18 years, are not under a sentence of death and are not 'certified to be insane or otherwise adjudged to be of unsound mind or detained as a criminal lunatic'.

A senator cannot be a member of the House of Representatives (section 40) and neither can any of the following persons be a member of either House:

- a foreigner
- a holder of public office, a member of the judiciary or of the defence force without dispensation of Parliament
- a person who, having a contractual relationship with the Government of Jamaica, does not declare that interest
- one against whom a sentence of death has been imposed.
- an undischarged bankrupt
- a person of unsound mind
- any person convicted of an electoral offence.

The Constitution also provides for the appointment of a Speaker and Deputy Speaker to the House of Representatives and of a President and a Deputy President to the Senate. The eligibility of the persons who may be so appointed is set out in sections 42 and 43.

The Clerk and Deputy Clerk of the Senate and the House of Representatives respectively are appointed under the Constitution. They are public officers, responsible for the day-to-day administration of the House of Parliament. Sections 48–62 of the Constitution prescribe the power and procedures of Parliament. Section 48 provides that:

> 'Subject to the provisions of this Constitution, Parliament may make laws for the peace, order and good government of Jamaica.'

This is an important provision, which opens the door for laws passed by Parliament and which are ultra vires the Constitution to be subject to judicial review.

The sections in this part also deal with the immunities and privileges of Parliament, alteration of the Constitution, submission of Bills to the Governor General for assent, procedures for voting, quorums of sittings and restrictions on the Senate with respect to money Bills and other Bills.

The summoning, prorogation or dissolution of Parliament is done by the Governor General acting on the advice of the Prime Minister.

Section 65 provides for the holding of general elections within three months of the dissolution of Parliament. One of the reasons for the dissolution of Parliament is where a vote of no confidence has been passed against the Government.

Sections 66–8 establishes constituencies and set out the procedures for delimitation of their boundaries.

The Executive

Executive authority

Jamaica is a Constitutional Monarchy. Section 68 of the Constitution provides that 'the executive authority of Jamaica is vested in Her Majesty'.

In a speech made at a party conference in September 2003, the Prime Minister of Jamaica reiterated his commitment that Jamaica would become a republic in the near future. Similar expressions have been made by the Government of Barbados. In 2002, the Oath of Allegiance in Jamaica was changed from words swearing allegiance to 'Her Majesty, her heirs and successors' to 'the people of Jamaica'.

The executive authority of the Queen is exercised on her behalf by the Governor General.

The Cabinet

The Cabinet consists of the Prime Minister and such other ministers as he recommends to the Governor General for appointment under section 70 of the Constitution. By virtue of section 69(2):

> 'The Cabinet shall be the principal instrument of policy and shall be charged with the general direction and control of the Government of Jamaica and shall be collectively responsible therefore to Parliament.'

The business of the Cabinet is the responsibility of the Secretary of the Cabinet who is a public officer (section 92).

The Prime Minister

The appointment of the Prime Minister is done by the Governor General. Under section 70 it provides that the appointment is made, when the Governor General 'acting in his discretion, shall appoint the member of the House of Representatives who, in his judgment, is best able to command the confidence of a majority of the members of that House ...'. The Governor General may revoke the Prime Minister's appointment (section 71(1)). This revocation is one of the ways by which a Prime Minister's office becomes vacant. Others include resignation and dissolution of Parliament. A Minister's post becomes vacant for similar reasons and includes his non-appointment by the Prime Minister.

There has been no instance of a Governor General revoking the appointment of a Prime Minister in the Commonwealth Caribbean. It has occurred once, in Australia. No doubt, such an event would create a constitutional crisis.

Section 76 provides that the Prime Minister 'shall keep the Governor General fully informed concerning the general conduct of the government of Jamaica and shall furnish the Governor General with information as he may request with respect to any particular matter relating to the government of Jamaica'. This provision represents the codification of what is a convention in the relationship between the Queen and the British Prime Minister who holds regular meetings with Her Majesty, although the previous weekly meetings have been reduced to monthly meetings.

Parliamentary Secretaries and Attorney General

Sections 78 and 79 of the Constitution provide for the appointments of Parliamentary Secretaries and the Attorney General, respectively.

Parliamentary Secretaries are junior ministers who are 'to assist Ministers in the discharge of their functions'. The Attorney General is 'the principal legal adviser' to the Government and may, or may not, be a member of the Cabinet. These positions are appointed by the Governor General on the advice of the Prime Minister.

The Leader of the Opposition

The Leader of the Opposition is appointed by the Governor General who, in exercising his discretion, appoints:

> '... the member of the House of Representatives who, in his judgment, is best able to command the support of a majority of those members who do not support the Government, or, if there is no such person, the member of that House who, in his judgment commands the support of the largest single group of such members who are prepared to support one leader.' (section 80(1))

The Leader of the Opposition ceases to hold that office in the same ways as the Prime Minister and Ministers (see above). In addition, where in the judgment of the Governor General the Leader of the Opposition is 'no longer able to command the support' of those members of the House of Representatives who do not support the Government, he shall revoke the appointment.

If there is a vacancy in the office of Leader of the Opposition, either because 'no person is both qualified in accordance with this Constitution for, and willing to accept, appointment to that office', in any matter which requires that consultations be made with the Leader of the Opposition, the Governor General 'shall act in accordance with the advice of the Prime Minister'.

The Privy Council

Do not confuse this body with the Judicial Committee of the Privy Council, which advises Her Majesty in Council and which sits as a court.

Here the Privy Council means the body chaired by the Governor General and which, among its functions, makes recommendations to the Governor General on the exercise of the prerogative of mercy. Section 91 provides that where a person who has been sentenced to death, the Governor General may grant him a pardon on the recommendation of the Privy Council or in his discretion, if that recommendation is not obtainable in a timely manner. Section 90 covers situations when the Governor General may exercise the prerogative of mercy. These include substitution of a lesser penalty, a full or conditional pardon and substitution of a less severe punishment.

The Privy Council consists of six persons appointed by the Governor General after consultation with the Prime Minister. Section 82(2) provides that at least two of these persons should either hold or have held public office.

Permanent Secretaries

The Cabinet Secretary is a public officer who has charge of the business of the Cabinet. The Cabinet Secretary conveys the Cabinet's decisions.

Permanent Secretaries are the senior officers who supervise departments or ministries. The Minister under whose responsibility the particular portfolio falls exercises 'general direction and control' (section 93). The Permanent Secretary in the Ministry of Finance is the Financial Secretary.

The Director of Public Prosecutions

The office of the Director of Public Prosecutions is established under section 94 and is a public office. The officer appointed must be 'qualified for appointment as a Judge of the Supreme Court'. This means that he must have at least 10 years' experience at the Bar. The Director of Public Prosecutions has power:

- to institute criminal proceedings in any court, other than a court martial
- to take over any criminal proceedings instituted by any person or authority
- to discontinue any proceedings instituted or undertaken by him, at any stage, prior to judgment.

The Director of Public Prosecutions may exercise his powers 'in person or through other persons acting under and in accordance with his general or special instructions'.

Appointment to the office of Director of Public Prosecutions is made by the Governor General who may revoke the appointment acting on the advice of the Public Service Commission (section 96(3)). He enjoys security of tenure and may hold office until he attains the age of 60 years, or where he receives an extension of time, he may continue until the age of 65 years. A decision made by him will not be invalid because he had passed the age. The Director of Public Prosecution may, of course, resign his post. Otherwise, besides retirement and resignation, his security of tenure is contained in section 96(4):

> 'The Director of Public Prosecutions may be removed from office only for inability to discharge the functions of his office (whether arising from infirmity of body or mind or any other cause) or for misbehaviour and shall not be so removed except in accordance with the provisions of this section.'

The provisions referred to are to the effect that the Governor General shall appoint a tribunal to hear the cause relating to the removal of the Director of Public Prosecutions, before any such removal is done. The members of the Tribunal are to be appointed by the Governor General on the advice of the Prime Minister and must be persons who hold or have held 'office as a judge having unlimited jurisdiction in civil and criminal matters in some part of the Commonwealth or a court having jurisdiction in appeals from any such court'.

During the hearing by the tribunal of any matter relating to the suitability of the Director of Public Prosecutions, he may be suspended from performing his duties by the Governor General on the advice of the Prime Minister. The suspension may be revoked at any time and will cease to have effect if the tribunal recommends that he should not be removed (section 96(8)). We now move on to the third organ of government, the judiciary.

Role and Function of the DPP as a public officer

In recent times. in some of our jurisdictions, the role and function of the Director of Public Prosecutions have come into sharp focus through discussions in the media. Should the DPP appear before a Parliamentary Committee? Should the DPP's decision to proceed or not to proceed with a prosecution be influenced by any other constituted authority besides that of the DPP? Would a reference from such an authority fetter or prejudice the DPP in exercising his/her own discretion in determining when to proceed? What, if any, are the limits?

Throughout the Commonwealth Caribbean region, there have been examples of Directors of Public Prosecutions who have ensured the prosecution of politicians, police officers and other public officers fearlessly, consistent with the powers vested in them under the several Constitutions.

On the matter of the exercise of the DPP's discretion in prosecuting cases, there are two very interesting Jamaican cases you are to consider.

Lloyd Brooks v DPP (1994)

In this case, a preliminary enquiry was held before a Resident Magistrate against the accused, a medical practitioner. The Magistrate found that there was no sufficient basis for the matter to go before the Circuit Court for trial. The DPP decided that the matter should go to trial and sought to exercise his power to have this done. The accused appealed and his appeal was dismissed by the Privy Council. Among the findings by the Board were the following which turn directly on the powers of the DPP:

1 Under the Criminal Justice Administration Act, the DPP may prefer an indictment without seeking the direction of a judge. The DPP may also choose to seek a judge's consent or discretion.
2 The DPP's powers under section 94 of the Constitution are not subject to the control or power of any other person or authority. This, of course, points to the DPP's protection from political interference or influence.
3 The DPP is not a part of government nor is he a government official. In bringing proceedings, the DPP is subject only to the court and where proceedings are brought without seeking the consent or direction of a judge, ultimately for the matter to be heard, the court must consent.

Leonie Marshall v DPP (PC) (2006)

In this case, Ms Marshall, mother of deceased Patrick Genius, brought an application for judicial review in a case where the DPP had not given reasons for his decision not to prosecute police who hat shot and killed Mr. Genius in circumstances which became controversial and attracted great public interest.

The Jamaican Court denied Ms Marshall's application and she was given leave by the Court of Appeal to appeal to the Privy Council. The Privy Council dismissed her appeal and found, inter alia:

- judicial review of the DPP's exercise of discretion is an exceptional remedy which is to be exercised sparingly.
- as they are experienced prosecutors, the Court will attach weight to the decisions of the office of the DPP not to prosecute if they think there is little likelihood of success (In this case, their Lordships opined that self defence could very well succeed).

The review of decisions of the DPP in exercising discretion to prosecute, or not, may arise where it appears that

1 The DPP has acted outside of the Constitutional powers vested in him/her.
2 The DPP has acted contrary to settled policy
3 The decision was perverse, unreasonable or unusual and inconsistent with experienced or sound prosecutorial principles.

On the matter of giving reasons for a decision by the DPP, the Board made no ruling on the matter, save to say that reasons could be helpful.

You may also read the case of Janice Allen which challenged the DPP's decision not to re-open the prosecution of police officers who were charged with the killing of the teenage girl. You may also refer to the recent cases in Trinidad and Tobago where the DPP exercised discretion by issuing notices of discontinuance against over 200 persons who had been arrested and charged under the Anti-Gang Act. The DPP made the following statement in a speech at the Hugh Wooding Law School: "It is imperative to mount credible and reliable cases for gang related crimes."

The judiciary or judicature

Judges of the Supreme Court and of the Court of Appeal are appointed under sections 97–109 of the Constitution.

The Supreme Court is headed by the Chief Justice who, along with the Senior Puisne (pronounced 'puny') Judge and the other Puisne Judges, make up the judges of the court. The Chief Justice is appointed by the Governor General on the advice of the Prime Minister. Puisne Judges are appointed by the Governor General on the advice of the Judicial Service Commission; of which the Chief Justice is Chairman (section 111(2)).

Judges of the Supreme Court shall hold office until the age of 65 years. In the event of existing vacancies in the office of Puisne Judges, acting Puisne Judges may be appointed and during the period of acting they have the same powers as any Puisne Judge.

Judges may cease to perform their functions for the following reasons:

- Through retirement or resignation. (As in the case of the Director of Public Prosecutions, no decision taken by a Judge shall be invalid because he has attained the age of retirement.) A Judge may be granted an extension of time to 67 years, the extension being granted by the Governor General on the recommendation of the Prime Minister after consultation with the Leader of the Opposition.
- For inability to discharge the functions of his office ('whether arising from infirmity of body or mind or any other cause') or for misbehaviour.

There is a provision that the Governor General shall remove a Judge of the Supreme Court after the issue is referred by Her Majesty to the Judicial Committee of the Privy Council, which advises whether or not the Judge is to be removed. The issue of such removal is made to the Governor General by the Prime Minister in the case of the Chief Justice. In the case of Puisne Judges, the Chief Justice makes the recommendation after consultation with the Prime Minister.

Where a recommendation for the removal of a Judge is made to the Governor General, the Governor General shall appoint a tribunal on the advice of the Prime Minister, in the case of the Chief Justice or, on the advice of the Chief Justice, in the case of Puisne Judges. Members of the tribunal shall comprise persons who hold or have held judicial office in Jamaica or other Commonwealth country.

You should note that the qualifications of the tribunal are similar to those of the tribunal that is to be appointed to hear matters relating to the discipline of the Director of Public Prosecutions.

The tribunal is empowered to 'enquire into the matter and report on the facts thereof ' to the Governor General and recommends to him whether he should request a hearing by the Judicial Committee of the Privy Council.

During the enquiry by the tribunal, the Governor General may suspend the judge (where it is the Chief Justice, on the advice of the Prime Minister, or on the advice of the Chief Justice in the case of other judges). The suspension may be rescinded at any time, dependent on the outcome of the enquiry by the tribunal or the decision of the Judicial Committee.

The Court of Appeal

The Court of Appeal is established under section 103 and, like the Supreme Court 'shall have such jurisdiction and powers as may be conferred upon it by this Constitution or any other law'.

The Court of Appeal comprises the following:

- The President who is responsible for the arrangement of the Court's work and who presides at any sitting of which he is a part.
- The Chief Justice in his capacity as head of the judiciary. The Chief Justice 'shall not sit in the Court of Appeal unless there are at least four other judges sitting or unless he has been invited so to sit by the President of the Court'.
- Three other Judges.
- Such number of Judges, if any, prescribed by Parliament.

As in the case of the Supreme Court, acting Judges of Appeal may be appointed. These acting Judges usually come from the Supreme Court. (The practice has been for the Director of Public Prosecutions to be appointed to the Court of Appeal, where he enters the judiciary.)

The age limits and provisions for removal of Judges of the Court of Appeal are the same as for Judges of the Supreme Court.

Appeals to Her Majesty in Council

Appeals to the Judicial Committee of the Privy Council, referred to in the Constitution as appeals 'to Her Majesty in Council' are provided for in section 110. This is a provision that is under close scrutiny as discussions abound about the Caribbean Court of Justice and whether it is time for Commonwealth Caribbean States to abandon appeals to the Judicial Committee. You should pay close attention to these discussions and decisions. The headquarters of the Caribbean Court of Justice are located in Port of Spain.

Appeals lie to Her Majesty in Council 'as of right' in civil matters where the value claimed is one thousand dollars or more, in dissolution or nullity of marriage matters, civil or criminal matters relating to the interpretation of the Constitution or any other case prescribed by Parliament.

Leave to appeal to the Judicial Committee may be granted by the Court of Appeal in civil proceedings and 'where in the opinion of the Court of Appeal the question involved in the appeal is one that, by reason of its great general or public importance or otherwise', the court feels that a matter should be referred.

Special leave may be granted by Her Majesty in Council for appeals from the Court of Appeal in any civil or criminal matter.

We now turn to the Judicial Service Commission, which we shall examine briefly.

The Judicial Service Commission

Sections 111–13 establish the Judicial Service Commission and set out its composition. The Commission comprises the Chief Justice, who is the chairman, the President of the Court of Appeal and the Chairman of the Public Service Commission. In addition, there are three other members, the 'appointed members'.

Appointment of the members to the Commission is made by the Governor General acting on the recommendation of the Prime Minister after consultation with the Leader of the Opposition. Of the three appointees:

- one should hold or have held judicial office in Jamaica or other Commonwealth jurisdiction
- two should be from a list of six persons, none of whom is an attorney-at-law in active practice, submitted by the General Legal Council.

None of the 'appointed members' are to be holders of any public office, but they may be members of the Public Service Commission or the Police Service Commission. The appointed members hold office for three years and may be removed from office on the ground of illness or for misbehaviour. Where the appointed member is a Puisne Judge or a Judge of Appeal, his position is fixed until his office as a judge ceases for any reason.

Judges are appointed by the Governor General acting on the advice of the Judicial Service Commission'. The Commission also advises the Governor General on removal and disciplinary control of the judiciary. Appointments of Resident Magistrates, Judge of the Traffic Court, Registrars of the Supreme Court and of the Court of Appeal are also under the jurisdiction of the Commission. Before any disciplinary action or the removal of any judge or judicial officer is effected by the Governor General, the judge or officer may apply for his case to be referred to the Privy Council.

The organs: harmony at work?

You will have seen from the foregoing that each organ of the State is autonomous in that it has prescribed spheres of operation under the Constitution. Thus, one speaks of the independence of the judiciary the security of tenure of judges and the sovereignty of Parliament. In the case of judges, the methods for removal of a judge are stringent, but power rests in the Governor General to revoke the appointment of a judge once the constitutional provisions for doing so have been exhausted. The independence, therefore, is not without restraint and the level of inter-dependence is high. Think about those situations that require the advice of the Prime Minister either solely, or after conferring with the Leader of the Opposition. There is some harmony, provided each operates within the Constitution. The same can be said in reference to sovereignty of Parliament, as it is subject to judicial review when laws are made that may be inconsistent with the Constitution.

See, for example, such cases as Maharaj v. Attorney General of Trinidad of Tobago (No. 2) [1979] AC 385 and Hinds v. R [1977] AC 195, among others. Consider the relationship between the organs within the context of the separation of powers, judicial review and the Rule of Law, and you might even conclude that there is some discord at times.

Activity 4.1

Critical analysis

This activity is intended to assist you in the development of your critical analysis of issues.

You would be expected to discuss whether or not the existence of a written constitution is inconsistent with conventions. Do conventions foster uncertainty and arbitrariness? What if, for example, the Governor General/President appoints as Prime Minister someone he thinks enjoys the support of the majority, but that is not the wish of the legislators? Even though this is a 'codified convention', could the Governor General's/President's discretion be challenged?

Much of the relationship between the organs of the State is governed by constitutional conventions. Professor Fiadjoe's text Commonwealth Caribbean Public Law (1999) deals with the conventions of the constitution at pages 167–73. You should note carefully the points he makes concerning the fact that in the Caribbean there are written constitutions while, in the UK, with its unwritten constitution, conventions play a major role. You will observe that Caribbean constitutions have codified what are well-recognised conventions in the UK. These include the political leader appointed by Her Majesty to be Prime Minister, and the constitutional requirements for the Governor General or President, as the case may be, in the appointment of a Prime Minister.

Conventions, you will note, are well-recognised constitutional practices, and even with our written constitutions, we do have some 'non-codified conventions'. You should make a list of the codified and non-codified conventions.

Question: Do you think conventions are a help or hindrance to the administrative process? Give reasons for your answer. In your attempt to answer this question, consider Professor Carnegie's view, referred to in Fiadjoe's text at page 157, that it is unfortunate that 'conventions of the constitution did not die the death that might be expected given the adoption of a written constitution'.

Activity 4.2

Revision application

This exercise will enable you to have a good grasp of the most essential features of the three organs of the State, as your knowledge is increased through revision.

Here's the first question, for which you are provided with the answer.

It is (a) true/(b) not true that a citizen of the Commonwealth who has lived in Jamaica for a period of 12 months prior to the enumeration of voters can be enumerated to vote in a local or general election.

Answer: (a) True

Task

Now read the following statements and answer whether each is (a) True, (b) Not true. Delete the incorrect answer.

1 It is (a) True/(b) Not true that the Leader of the Opposition recommends to the Governor General for appointment to the Senate 8 of the 21 members of that Chamber.

Answer: (a) True; (b) Not true

2 It is (a) True/(b) Not true that the non-discriminatory nature of the Constitutions enables all persons to have the right to participate in the affairs of the State, so that a person of unsound mind or an undischarged bankrupt can be a member of the Houses of Parliament.

Answer: (a) True; (b) Not true

3 It is (a) True/(b) Not true that Jamaica is no longer a constitutional monarchy.

Answer: (a) True; (b) Not true

4 It is (a) True/(b) Not true that the head of the judiciary is the President of the Court of Appeal.

Answer: (a) True; (b) Not true

5 It is (a) True/(b) Not true that the Chief Justice is not a member of the Court of Appeal.

Answer: (a) True; (b) Not true

6 It is (a) True/(b) Not true that only after a finding by the Judicial Committee of the Privy Council will the Governor General revoke a judge's appointment.

Answer: (a) True; (b) Not true

7 It is (a) True/(b) Not true that the office of Director of Public Prosecutions is one of the organs of the state.

Answer: (a) True; (b) Not true

8 It is (a) True/(b) Not true that the Governor General has the power to appoint any member of the House of Representatives to be the Prime Minister.

Answer: (a) True; (b) Not true

9 It is (a) True/(b) Not true that the Governor General also has the power to appoint a member of either House to be the Leader of the Opposition.

Answer: (a) True; (b) Not true

10 It is (a) True/(b) Not true that the Privy Council performs different functions from the Judicial Committee of the Privy Council.

Answer: (a) True; (b) Not true

Feedback

You should have deleted the following incorrect answers:

1 (b);	2 (b);	3 (b);	4 (b);	5 (b);
6 (a);	7 (b);	8 (b);	9 (b);	10 (a).

How did you fare? If you missed any of these, check your facts again.

Separation of powers

Historical background

Today we take it for granted that there are three organs of government, namely, the executive, the legislative and the judicial. These divisions were conceived by the Greek philosopher, Aristotle, who lived in the 3rd century bc. He called them the deliberative, the magistracy and the judicial.

The 17th-century English philosopher, Locke, also divided the system of government into three functions, prioritising each function respectively, as legislation, executive and 'federative'.

The descriptions as we know them are attributed to the 18th-century French philosopher, Montesquieu. His famous words on the fundamental nature of the doctrine in the preservation of the Rule of Law are set out below:

> 'Political liberty is to be found only when there is no abuse of power. But constant experience shows us that every man invested with power is liable to abuse it, and to carry his authority as far as it will go ... To prevent this abuse, it is necessary from the nature of things that one power should be a check on another ... There would be an end to everything if the same person or body ... were to exercise all three powers.'
>
> L'Esprit de Lois, Chap. IX, pages 3–6

The learned writers O. Hood Phillips and P. Jackson, in Constitutional and Administrative Law (Sweet & Maxwell, 1987) express the view that while Montesquieu's opinion is a laudatory one, the purpose of which is designed to prevent tyrannical or authoritarian rule, if taken to its extreme, it would be impractical. According to them (at page 6):

> 'A complete separation of powers, in the sense of a distribution of three functions of government among three independent sets of organs, with no overlapping or co-ordination, would (even if theoretically possible) bring government to a standstill.'

Hood Phillips and Jackson cite a comment from another 18th-century English legal writer, Blackstone, who said that 'wheresoever these two powers are united together there can be no liberty'.

The two powers to which he referred are the making and the enforcing of laws.The United States Constitution is regarded as that which best enunciates the doctrine of separation of powers. The three organs of government, while operating separately, are connected by a system of checks and balances. For example, the US President may veto a decision taken by Congress, but his veto may be over-ridden by a two-thirds vote of the House and Senate. Each cabinet or judicial appointment the President wishes to make must be confirmed by the Senate and in recent times there have been some interesting hearings after which appointees are rejected. The process is a remarkable one.

Separation of powers and Commonwealth Caribbean Constitutions

The fact that our written constitutions reflect to some extent the ethos and principles of the unwritten British constitution means that if the doctrine of separation of powers is applicable in Britain, then we should find it in our Caribbean constitutions as well. While our scholars and judges are agreed that we do have the doctrine in our legal system, the extent to which it applies has been viewed differently. Professor Fiadjoe indicates that the leading case of Hinds v. R [1977] AC 195, [1976] 2 WLR 366, [1976] 1 All ER 353 (P.C.), (1975) 24 WLR 326 has undoubtedly put the question of application to rest. His view on the extent of that application is that:

> 'What is clear is that the Caribbean constitutions adopt a halfway house between the doctrine as understood in the constitutional law of the USA and as applied to the British Constitution. Most commentators would agree that, in the UK, separation of powers means little more than an independent judiciary, there being no separation of powers strictly speaking between executive and the legislative.'
>
> Fiadjoe, Commonwealth Caribbean Public Law, (1999) page 158

Fiadjoe refers to an article by the distinguished scholar and former Chancellor of the University of the West Indies, Sir Allen Lewis, who wrote that the doctrine of separation of powers as it applies in the United States of America is unsuited to our legal system. Sir Allen suggested that:

> 'For practical purposes, it is essential, if developing countries are to be moved forward quickly, that there be the utmost trust and cooperation between the legislature and the executive and the administration to facilitate implementation of the government's economic and social policies.'
>
> Quoted in Fiadjoe at page 160

One agrees wholeheartedly with Sir Allen and might add that what he says must indeed be so, and is it not more consistent with our temperament as a people?

The cooperation that must exist between the three arms of government is intrinsic to the Rule of Law. Again, we are indebted to Professor Fiadjoe who has given us the reference to the insightful judgment of Saunders J in the High Court of Anguilla, where his lordship said, in part, on the efficacy of the doctrine and the need for 'a certain comity' between the three branches:

> 'For our democracy to operate effectively, it has been said that a certain comity should exist between the three branches. Each should respect the role and function of the other. The court is subject to and must enforce laws passed by Parliament that are intra vires the Constitution. The executive should respect and obey the decisions and accept the intimations of the court. If this comity does not exist, then the wheels of democracy would not turn smoothly. A jarring and dangerous note will resonate from them.'
>
> Saunders J, in Benjamin et al v. Minister of Information et al, unreported case decided in 1998, Fiadjoe at page 161

The views expressed by his lordship underscore the value of the doctrine of separation of powers to the Rule of Law, enshrined in our constitutions by the written provisions and the conventions that are intrinsic to them. We see this working well in the judgment of Floissac CJ in the OECS Court of Appeal decision of J Astaphan & Co. [1970] Ltd. V. The Comptroller of Customs and AG of Dominica, the facts of which are given at pages 162–5 of Fiadjoe. You should read those pages carefully and note that Floissac CJ relied on two Privy Council decisions from the region, namely the well-known Hinds v. R, as well as John v. DPP [1985] 32 WLR 230. We will look at these two very important decisions next, and thereafter, rest our case!

Hinds v. R [1977] AC 195, [1976] 2 WIR 366, [1975] 24 WIR 326, [1976] 1 All ER 353, PC

In 1974 the Parliament of Jamaica passed the Gun Court Act 1974 under which a Gun Court was established to deal specifically with gun crimes. The court was to sit in three divisions: a Resident Magistrate's Court Division, comprising a Resident Magistrate; a Circuit Court Division comprising a Supreme Court Judge; and a Full Court Division, comprising three Resident Magistrates. The Act provided that all trials would be held in camera, and that for certain offences the Gun Court should impose a mandatory sentence of detention at hard labour. It also provided that the Full Court Division had jurisdiction over the whole island, a jurisdiction which, prior to the Act, was exercisable by a Circuit Court Judge, and was what maintained at the time the Constitution came into force. A Review Board was also set up to advise the Governor General on mandatory sentences. Only one member of the Board was a member of the judiciary.

The defendants were convicted in the Resident Magistrate's Division and were given mandatory sentences of detention at the Governor General's pleasure. They appealed to the Court of Appeal against their convictions and sentences on the grounds, inter alia, that the Gun Court Act was in conflict with the Constitution of Jamaica and, therefore, void. It was held by the Judicial Committee of the Privy Council as follows:

- The provisions of the Act extending the geographical boundaries through the Circuit Court and Resident Magistrate's Court Divisions were not contrary to the Constitution.
- The presumption regarding in camera trials could have been rebutted by evidence of bad faith by Parliament but the appellants had adduced no such evidence.
- The principle of separation of powers was implicit in the Constitution and Parliament had no power to transfer from the judiciary to the Review Board established under the Act, the Board not being comprised of a majority of persons who were qualified to exercise judicial powers and the provision establishing the Board was therefore contrary to the Constitution was null and void and the sentences passed under it were unlawful.
- The inconsistent provisions of the Act would be severed and the valid provisions could subsist.

The appeals against conviction were dismissed, sentencing being remitted to the Court of Appeal.

The Separation of Powers doctrine is alive and well as the recent case of Adrian Nation and Kerreen Wright v Director of Public Prosecution and Attorney General of Jamaica (Supreme Court, unreported, July 2011) has demonstrated.

In 2000 Jamaica's Bail Act came into force. This Act, described by Marsh J as 'revolutionary' provided that every person who is charged with a criminal offence was "entitled to be granted bail". In July 2010, Government responded to the need to reduce violent crimes by introducing sic pieces of legislations, referred to as "the Anti-Crime Bills", among them being The Bail Amendment Act, 2010 and The Bail (Interim Provisions for Specified Offences) Act, 2010.

In Essence, these "Anti-Crime Bills" sought to implement more draconian measures, including restrictions on the admissibility of accused persons to bail. The burden of proof in such matters was shifted from the prosecution to the accused. The period in which an accused person could be held without being admitted to bail was extended from twenty four hours to a minimum of seven days and a maximum of fourteen days when a person in custody should be brought to court. The amendments provided for up to 60 days before the right to bail became "absolute" in violation of Section 22 of the Bail Act which provided for the twenty four hours within which an accused person who is arrested or charged should be brought before the court to have his bail considered. A right of appeal was granted to the prosecution against an order for bail to an accused person.

The claimants, Nation and Wright had both been arrested and charged for murder. Their applications for bail before a Resident magistrate were refused on more than one occasion, the amendment to the Bail Act being advanced as the reason for the Magistrate's position. Eventually bail was offered to them but they brought this action before the Full Court on the grounds that their constitutional rights had been impugned.

Their Lordships, Justices Marsh, Brooks and Pusey heard their application in which the Director of Public Prosecutions and the Attorney General were the respondents.

Both defendants vigorously opposed the application, and in doing so cited numerous authorities as well as public interest and Parliament's power to pass laws for the "peace, order and good government" of the nation.

Section 3 of the Bail Act 2000 provided that every person is entitled to bail by a court Justice of the Peace or a police officer. A person charged with an offence should not be held in custody for more than twenty four hours without the question of bail being considered. Any person charged with murder, treason or treason felony may only be granted bail by a Resident Magistrate or a judge (judge of the Supreme Court).

Section 4 (4) of the Bail Act 2000 sets out those circumstances and the considerations to be taken into account, which may preclude an accused person from being granted bail. These include those circumstances where the Court, a Justice of the Peace or police officer "is satisfied that there are substantial grounds for believing that the defendant, if released on bail would –

- **i** fail to surrender to custody
- **ii** commit an offence while on bail
- **iii** interfere with witnesses or otherwise obstruct the course of justice, whether in relation to himself or any other person..."

There are several other considerations, but they need not detain us here.

Marsh J posited the main issue to be determined as follows:

"If the effect of the Amending Acts was to remove from the person charged with an offence or detained, an entitlement to bail, then the question which falls to be answered is whether Parliament was acting in compliance with authority provided it by the Constitution when these Acts were passed". (para 33)

Their Lordships thoroughly examined cases form the Commonwealth Caribbean as well as from other jurisdictions with "Westminster Model" and common law backgrounds. They were unanimous in finding that the proposed amendment were encroaching upon the function of the judiciary and were in violation of the Constitution. One such case they cited is Benjamin et al v Ministry of Information et al, an unreported case from Anguilla. Heavy reliance was also placed on the very significant case, Hinds v R, with which you are no doubt familiar. Marsh J said, at paragraph 63 of Nation and Wright:

"(The Acts) could not properly amend the actions of the Constitution which they were intended to. The situation is not ameliorated by the fact that the provision is interim and set to last for only a year. It still has the effect, while it is in existence of trespassing on what is the "domain of the judiciary".

Brooks J found the amendments to be as offensive when he said that Section 3 of the Bail (Amendment) Act which provided that an accused should remain in custody until the outcome of any appeal from the prosecution, when he said:

"I find that this provision also offends the principle of separation of powers. It is the Court which should decide, if the prosecution indicates an intention to appeal, whether it will order the defendant to remain in custody pending the appeal. That authority may not be removed by ordinary legislation." (para 149)

Pusey J spoke emphatically when he said at para 182 "The responsibility of safeguarding the fundamental rights granted under Jamaican Constitution resides in the independent judiciary."

Their Lordships were therefore unanimous in finding the offending provisions to be unconstitutional and therefore void.

Rule of Law and the role of the police

What is the Rule of Law?

The historical foundation of the Rule of Law is of some antiquity and is closely aligned with fundamental rights. Aristotle saw the concept as fundamental to good government and declared in his Politics that 'the Rule of Law is preferable to that of any individual'. Both the American Declaration of Independence (1776) and the Declaration of the Rights of Man, which prefaced the French Constitution (1791), had been influenced by 'Enlightenment' philosophy propounded by such writers as John Locke. The American Declaration of Independence declares that all men are created equal and that life, liberty and the pursuit of happiness are among their inalienable rights. Based on the principles of 'freedom, fraternity and equality', which influenced the French Revolution, it was understandable that the French post-Revolution Constitution would seek to uphold the Rule of Law.

The Universal Declaration of Human Rights, which was adopted by the General Assembly of the United Nations in 1948 and the European

Convention for the Protection of Human Rights, which came into force in 1953, are modern pronouncements on the Rule of Law and which have binding effect on their signatories. The Universal Declaration of Human Rights makes reference to 'the Rule of Law' and in 1959 the International Commission of Jurists meeting in New Delhi produced the Declaration of Delhi, which sought to define the 'Rule of Law'. The Declaration of Delhi identified four fundamentals of the 'Rule of Law' as follows:

1 The legislature, whose responsibility is to ensure that citizens enjoy good government, free from arbitrary and oppressive laws and ensuring that the principles of the Conventions on Human Rights are upheld.
2 The executive, whose responsibility is to ensure that those to whom functions are delegated are subject to independent judicial review and that aggrieved citizens have a remedy against the state or government.
3 The criminal process, which is to ensure that accused persons are subject to a fair trial, grounded in a presumption of innocence and are guaranteed representation in a predictable legal process.
4 The judiciary and the legal profession, the former to be independent and the latter to be organised and autonomous.

Dicey and the Rule of Law

The most famous proponent of the concept of the Rule of Law was Professor Dicey, who first mentioned it in his book, The Law and the Constitution, in 1885. Dicey's views have been subject to much criticism, especially that they are too absolute, but the principles behind them have survived, as we shall see. In essence, Dicey formulated three principles, as follows:

> 'No man is punishable or can be lawfully made to suffer in body or goods except for a distinct breach of law established in the ordinary legal manner before the ordinary Courts of the land ...'
>
> '... no man is above the law ... whatever his rank or condition [he] is subject to the ordinary law of the realm and amenable to the jurisdiction of the ordinary tribunals.'
>
> 'The general principles of our constitution ... are with us the result of judicial decisions determining the rights of private persons in particular cases brought before the Courts ...'

Extracted from Dicey, The Law and the Constitution, 10th ed., pages 188–203

On the last of the Dicey's three points, you should note that he was referring to an unwritten British Constitution. We will now examine how the Rule of Law is embodied in our written constitutions.

The Rule of Law in Commonwealth Caribbean constitutions

We start with Professor Fiadjoe's laudable submission on how the Rule of Law functions in our constitutions:

> 'In West Indian public law, it is submitted that the Rule of Law has come to mean the exercise of State power according to law and the subjugation of state power to the constitution. The phrase "the Rule of Law" is thus a useful compendium to define the bundle of citizens' rights or legitimate expectations to hold the State accountable for its actions.'

Commonwealth Caribbean Public Law, 1999, pages 121–2

The emphasis, you should note, is on accountability. Yes, indeed, accountability of those who are vested with powers of decision making, thus ensuring that even the humblest among us is protected by the law, which is what constitutes the Rule of Law. As you progress in your study of the fundamental rights provisions and how judicial review of administrative action ensures the protection of these rights, it will certainly lead you to conclude, as Professor Fiadjoe has, that accountability is essential in ensuring the Rule of Law. Let us now examine some cases demonstrating this position.

How the Rule of Law ensures accountability

You will have gleaned from earlier comments on the various thinkers and the tenets of the various human rights conventions that an underlying feature of the Rule of Law is that no one is above the law. This principle is one you will also appreciate as important to judicial review when you examine that subject later. It might be said that the concept of the Rule of Law and judicial review of administrative action are twins in the maintenance of right and justice in society.

There is a wide body of cases illustrating the fact that the Rule of Law is alive and well in our jurisdictions. You are already familiar with the case of Hinds so we will not repeat it here, but you should ensure that you understand it well. See below for details of Collymore, which also demonstrates the application of the Rule of Law.

Executive authority and the Rule of Law

In his text, Professor Fiadjoe cites several cases, which illustrate that the executive arm of government, including the Governor General, is not above the law, as Dicey had said (see pages 122–7 of Commonwealth Caribbean Public Law, 1999). We will look at one of those cases here:

Hochoy v. Nuge (1964) 7 WLR 174

Sir Solomon Hochoy was the first Governor General of Trinidad and Tobago. By virtue of powers conferred on him under section 2 of the Commission of Inquiry Ordinance he appointed a Commission of Enquiry to enquire into certain matters. The respondents, a trade union and others sought a declaration that the appointment was ultra vires and therefore null and void and no effect. They were successful and the Governor General appealed, relying on the point that, in his capacity as the Queen's representative, he was immune from suit and the court had no jurisdiction over him. The Court of Appeal dismissed the Governor General's appeal.

After examining the issues Wooding CJ underscored the importance of ensuring that all persons, irrespective of rank, must conduct themselves within the law, and where they fail to do so, are subject to the law. Consequently, his lordship sought to disabuse from the mind of the executive arm that there were any special privileges to its benefit if it acts in breach of the law. His lordship said, at page 177:

> 'In my opinion, examination of the cases will show that, while the courts have been astute to preserve the immunity from liability of officers of state in the due performance of acts of a political character, they have never conceded that any such officer may be immune from suit. The reason is that immunity from suit is personal to the sovereign and stems directly from the ancient doctrine that no Lord could be compelled to answer in his own court.'

A similar approach was taken in the Guyanese case IRC and AG v. Lilleyman [1964] WLR 496.

See also Sugar Producers Federation v. Phillips [1965] 9 WLR 120 where the Governor General's exercise of a statutory power was struck down, there being no evidence before the court that he had exercised the power to appoint a commission of enquiry in circumstances that warranted the appointment.

Legislative authority and the Rule of Law

Again, Collymore is a useful case to consider under this heading, as is Bribery Commission v. Ranasinghe, both of which you should be familiar with.

A feature of Commonwealth Caribbean constitutions is a provision to the effect that Parliament may pass laws for 'peace, order, and good government'. We have seen that the courts will sever provisions that are inconsistent with the constitution as in Hinds. In the case of written constitutions, the boundaries within which Parliament must operate are clearly defined and the courts seek to preserve these boundaries. Besides the cases with which you are already familiar we will look at two recent cases.

Professor Fiadjoe points out that 'the courts are not too quick to strike down legislation, except for strong and compelling reasons. This is very much in keeping with the philosophy that the legislation primarily belongs to the elected representatives of the people' (Commonwealth Caribbean Public Law, 1999, page 130).

He refers to one of the cases we will examine as clearly reflecting this principle:

King v. AG of Barbados [1994] 1 WLR 1560 (PC)

The appellant was a clerical officer in the Ministry of Education. Her appointment was made under the Civil Service Establishment (General) Order 1990 pursuant to section 2 of the Civil Establishment Act 1948. In 1991, as part of its decision to stabilise the Barbadian economy, the Barbados Parliament passed the Public Service Reduction of Emoluments Act 1991 by which the emoluments of public officers were reduced by 8 per cent. Miss King claimed that the Act was unconstitutional in that it deprived her of her right to property in her emoluments, contrary to section 16 of the Constitution. This section provides that no person's property shall be compulsorily taken possession of without due process of law and without compensation. The Privy Council dismissed Miss King's appeal on the ground that she had no right to a minimum salary and, consequently, no right to any property of hers had been infringed.

No doubt, their lordships saw the public interest overriding Miss King's interest, which in the event, the Court, including the Court of Appeal in Barbados, held not to have been affected by the legislation. See also the interesting case of Morgan v. AG of Trinidad and Tobago (1987) 36 WLR 396, also a decision of the Privy Council.

The next case we will examine is also an appeal to the Privy Council and comes from Antigua and Barbuda. Here the appellant was successful:

Hector v. Attorney General of Antigua and Barbuda & Others (1990) 37 WLR 216

Leonard Hector appealed to the Privy Council from a decision of the Court of Appeal of the Eastern Caribbean States, which had allowed the appeal of the Attorney General from the High Court's decision in his favour. A 1976 amendment of the Public Order Act 1972 made it an offence, inter alia for any person who in any public place or at a public meeting:

> 'prints or distributes any false statement which is likely to cause fear or alarm in or to the public, or to disturb the public peace, or to undermine public confidence in the conduct of public affairs ...'

Mr Hector had published an article in The Outlet newspaper of which he was the editor. He was prosecuted under the provisions of the 1976 amendment and he challenged the prosecution.

The Judicial Committee viewed aspects of the legislation as repugnant, finding that the words 'or to undermine public confidence in the conduct of public affairs', 'offend against the Constitution and cannot therefore have any effect' (page 221). As their lordships said:

> 'In a free democratic society it is almost too obvious to need stating that those who hold office in government and who are responsible for public administration must always be open to criticism. Any attempt to stifle or fetter such criticism amounts to political censorship of the most insidious and objectionable kind.'

Here again we see the triumph of enlightened, public policy considerations.

Judicial authority and the Rule of Law

We shall examine the leading regional authority of Maharaj v. Attorney General of Trinidad of Tobago (No. 2).

Maharaj v. Attorney General of Trinidad of Tobago (No. 2) [1979] AC 385, [1978] 2 WLR 902 (PC)

The appellant Ramesh Lawrence Maharaj, was a well-known barrister (and later well-known politician), who was committed to prison for seven days on a charge by a High Court Judge, Maharaj J, for contempt of court. He applied to the High Court to have the order set aside on the ground that he was being deprived of his liberty without due process of law. His motion was dismissed some six days later by another High Court Judge, Scott J, and he was ordered to serve his term. Mr Maharaj served the term and appealed to the Court of Appeal from the High Court's ruling. While that appeal was pending, he obtained leave to do so and appealed to the Privy Council against the committal order. The ground of this appeal was that there had been a fundamental breach of natural justice as the judge had not communicated to him exactly what he had done, neither had he been given a chance to explain or excuse his conduct. The appeal to the Court of Appeal was subsequently heard and Mr Maharaj's action failed as the Court of Appeal held that the judge's failure to specify the nature of the contempt did not violate section 1 of the Constitution, which protected the citizen from infringement of his rights by the state. The Privy Council ruled in favour of the appellant and held:

- The Constitution gave the High Court original jurisdiction to hear matters brought by any person claiming that his fundamental rights have been infringed. Consequently, the High Court had jurisdiction to hear whether the procedure adopted by the Court in committing the appellant to prison contravened his constitutional rights.
- The Constitution protected individuals from having their rights infringed by the state or a public authority and the actions of the court in committing the appellant to prison without attention to natural justice requirements constituted a breach of the common law and contravened his rights under the Constitution, entitling him to obtain redress.
- Section 6 of the Constitution created a remedy for persons whose rights were contravened and the appellant would be granted a monetary compensation as he had suffered loss of earnings during his detention, as well as inconvenience and distress.

In this case, we see the Judicial Committee doing what the High Court had been reluctant to do, that is, to exercise jurisdiction over another High Court judge. In the interest of justice and in preserving the constitutional safeguards in respect of an individual's fundamental rights, the Board was prepared to take this bold step. Lord Diplock, in delivering the judgment of the majority, said:

> 'The order of Maharaj J committing the appellant to prison was made by him in the exercise of the judicial powers of the State; the arrest and detention of the appellant pursuant to the judge's order was effected by the executive arm of the State. So if his detention amounted to a contravention of his rights ... it was a contravention by the State against which he was entitled to protection.'

State institutions, including the police, and the Rule of Law

The police, whose motto is "to serve and protect" have come under scrutiny, whether as a result of perceived excesses as in the aftermath of the Rodney King Riots in the United States in 1992, or in the perceived brutality meted out to thousands in the "Arab Spring" uprisings of 2011. Here in the Caribbean, the cries of "police brutality", have been no less strident, especially as our government continue to fight the scourge of criminal activities and introduce curfews, and states of emergencies among crime fighting measures.

Recently, following the arrest of a number of police officers in Trinidad and Tobago for alleged excesses against a group of men they had detained, the Commissioner of Police described the matter as "tragic and unfortunate" and added that police officers are expected to conduct themselves, "in a way which upholds and observes the rule of law and demonstrates professionalism and confidence." (taken from news reports). The surrounding circumstances had attracted widespread national attention based on the reports of the nature of the excesses allegedly committed against the men; the subsequent protest by the villagers who knew the men and the submission of a report to the Director of Public Prosecutions who ruled that the officers be arrested. The need to regulate public officers to prevent excess and abuse is well recognised.

Professor Fiadjoe puts it succinctly when he says:

> 'Numerous examples exist here of the courts' desire to rein in State power, where unfairly exercised, from immigration officers, to customs collectors, police officers, officers of the Crown and broadcasting authorities.'
>
> Commonwealth Caribbean Public Law, 1999, page 133

We first examine a case involving the police:

Thornhill v AG [1974] 27 WIR 281 (High Court, TT)

The applicant was wanted by the police in connection with investigations being conducted by them into some serious crimes. On one occasion, T was involved in an incident with the police during which there was an exchange of gunfire. He was arrested and charged for offences arising from this incident. Intensive investigations ensued, including identification parades. He was subsequently charged with a number of offences, for which he gave statements to the police. T later alleged that the police denied him access to counsel who had sought to interview him. His action before the High Court included the ground that he was denied access to counsel, thereby contravening his constitutional rights; the statements given by him to the police were consequently unconstitutional, null and void. He also claimed not to have been informed promptly of the charges against him and that he was not brought promptly before a judicial authority. T argued before the court that his rights, which he claimed, were to be found in the Constitution. Georges J held that T's right to have prompt access to legal advice is a common law right that existed before the Constitution, which recognised its continuity post-constitutionally. The applicant succeeded on all grounds, except on the voluntary nature of the statements given, as the court found no evidence that they had not been voluntary. The actions of the police were found to be improper.

Let's look at another case involving a state authority; this time the issue is government's acquisition of property.

San Jose Farmers' Cooperative v. Attorney General (1991) 43 WIR (CA, Belize)

San Jose Farmers' Cooperative appealed to the Court of Appeal from the ruling of the Chief Justice. The issues turned on a purported acquisition of land by government under the Land Acquisition (Public Services) Act and whether such acquisition contravened a constitutional provision against compulsory acquisition without compensation within a reasonable time.

The Court of Appeal held that a provision under the Act to compensate a landowner over a 10-year period was not payment within a 'reasonable time' in accordance with a constitutional provision. It was also held that while it was not the court's role to usurp Parliament, at the same time it must bring laws into conformity with the Constitution. Hence, the court would strike out the repugnant clause from the legislation.

As you have seen from the foregoing, there is indeed no one above the law, not the police, nor the Governor General or a High Court judge. This is what makes for the full effect of the Rule of Law.

Activity 4.3

Research

At the end of this exercise, you should have developed a better understanding of the Rule of Law, arising from your own analysis.

Select two from the following list of cases:

- Pratt and Morgan v. AG of Jamaica [1993] 43 WIR 340
- Lennox Phillips et al v. A.G. of Trinidad and Tobago [1992] 1 AG 545 (PC)
- Williams Construction Ltd v. AG of Barbados [1995] 1 WLR 102, (1994) 45 WIR 94 (PC)

1. Identify the facts of the case.
2. Identify the main issues of the case.
3. What is the ratio of the case?

4 How does the Court treat the Rule of Law concept in relation to constitutional rights?

5 Do you perceive a consistent approach by the court in the cases you have chosen? Support your answer with reference to the case itself.

Feedback

This exercise should challenge you in a positive way.

The supremacy of the Constitution

In this section, the Constitution of Jamaica is examined. You should, therefore, consult your own Constitution and see whether it is similar to or different from, the Jamaican Constitution on the subject of supremacy.

Section 2 of the Jamaican Constitution declares the Constitution to be the supreme law, as follows:

> 'Subject to the provisions of sections 49 and 50 of this Constitution, if any other law is inconsistent with this Constitution, the Constitution shall prevail and the other law shall, to the extent of the inconsistency, be void.'

Section 49 contains provisions for alteration to the Constitution. Section 50 provides that an Act of Parliament shall have superior status over the Charter of rights which came into force in July 2011 and 'shall not be void to the extent of any inconsistency' with those provisions and shall, 'notwithstanding such inconsistency, prevail over those provisions'. The Act passed under this section must have received 'not less than two-thirds of all members of that House'. You would have met this point before, regarding the entrenchment of the fundamental rights provisions in the various Constitutions in the region.

Section 48 of the Constitution provides that 'Parliament may pass laws for the peace, order and good government of Jamaica'.

While section 2 declares the Constitution to be the Supreme Law, section 48 vests the authority to pass laws in the Parliament. This brings to the fore the issue of parliamentary sovereignty. Both sections are, in fact, complementary, provided that Parliament passes laws that are not inconsistent with the Constitution, in which event such laws would be void. We have an example of a law passed by Parliament being considered void in some provisions which the court severed, as a result (see below).

The earliest regional authority on the subject of the supremacy of the Constitution is the case of Collymore and Abrahams v. The Attorney General.

Collymore and Abrahams v. Attorney General [1970] AC 538, [1969] 2 All ER 1207 (PC), [1967] 12 WIR 5 (CA)

In Collymore, the appellants were members of a trade union. They were unsuccessful in their application to the High Court to declare as ultra vires an Act called the Industrial Stabilisation Act 1965. The preamble to the Act stated its aim to be, among other things, (i) for the compulsory recognition by employers of the trade unions and workers organisations, and (ii) for an expeditious settlement of trade disputes.

The Act also provided that it was unlawful for a worker to engage in industrial action, unless the Minister of Labour failed to refer the dispute to the Industrial Court.

For our purposes, one of the points on which the appellants based their action was that the Act was repugnant to the Constitution. They also argued that certain of its provisions abrogated, abridged or infringed the fundamental rights provisions of the Constitution, particularly freedom of association.

Wooding CJ, in considering the appellants' case, referred to section 36 of the Constitution, which provided that 'Parliament may make laws for the peace order and good government of Trinidad and Tobago' and said:

> 'In my judgment, the section means what it says. And what it says and says very clearly, is that the power and authority of Parliament to make laws are subject to its provisions. Parliament may therefore be sovereign within the limits thereby set, but if and whenever it should seek to make any law such as the Constitution forbids it will be acting ultra vires.'

His lordship went on to hold, inter alia, that the Supreme Court is the guardian of the Constitution. It was therefore in its competence and it was its right and duty to make binding declarations, if and whenever warranted, that an enactment passed by Parliament is ultra vires and void. You need not concern yourself with the industrial relations aspect of the judgment, but should note that this case also makes a significant ruling on the point of judicial review of legislative action and underscores the principle of separation of powers. (The appellants appealed on the ruling of the court on the industrial relations points, but the Privy Council upheld Wooding CJ's judgment on all points.)

You should bear in mind, as Professor Fiadjoe points out in Commonwealth Caribbean Public Law (1999), that although 'Collymore itself made no such express assertion of constitutional supremacy .... Yet, the logical effect of Collymore is to accept the fact that Parliament's sovereignty is limited by the Constitution' (page 6).

In support of this conclusion, the learned writer refers to the dictum of Fraser JA in Collymore. There, the learned judge, while recognising that Parliament's law-making power is absolute, said that such laws when made must be consistent with the Constitution, which, even if Parliament were to amend it, the amendment must also be consistent with the constitutional provisions for doing so. His Lordship said:

> '[N]o question of sovereignty of Parliament arises, ... Parliament can amend the constitution only if the constitutional prescriptions are observed and providing Parliament fulfils the requirements of the constitution its power is sovereign and supreme.'

The important case of Hinds v. R, referred to on page 59, is widely held as having put to rest any lingering doubts caused by any real or perceived limitations of the Collymore case on the question of the supremacy of Commonwealth Caribbean Constitutions. The facts of the case are set out in the section on the separation of powers doctrine. You should read the facts and observe the principles of that case very carefully.

Another interesting case, which precedes both Collymore and Hinds, and which is also a Privy Council decision is Bribery Commissioner v. Ranasinghe [1965] AC 172, [1962] 2 WLR 1301, [1964] 2 All ER 785 (PC). Professor Fiadjoe's note on the case is most helpful. As he points out, in Ranasinghe 'the Judicial Committee of the Privy Council therefore adhered to the principle that there is no doctrine that a sovereign Parliament can ignore the constitutional restrictions on its law making powers' (page 8 of Commonwealth Caribbean Public Law, 1999).

The facts in Bribery Commissioner v. Ranasinghe (an appeal from Ceylon, now Sri Lanka) are as follows. A section of the Constitution provided that there were several powers granted to Parliament, including the making of laws for the peace, order and good government of the island, and power to amend and repeal laws (with certain restrictions). There was also a provision that 'Every certificate of the speaker therefore shall be conclusive and shall not be questioned in any court of law'.

The Bribery Commission, against which the respondents appealed, was appointed under the Constitution and held judicial office when sitting. Their appointment was made by the Governor General on the advice of the Minister of Justice, and not by the Judicial Services Commission as required by the Constitution. The Privy Council held that decisions made by the tribunal, which itself was not properly constituted, were null and inoperative and were ultra vires an empowering legislation.

Their Lordships reinforced the point that the sovereignty of Parliament is not affected by the supremacy of the Constitution, provided Parliament follows the required procedures for amendment as set out in the Constitution itself.

This case was referred to in Collymore as a precedent. See Collymore v. Attorney General (1967) 12 WLR 5 at page 35 in the judgment of Fraser JA, who saw the case as 'clear authority' for the view that 'if Parliament fails or omits or neglects' to fulfil the requirements of the Constitution 'any person who alleges that he has been, or that he is, or that he is likely to be prejudiced by such contravention may seek recourse to the High Court and pray its relief' (per Fraser JA).

So, you might ask, is there any tension between constitutional supremacy and parliamentary sovereignty? That is, indeed, a pertinent question. The cases we have looked at above suggest that the tension will only manifest itself if Parliament seeks to exercise its sovereignty in a manner that is ultra vires the Constitution.

Activity 4.4

Teamwork

At the end of this exercise you will have benefited from revision and should have a good understanding of how constitutional supremacy and parliamentary sovereignty are inter-related.

You and a study partner or two should each take one of these cases:

- Collymore and Abrahams v. Attorney General [1970] AC 538, [1969] 2 All ER 1207 (PC), [1967] 12 WIR 5 (CA)
- Hinds v. R [1977] AC 195, [1976] 2 WIR 366, [1975] 24 WIR 326, [1976] 1 All ER 353 (PC)

1. Identify the ratio decidendi of the case on the points of constitutional supremacy and parliamentary sovereignty.
2. Examine the court's treatment of the topic of constitutional supremacy and how this affected their review of the legislation in issue.
3. Share your findings with each other and keep your notes for further study.

Feedback

You are reminded that the ratio decidendi of a case is, literally, the reason the judge gives for coming to a decision. Both these cases must be read closely. When you have completed the exercise, you should be equipped to answer any question on the subject.

Locus standi

The term locus standi, which can otherwise be referred to as 'standing', means literally 'a place to stand on'. According to Jowitt's Dictionary of English Law (Sweet & Maxwell, London, 1977), 'To say that a person has no locus standi means that he has no right to appear or be heard in such-and-such a proceedings.' The issue often turns on (1) whether the proper person has brought the action and (2) whether the proper party has been sued. In public law, the concern is largely with (1) as the cases are usually brought to protect a public right or interest.

In essence, then, as was said by Peterkin J in R v. Mbafeno et al ex p. Pierre (1966) 10 WIR 368, the requirement is that one should have locus standi to be eligible to be granted relief by the court:

> 'Therefore he has to show that he is one who is wrongly deprived of or refused something to which he is legally entitled or upon whom a legal burden is cast, and not merely one who is dissatisfied with an act or decision [author's emphasis]. In short, he must have a locus standi to apply for an order of certiorari to impugn the order or decision with a view to having it quashed.'

In that case, the facts were as follows: under the Commission of Enquiry Ordinance in Trinidad and Tobago, the Governor General appointed a Commission to enquire into the nature and extent of subversive activity within the country, with particular emphasis on the trade union movement, the public service and youth organisations. The applicant, a solicitor, was summoned to appear before the Commission but he declined to do so. He later sought to have the Commissioners' report quashed. On the question of locus standi the court found that the applicant had failed to show that he was a person who was wrongly deprived of or refused something to which he was entitled.

What was said by Peterkin J in the Mbafeno case with respect to the discretionary remedy of certiorari is also true of other remedies sought by an applicant; he must show that he has locus standi.

In Commonwealth Caribbean Public Law (1999), Professor Fiadjoe illustrates with reference to a number of regional and other decisions that there are 'conflicting signals' from the courts on the issue of locus standi. Some judges have adopted a restrictive approach, while others have adopted a liberal approach to the matter, the latter approach appearing to be that which best addresses public interest issues. Professor Fiadjoe agrees with the liberal approach and finds support for it in the judgment of Mitchell J in Payne v. Attorney General of St Kitts (1982) 30 WIR 88 where the learned judge expressed the view that there are many categories of issues which give rise to the court's determination that one has locus standi and may therefore bring an action in respect of those issues. His Lordship said:

> 'The relevant interest required by the Constitution may be moral, religious or otherwise once it is ascertainable and therefore not too remote. The interest may be a social interest as embracing the efficient working of the legal order in the society, national security, the economic prosperity of society, the protection of religious, moral, humanitarian and intellectual values or it may be a private interest which is a personal or a family interest or an economic interest or a political interest and that list is not complete.'

Professor Fiadjoe clearly disagrees with the restrictive approach to standing as it emphasizes the rigidity and formality of procedural questions as against the approach which better protects the general public interest. He concludes that the tendency is towards the liberal approach which augurs well for the systems of justice and the protection of citizens' rights.

In Payne the relevant question, for our purposes, turned on whether the respondent, an elected member of the House, could bring proceedings seeking a declaration concerning certain statutes that were passed in the House of Assembly of St Christopher and Nevis in 1981. This was after the UK Parliament had passed the Anguilla Act in 1980 by which Anguilla ceased to be a member of the Associated State of St Christopher Nevis and Anguilla. Payne's argument was that the leading of the Bills as being passed in 'Saint Christopher and Nevis' was irregular.

Although Mr Payne's 'relevant interest' in bringing the matter was acknowledged by the court, his action failed on the substantive issue, the Court of Appeal of Eastern Caribbean States holding that 'Saint Christopher and Nevis' was the proper description of the State and the Bills were therefore correctly headed.

We have seen that although it is fundamental that one should have standing in order to initiate and sustain a matter successfully before the courts, that in matters of public interest, the courts have been willing to extend the situations that give rise to that standing. Once again, we turn to Professor Fiadjoe in support of this position. He cites the case of R v. Secretary of State for Foreign Affairs ex p. World Development Movement Ltd [1995] 1 All ER 611, where the court extended the concept of locus standi in a matter of considerable public interest. The bases upon which the court took that approach are stated by Professor Fiadjoe and are as follows:

- 'The merits of the challenge
- The importance of vindicating the Rule of Law
- The importance of the issue raised
- The likely absence of any other responsible challenge
- The nature of the breach of duty against which relief was sought; and
- The prominent role of the applicants in promoting and protecting aid to developing nations.' (page 153)

In the case, a non-partisan pressure group sought review of a decision by the Foreign Secretary to approve an aid and trade project in Malaysia. This was being done at the urging of a consortium of construction companies but against the advice of the Overseas Development Administration, which examined being done the project and concluded that it was uneconomic. The Foreign Secretary decided to proceed with the project, nevertheless, on the ground that it would affect the UK's credibility negatively, to do otherwise. The applicants campaigned against the project and sought judicial review. The Foreign Secretary contended, inter alia, that the applicants had no locus standi. For the reasons stated earlier the Queen's Bench Division of the Court held that they did.

If the restrictive approach had been taken, it is likely that the applicants would not have succeeded, as their interest could be regarded as not being 'direct' in the strict sense.

In conclusion, let us look at the recommendations of the Working Paper on Public Interest Litigation made by the Law Commission of Trinidad and Tobago in 1997. These recommendations are found at pages 153–4 of Professor Fiadjoe's text. Suffice it to say that they are in favour of the liberal approach to standing and uphold the view that the public interest and the Rule of Law must be unrestricted, albeit within a system of clearly defined guidelines. Paragraph (d) at page 154 of Fiadjoe, is most helpful in setting out what the court should consider, as follows:

> '(d) The Court, in exercising its discretion should take into account the principles which have emerged in the case law espousing a liberal standing such as, inter alia;
>
> - the need to screen out the mere busybody
> - the importance of vindicating the Rule of Law
> - the importance of the issues raised
> - the likely absence of any other responsible challenger with a more direct interest in the matter
> - the genuine interest of the applicant in the matter
> - the expertise of the applicant and the applicant's ability adequately to present the case
> - the nature of the breach of duty against which relief was sought
> - the allocation of scarce judicial resources.'

The recommendations also provide that it is in the public interest plaintiffs should advertise their action to give opportunity to persons 'more directly affected' an opportunity to participate or bring the action, should they so desire.

Activity 4.5

Revision and evaluation

At the end of this exercise you will have revised this section on locus standi and should be able to identify the advantages of the liberal approach to locus standi.

You should place an x in the box provided, indicating whether the following statements are 'true' and 'false'. The first one is done for you.

1. A plaintiff must have locus standi if he seeks to bring an action before the court for judicial review. True (√) False ( )
2. In determining whether a party has locus standi, the better view is that the court must ensure that the correct procedure has been followed. True ( ) False ( )
3. The requirement that a plaintiff should have locus standi effectively bars busybodies. True ( ) False ( )
4. The restrictive approach to locus standi limits litigants in the pursuit of public interest issues. True ( ) False ( )
5. The liberal approach to locus standi is a triumph for the protection of citizens' rights. True ( ) False ( )

Feedback

2 False (√). 4 True (√).
3 True (√). 5 True (√).

The ultra vires doctrine

Ultra Vires is a Latin term meaning 'acting in excess or outside one's powers or area of authority'. An Ultra Vires situation can also occur when a piece of legislation attempts to take away or infringe a right given to an individual under the Constitution.

The idea of acting in excess of, or contrary to, the authority or power vested in one's self is not limited to individuals but also applies to:

- institutions
- boards (for example, a Board of Directors or a Board of Inquiry)
- a statutory enactment (a piece of legislation).

Example of ultra vires

Below is an example of a case from Trinidad and Tobago, which is most popular for the decision given by the Privy Council and which decision established the principle that public servants are no longer dismissible at pleasure.

Thomas v. Attorney General (1981) 32 WIR 375

In Thomas v. Attorney General, the plaintiff, a police officer, was charged with the disciplinary offences of neglect of duty and failure to carry out the instructions of a senior officer contrary to regulation 74 of the Police Service Regulations 1966. The plaintiff challenged the disciplinary proceedings and the validity of the order removing him from the public service.

The Attorney General who was the defendant in the proceedings, initially maintained that the regulations were valid; but conceded before the Privy Council that regulation 74 was ultra vires.

Chapter VII of the Police Service Regulations of 1966, which is labelled 'Conduct', sets out those acts that might be considered acts against the discipline of the police service and which may attract punishment.

Lord Diplock in his judgment said, 'The relevant regulation-making power under section 102 of the Constitution pursuant to which Chapter VII of the Regulations purported to be made was the power of the commission with the consent of the Prime Minister to regulate its own procedure. Laying down codes of conduct to be observed by police officers is not comprised in regulating the commissions own procedure ... Before this Board it has been conceded by the Attorney General that a regulation under section 102 of the Constitution did not provide a legally appropriate way of doing this and Chapter VII of the regulation is qua regulation, ultra vires.'

Judicial review

Judicial review may be defined as the review by the High Court of the decisions, acts and omissions of public bodies or their officers. The aim of judicial review is to keep the actions of public bodies and officials within the confines of the law from which they derive their power. The court that exercises the power of judicial review is the Supreme Court of the High Court, which is a superior court of record. The Supreme Court of the High Court sits as a court of original jurisdiction, a court of appeal and a court of review. Below are examples of public bodies that are subject to judicial review by the Supreme Court of the High Court:

- the Ministry of Education
- the Ministry of Health
- the Fire Service
- the Mayor and City Council.

Note: These may also be called statutory or public bodies.

Below are examples of public officials who are subject to judicial review by the Supreme Court of the High Court:

- the Governor
- the Commissioner of Inland Revenue
- the Minister of Health
- High Court judges
- the Commissioner of Police
- Magistrates.

Note: Judges and magistrates are also known as public tribunals as well as public functionaries.

Note: The terms 'Supreme Court' and 'High Court' are used interchangeably and both mean the 'Supreme Court of the High Court'.

Supervision of tribunals, arbitrations and other bodies

The Supreme Court sitting as a Court of Appeal

When the Supreme Court sits to hear an appeal against the decision or sentence of a lower court it is exercising both its inherent jurisdiction at common law and its statutory jurisdiction under the High Court Act.

The Supreme Court sitting as a Court of Review

When the Supreme Court sits as a Court of Review it is exercising its inherent jurisdiction, which is vested in it at common law and which enables it to function in its supervisory capacity to review the actions of statutory or public bodies or their officials.

When the court is exercising this supervisory function it is also exercising its original jurisdiction to hear applications for a review of the actions or omissions of a public (statutory) body, tribunal or its functionaries (officials).

What is a public body?

A public body is a body vested with the responsibility of performing a public function.

What is a statutory body?

A statutory body is a body created by statute or by parliamentary enactment and which derives its power from that statute. A statutory body may also be called a public body.

The inherent jurisdiction of the High Court

- A power vested in the High Court at common law.
- A power not limited to powers vested under statute.
- A power that vests the court with the authority to apply its discretion outside of the requirements of statute.

When does a public law issue arise?

A public law issue may arise when a public or statutory body, tribunal or functionary acts or fails to perform a public duty, which it owes to the individual.

Locus standi: who can sue and who to sue

Locus standi (See page 65 on this topic) may be defined as having the interest under the law, which entitles one to bring an action or challenge a decision. For the purpose of this lesson locus standi will be examined only with respect to public law matters.

If a person wishes to bring a matter against a public body into court he must, if he lives in Guyana or other Caribbean Jurisdiction, apply to the Attorney General to be allowed to approach the High Court. It is only if his application is accepted by the Attorney General that he can then proceed to apply to the High Court to have the matter heard there.

This procedure is known as the 'relator action'. In order to satisfy the Attorney General that his case merits the grant of permission to be heard in the High Court the Applicant must show that:

- he has locus standi
- he has a good prima facie case
- the body against whom the claim is being brought is a public body that has done something it ought not to do or failed to do that which it ought to do
- the applicant must also show that he or those whom he seeks to represent has/have been affected by the acts or omissions of the public body.

The grounds for judicial review

The main grounds upon which the courts will now interfere to assert their supervisory role are:

- where the powers exercised are ultra vires the powers of the tribunal, body or official
- where there has been improper delegation of that power
- where there has been infringement of the rules of natural justice and legitimate expectation. Natural justice is one of the cardinal principles in administrative law. The concept underscores that a litigant or a person aggrieved has certain rights which have developed overtime to ensure fairness in the way his or her case is handled. These include freedom against bias, the right to be heard and "legitimate expectation". Legitimate expectation is a fundamental public policy concept. It is that expectation which a citizen has that

public bodies including governments, public officers and persons in authority will conduct themselves, make regulations or pass laws which are consistent with well established norms, values, practices and legal principles. For further reading, see recommended text, Commonwealth Caribbean Public Law by Professor Albert Fiadjoe.
- where there has been an abuse of discretion
- where there has been an error of law or fact appearing on the face of the record.

Any of the above (except the fifth point) may have been done as a result of any of the following:

- improper motive in the exercise of power or
- that the powers were exercised
  - in an arbitrary manner or
  - capriciously or
  - that the acts of the tribunal or official were motivated by bias.

Remedies available under judicial review

- Certiorari is available in cases where there has been excess of jurisdiction, want of jurisdiction, abuse of powers.
- Declaration is a discretionary remedy, which takes the form of a statement by the High Court that an individual possesses a particular legal status, right or obligation.
- Injunction is another discretionary order of the High Court, which prevents a tribunal, official or statutory body from performing a particular act.
- Mandamus is the Latin word for 'we command'. It is a prerogative order of the High Court instructing an official, or tribunal to perform a specified public duty relating to its responsibilities, for example, an instruction that the tribunal of official hear a particular dispute.
- Prohibition is a remedy granted by the High Court and which bars an inferior tribunal, official or administrative body from the performance of a particular act.
- Damages is a form of compensation in money terms, which is granted by an order of the High Court. Such an order seeks to put the individual back into the position that he or she was before the commission of the wrongful act of which the individual has complained. (Note: In Guyana, the remedy of damages is not available at judicial review.)
- Habeas corpus is a Latin term meaning 'let us have the body'. It is an application for an order of the High Court against an inferior tribunal official or statutory body (usually the Commissioner of Police) to produce (usually in court) a person being held in breach of that individual's constitutional and/or fundamental rights.

Breach of one's fundamental rights

Contained in all the Commonwealth Caribbean Constitutions is a Fundamental Rights section. These provisions were amended in the Jamaican Constitution by a Charter of Rights which came into force in July, 2011. You should note the extent to which the Charter is more expansive in its ambit or scope, than the Fundamental Rights provisions.

In the Guyana Constitution the fundamental rights section is found between articles 138–54, Barbados, sections 11–27. The fundamental rights stated in all of the Commonwealth Caribbean Constitutions offer protection to every citizen and are also justifiable. This means that one can seek enforcement of one's fundamental rights in a court of law.

Below is a list of some of the rights that are protected by and enshrined within the fundamental rights section of Commonwealth Caribbean Constitutions:

- the right to life
- the right to freedom of worship
- the right to protection against arbitrary search and seizure
- the right to freedom of expression
- the right to protection from deprivation of property.

Activity 4.6

Check the Constitution of your country to discover where the fundamental rights provisions are located. Then make a list of all the rights of the individual, which are protected under the fundamental rights section of your Constitution, then compare them with those found within the Constitution of any other Commonwealth Caribbean territory of your choice.

Let us now consider the court's attitude towards breaches of any of the fundamental rights provisions of the Constitution. The case below illustrates the court's power to declare that a piece of legislation is invalid and set it aside for being unconstitutional.

Inland Revenue Commissioner and Attorney General v. Lilleyman and Others (1964) 7 WIR 464

Lilleyman was the first Guyanese case on fundamental rights breaches to be reported in the West Indian Law Reports. It was determined on appeal by the British Caribbean Court of Appeal. Here, a challenge was brought against legislation imposing compulsory savings on the citizenry. The legislation was held to be unconstitutional in that:

- the levy under the National Development Savings Levy Ordinance 1962, No. 16 [B.G.], is in the nature of a forced loan, and is neither a tax nor a due, and is therefore not protected by article 12(3)(a) of the Constitution; the Ordinance is subsequently ultra vires the legislature
- the power to legislate for the peace, order and good governance of the country does not authorise the enactment of a law, which contravenes the provisions of the Constitution that gives such power, even though such a law has been duly passed by the legislature
- that money was property within the meaning of article 12(i) of the Constitution.

The case also involves the protection of the individual's right to property (money), which is enshrined in what is now article 142 of the 1980 Constitution of Guyana under the fundamental rights section: put simply, the government sought to compulsorily acquire the property of citizens through forced loans to the government in the form of a levy, which was created by parliamentary enactment.

The court held that despite the fact that this move to take people's money was supported by statute it was nevertheless bad for being contrary to article 12 of the 1960 Constitution of Guyana.

The case that follows is an important one for examining the protection afforded the individual by the court and which protection extends also to breaches occasioned by the court itself.

Maharaj v. Attorney General of Trinidad and Tobago (No. 2) [1978] 2 All ER 670

In the Trinidadian case of Maharaj, Mr Maharaj, a barrister, was committed to prison by a High Court Judge to serve seven days for contempt of court. On the same day the appellant applied ex parte by a motion to another High Court judge claiming ... redress for alleged contravention of his right under section 1(a) of the Constitution of Trinidad and Tobago not to be deprived of liberty except by due process of law.

The redress claimed was, inter alia, an order for immediate release from prison pending final determination of the motion and damages for wrongful detention and false imprisonment against the respondent, the Attorney General as representative of the State. The judge ordered that the appellant be released from prison forthwith.

On the substantive hearing of the motion, a third judge (Scott J) dismissed the motion and ordered the appellant to serve the remaining six days of his sentence, which he served.

He appealed against the decision of the Court of Appeal. While the appeal was pending he obtained special leave to appeal to the Judicial Committee of the Privy Council against the committal order made on 17 April. On 27 July 1976 the Judicial Committee allowed that appeal on the ground that the judge who made the committal order had failed to specify sufficiently the nature of the contempt charged against the appellant before committing him to prison and held that in consequence the committal order was invalid.

On 29 April 1977 the Court of Appeal dismissed the appeal relating to the motion on the ground that although a High Court judge had jurisdiction under section 6 of the Constitution to grant the appellant redress for contravention of his constitutional rights, which resulted from something done by another High Court judge acting in his judicial capacity, the failure of the judge to inform the appellant of the nature of the contempt charged did not contravene his rights under section 1(a) of the Constitution.

The appellant appealed to the Judicial Committee of the Privy Council against the decision. It was held that:

- Because the motion was an inquiry into whether the procedure adopted by Maharaj J before committing the appellant to prison was a breach of his fundamental rights, Scott J had jurisdiction to entertain the motion.
- Maharaj J. acted in breach of the common law procedure for committing a person to prison for contempt and that when the Constitution came into being this procedure became entrenched into it thereby protecting the right of the appellant under section 1 and sections 1, 2 and 3 thereof to due process of law.
- By the operation of section 1 the Constitution created a remedy against interference with the rights or freedoms protected by section 1. The appellant was therefore entitled to any other available remedy. Flowing from this was:
  - his right to apply to the High Court for redress under section 6(1) with respect to his imprisonment ...

Breach of a provision of the Constitution other than fundamental rights

Separation of powers

All Commonwealth Caribbean Constitutions contain sections that lay down certain principles that operate outside of the fundamental rights section.

One of these principles deals with the separation of powers whereby it is decreed that the three organs of the State, that is, the legislature, the executive and the judiciary cannot perform the functions of each other. This is known as the doctrine of the separation of powers.

In the Guyana Constitution, articles 155–82 deal with Parliament, which is the legislative arm of the State. Articles 183–90 deal with the President who, together with his cabinet, constitutes the executive arm of the State. Article 190 deals with the judiciary.

Check the Constitution of your territory to discover which sections, articles or parts deal with the three organs of State.

Nowhere is the doctrine of the separation of powers more powerfully illustrated than in the Caribbean locus classicus of Hinds v. R, wherein the provisions of the 1974 Act came under scrutiny by the Jamaican Court of Appeal.

The five appellants were each convicted by a Resident Magistrate Division of the Gun Court of being in unlawful possession of firearms and ammunition contrary to section 20 of the 1967 Act.

In accordance with section 8(2) of the 1974 Act they were sentenced to detention and hard labour. They appealed, contending inter alia that: the provisions of the 1974 Act relating to mandatory sentences of hard labour during the Governor General's pleasure, acting with the advice of the Review Board, were unconstitutional in that they interfered with the right of a convicted person to have his sentence determined by the court, i.e. that the Board so constituted to include one judge sitting together with persons who were not a part of the judiciary was really an executive body performing judicial functions contrary to the doctrine of separation of powers.

It was held, inter alia, that sections 8(2) and 22(1) of the 1974 Act purported to transfer from the judiciary to an executive body not appointed under Chapter VII of the Constitution a complete discretion to determine the severity of punishment to be inflicted on a certain class of offender, that is, persons convicted of gun-related offences.

The combined effect of those sections was to give the Review Board the power to fix the duration of a sentence not previously fixed by anyone else.

Those sections had been enacted after the coming into force of the Constitution and were inconsistent with the provisions of the Constitution. It followed that sections 8(2) and 22(1) were void under section 2 of the constitution.

Breach of the provision of some statute other than the Constitution

We will now discuss a case that illustrates what can happen when an individual or a group of individuals act in breach of a provision in a statute. See discussions related to the recently decided case of Nation and Wright v DPP and AG under the section dealing with 'Separation of Powers'. This is an example of a statute running afoul of the Constitution. The same is true for Hinds v R.

Collymore v. Attorney General [1967] 12 WIR 5

In the Trinidadian case of Collymore v Attorney General the appellants had acted in breach of section 34 of the Stabilisation Act, which prohibited a worker from taking part in a strike in connection with any trade union unless the Minister of Labour failed to refer the dispute to the Industrial Court.

The appellants being members of the Oilfield Workers Trade Union unsuccessfully moved the High Court to declare as ultra vires the Industrial Stabilisation Act of 1965.

The appellants in their motion alleged that apart from being otherwise repugnant to the constitution, certain provisions of the Act infringed the right of free collective bargaining and the right to strike.

These rights, they alleged, were common law rights, which were accordingly encompassed in the right to freedom of association, which is specifically recognised and declared in the fundamental rights section of the Constitution.

It was held, inter alia, that the right of free collective bargaining and the right to strike were not included in the fundamental freedom of association recognised and declared by section 1(i) of the Constitution and were consequently not protected under the provisions of sections 2 and 6 of the Constitution.

Please note: The disability under which the oil workers laboured was two-fold:

1 The rights (the right to strike and the right to free collective bargaining), which they sought to enforce were not protected under the fundamental rights section of the constitution and

2 no statutory enactment was created to enforce the alleged common law right to free collective bargaining and the common law right to strike.

This fact rendered the alleged rights unenforceable at law.

End Test

As part of your local Community Council's study of constitutional issues, you have been asked to address the next monthly meeting on 'The separation of powers doctrine: aid or restraint to governance?' Prepare for and write notes on your presentation. **45 minutes**

1 Mr La Guerre is a well-known opposition politician who has served as Deputy Prime Minister and Minister of Foreign Affairs in a previous government in Albion, a Commonwealth Caribbean State. Recently, in a wide-ranging speech delivered to a convention of the Confederation of Trade Unions, Mr La Guerre spoke out against what he described as 'the erosion of the Rule of Law' in Albion. He declared that the government had lost the will to govern, the police were being given 'a straw basket to carry water' as they were so woefully under-equipped and that the citizenry felt exposed as their fundamental rights were being eroded.

Examine the matters referred to by Mr La Guerre as examples of the erosion of the Rule of Law and write a critical analysis of the Rule of Law as it operates in your country. **45 minutes**

2 Mohan and Sherine are revising for their CAPE Law examinations. As usual, they are having a lively discussion on today's topic, supremacy of the constitution.

Sherine: I think I'll just concentrate on Hinds, know that case well, and I'm safe...

Mohan: I don't believe I'm hearing right! You seem to think that if you read Hinds alone you can answer everything in public law? Are you crazy? What about Collymore?

Sherine: There you go again being hyper! All I'm trying to say is that Hinds sets some very important precedents, and not just on the supremacy point. And, you can rest assured, it's not the only case I'll read. Of course, there's Collymore, Ranasinghe et cetera!

Mohan: OK, OK. Now that you explain yourself, I guess I understand what you mean.

Sherine: Thanks a lot! Provided we get it in our heads that we have authorities on the point that the Constitution is the supreme law!

Discuss the extent to which the Constitution of your state is the Supreme Law:

3 a Analyse the efficacy of the cases of Collymore and Hinds in demonstrating this supremacy.

b Assess the relationship between the privacy of the Constitution and Parliamentary Supremacy.

4 The Minister of Commerce of a Commonwealth Caribbean State issues an order that at the end of the next four weeks the licensing and importation regime for reconditioned vehicles imported into the country by used car dealers will be changed. All such vehicles must now be more than three years old at the date of arrival. This position reverses the previous one, which had allowed vehicles aged six years and under to be imported. Mr Subasingh is a member of the public who wants to have the Minister's order rescinded on the grounds that:

a it will prevent poor people from ever being able to afford a decent motor car

b the Minister's order is arbitrary and is in breach of a promise made by him in a speech to the Used Car Dealers Association some months earlier that there would be no change in the government's promise concerning the importation of reconditioned vehicles.

Advise Mr Subasingh on whether or not he can successfully approach the court as a person who has locus standi to bring the action.

End Test Feedback

1 Your presentation should include the following:

- definition or description of separation of powers doctrine
- aims and objectives of separation of powers (to prevent an abuse of power by officers of government to prevent corruption, etc.)
- brief background on the development of the doctrine of separation of powers
- advantages of separation of powers (give examples)
- disadvantages of separation of powers (give examples)
- conclusion: to what extent is it an aid or restraint to governance?

Case: Hinds v. R.

2 You are expected to:

a define the term 'Rule of Law' and give a brief history of its development, e.g. US and French Constitutional provisions, conventions on human rights (e.g. UN), Declaration of Delhi, theories of the concept, for example, the Diceyan view

b discuss how the Rule of Law is evident in a chosen Commonwealth Caribbean jurisdiction

c identify each issue raised by Mr La Guerre and show how each is fundamental to the Rule of Law; that is, the role of government, the police and protection of citizen's rights

d illustrate how the concept of the Rule of Law functions by reference to decided cases, as an example of practical application, for example, Hochoy v. NUGE (1964) 7 WIR 174, Sugar Producers Federation v. Phillips (1965) 9 WIR 120, Lennox Philips et al v. AG [1992] 1 AC 545, Pratt and Morgan v. AG of Jamaica (1993) 43 WIR 340, Collymore v. AG (1967) 12 WIR 5, d Hinds v. R, San Jose Farmers Co-op Society v. AG (1991) 43 WIR 63.

There are numerous other cases from our jurisdictions, including Maharaj and Thornhill, so you are not without a wealth of judicial authorities. You should feel free to select cases from among these authorities. Enjoy your research!

3 Your answer should consist of the following tasks:

a discuss what is meant by the term constitutional supremacy and say whether or not your constitution has a supreme law clause and, if so, what section

b describe the principles emanating from the cases of Collymore and Hinds in respect of the supremacy of the constitution

c explain what is meant by the term parliamentary sovereignty and say how it relates to constitutional supremacy

d refer to the cases that show the tension between parliamentary sovereignty and constitutional supremacy.

4 You must begin by defining locus standi and the approaches to it.

The guidelines proposed by the Law Commission of Trinidad and Tobago should assist you. Is Mr Subasingh being a busybody? Can he be said to a person affected by the Minister's ruling? If he does not bring the action, can or will anyone else? See the dictum of Peterkin J in the Mbafeno case.

Payne and R v. Secretary of State should be helpful. This matter calls for a discussion of the restrictive and the liberal approaches.

5 Criminal liability

General objectives

On completion of this chapter, you should:

- develop an appreciation of the basic principles of criminal law
- understand the provisions governing criminal liability and defence in jurisdictions of Commonwealth Caribbean countries.

Specific objectives

You should be able to:

- outline the basic principles of criminal liability
- distinguish the various types of offences common to Commonwealth Caribbean countries
- explain the elements of stated offences
- evaluate sentencing practices in Commonwealth Caribbean countries.

Introduction

In chapter 4, we examined the principles of public law. You became aware of the major similarities and differences among the constitutions of Commonwealth Caribbean States. You can now appreciate the special characteristics and general principles of administrative law.

In chapter 5, we turn our attention to the basic principles and practices of criminal law. This chapter will help you to become familiar with ways of establishing criminal liability. You will learn the subtle differences between how criminal law is applied across Commonwealth Caribbean jurisdictions. On completion of chapter 5, you will be able to analyse issues in law related to offences against the person and be able to evaluate the main dimensions of a case involving criminal liability. On completion of this chapter, you should be able to put up an efficient and reliable defence, using the provisions for defences under criminal law.

Content

- Criminal liability
- Offences against the person
- Sexual offences
- Select defences
- Sentencing

Criminal liability

Let us begin by establishing what is meant by criminal liability. There are two elements that are crucial in determining criminal liability. These are the actus reus and mens rea of a crime. The correlation of these two elements is essential as the learned writers of Smith and Hogan Criminal Law suggest very early in that leading text. They put it thus:

> 'It is a general principle of criminal law that a person may not be convicted of a crime unless the prosecution have proved beyond reasonable doubt both (a) that he has caused a certain state of affairs which is forbidden by criminal law, and (b) that he had a defined state of mind in relation to the causing of the event or the existence of the state of affairs. The event or state of affairs is called the actus reus and the state of mind the mens rea of the crime.'
>
> Smith and Hogan 10th ed., 2002 (page 28)

Now look back at this quotation and underline the following words or groups of words:

- 'a certain state of affairs'
- 'forbidden by criminal law'
- 'defined state of mind'
- 'causing of the event'
- 'existence of the state of affairs'.

You will be going back to these words or groups of words, which you have just underlined, but after we look at the two elements, which must coexist before one is deemed guilty of a crime. These are actus reus and mens rea. Let's look at the definitions of each:

1 The actus reus refers to the conduct of the accused and includes acts or omissions, consequences and surrounding circumstances, that is, 'the state of affairs' must be such as to be able to attribute responsibility to the accused.
2 The mens rea refers to the accused's state of mind and includes intention, recklessness, gross negligence and knowledge, that is, the accused's 'defined state of mind' must have 'caused the event'.

Look at the following cases, which illustrate the actus reus and the mens rea.

Actus reus cases

R v. Deller (1952) 36 Cr. App Rep 184

D induced P to purchase a car, representing, inter alia, that the car was free from encumbrances, when to his knowledge it was not as he had placed a lien against the car. He did not know that the document granting the lien was probably void as an unregistered bill of sale. D thought he was lying, but it turned out that his representations to P were true. D's conviction for obtaining money by false pretences was quashed by the Court of Criminal Appeal. Even though he had the mens rea, the actus reus had not been established.

R v. Dyson [1908] 2 KB 454

In November 1906 and again in December 1907, D inflicted injuries on a child who died on 5 March 1908. D was indicted for manslaughter. The child's death had occurred at a time longer than that required for D to be found guilty of manslaughter. His conviction was quashed in the absence of an actus rea of the crime.

Mens rea cases

R v. Faulkner (1877) 13 Cox Crim. Cases 550

D, a seaman, went into the hold of a ship to steal rum from the cargo. He lit a match to see what he was doing. The match accidentally lit the rum, resulting in the burning of the ship. D was convicted for 'feloniously, unlawfully, and maliciously' setting the ship on fire. The Court of Criminal Appeal quashed D's conviction on the ground that it was wrong for the jury to have been instructed that D acted maliciously in burning the ship, if he was attempting to commit another crime. (The prosecution had not shown that the burning of the ship was a probable or foreseeable cause of D's action.) There was therefore no mens rea on D's part affecting the burning of the ship.

In another case Hyam v DPP (1973) 3 ALL ER 842, (1973) 3 WLR 475, D, wishing to frighten B, her rival for X's affection, puts blazing newspaper through the letter-box of B's house, causing the deaths of two of B's children. The jury found B guilty of murder. The judge directed them that D was guilty if they found that D knew that her action would result in at least serious bodily harm. (In R v. Moloney [1985] A.C. 905, the House of Lords held that the mens rea of murder is to cause death or serious bodily harm. The jury must therefore be clearly instructed in this regard.)

From looking at these cases, and your further reading, you will see how important it is that the actus reus and the mens rea of a crime are present before criminal liability will be determined against an accused.

Where the actus reus exists without the presence of mens rea or vice versa, there is no criminal liability. Here's a Latin maxim, which sums up the principle: actus non facit reum nisi mensit rea. This means that the intention and the act must coincide to constitute a crime. The case that illustrates this point is Thabo Meli v. R [1945], where the defendants got the deceased into a drunken state, then hit him on the head, intending to kill him. They succeeded in hitting him unconscious, but believing him to be dead, they threw him over a cliff. He died from the fall and exposure and not from the beating. The defendants were convicted. The prosecution needed only to establish that at some time during the chain of events, the accused had formed the mens rea for murder. It was clearly evident in this case.

Activity 5.1

Actus reus

This activity will help you to identify the circumstances in which an accused will be found to have the actus reus of a crime.

Read the problems that follow, then write in the space provided 'actus reus of a crime' or 'no actus reus of a crime', as appropriate.

The first one is done for you:

1. D buys a pound of compressed leafy substance, which he believes to be marijuana. At the airport, D is stopped and confesses to having the drug. It is later found that the substance is a medicinal herb called 'cerasee' and not marijuana. Actus reus of a crime
2. Marcia believes she is pregnant and goes to a doctor for the purpose of procuring an abortion. Abortions are illegal in her country. The doctor administers a medicine to Marcia and finds that Marcia is not pregnant.
3. Harold enters Mr Jones's house at night, with the sole purpose of stealing a painting. He believes Mr Jones is not at home. To Harold's surprise, Mr Jones is home. In attempting to escape, Harold bounces into a mantelpiece, breaking several pieces of crystal and a Ming vase.
4. X has sexual intercourse with Y whom he believes to be 18 and who tells him she is 18. Y is, in fact, 14.

Feedback

2. No actus reus of a crime.
3. Actus reus of a crime.
4. Actus reus of a crime.

How did you do? If you missed any, revise the section. The reasons for each answer are given:

1. A would be guilty of attempting to be knowingly involved in dealing with a prohibited drug.
2. As Marcia is not pregnant, there can be no actus reus.
3. Harold has committed the actus reus of attempted burglary. He would be liable also for criminal damage of the Ming vase. He therefore has committed two offences.

4 This would be a crime of strict liability (see chapter 3). The real issue is that X has had sexual intercourse with a minor, prohibited by statute.

Activity 5.2

Mens rea

Let us now deal with the mens rea. Once again, you will attempt the following problems, writing in the space provided 'mens rea of a crime' or 'no mens rea of a crime', as appropriate.

The first one has been done for you.

1 A throws a stone into a crowd, intending to hit B. The stone misses B, but catches C, hitting him in the eye, resulting in blindness. Mens rea of a crime

2 D is suspected of several recent burglaries in the community of Tranquillity. One night, the police apprehend a man who is seen in Miss Duff's yard crouching under a tree. In his bag they find several implements including a torch, a crowbar and pliers.

3 X sharpens a machete and leaves with it, intending to kill Y. Y disarms him, whereupon X hits him on the head with an iron rod. Y does not die.

4 A arranges with B, a bank teller, that he is going to hold up the bank where B works. B gets cold feet, but is unable to get a message to A. A robs the bank and is arrested. He reveals B's part in the plot.

Feedback

2 Mens rea of a crime.

3 Mens rea of a crime.

4 Mens rea of a crime.

How did you do this time? Check your answers against the reasons given below:

1 By throwing a stone into a crowd A is reckless. Even though he misses the intended victim, he could have foreseen danger to C.

2 The circumstances are such as suggested that D has formed the mens rea of a crime.

3 X clearly forms the mens rea of a crime (murder). It results in grievous bodily harm to Y.

4 B has the mens rea of a crime, facilitating A in the hold-up. A does not know of the change of heart by B.

Examples

Mary, Mrs Brown's household helper, takes a watch from Mrs Brown's dresser and puts it in her bag. As she is about to leave the house, Mrs Brown says, 'Oh, Mary, I forgot to tell you to take the watch on the dresser. It is yours.'

In this example Mary's taking of the watch demonstrates the mens rea and the actus reus of theft. The state of affairs or event is present in her taking the watch. She then puts it in her bag, evidencing a 'defined state of mind'. However, when Mrs Brown tells Mary the watch is hers, both the actus reus and mens rea of theft are destroyed as you cannot steal from yourself. (This will become clearer later when we look at theft.)

Mary takes the watch and leaves with it. Later that evening Mrs Brown is looking for the watch to wear to a reception and discovers it missing. Mrs Brown calls the police who go to Mary's house and find the watch in a bag, under Mary's bed.

In this second example the state of affairs or event coincides with the state of mind. By taking the ring away to her home, and hiding it, Mary's intention seems clearly to be to deprive Mrs Brown permanently of it. She would be liable for the theft of the watch.

Activity 5.3

This activity will help you to identify how the actus reus and mens rea must coincide for criminal liability to arise.

Read each scenario, then put a '√' in the appropriate box. The first one is done for you.

1. Fred and Barney want to attend a cricket match without paying the entrance fee. They scale the back fence and, seeing two empty seats, they watch the match. We have both the actus reus and the mens rea of a crime. Yes (√) No ( )
2. Fred and Barney want to attend the cricket match. They climb a tree overlooking the field and watch from there. We have both the actus reus and mens rea of a crime. Yes ( ) No ( )
3. Unknown to B, A is already dead when he sneaks into A's room and injects him with a deadly poison. We have both the actus reus and mens rea of a crime. Yes ( ) No ( )
4. X, the householder, badgers Y to have sexual intercourse with her. She always refuses but says to him one day, 'We will see what happens'. That night, X goes to Y's room and has sexual intercourse with her, despite her protests. We have both the actus reus and mens rea of a crime. Yes ( ) No ( )
5. Jack and Jill are in a fight at the well. Jill hits Jack on the head with her pail, as a result of which he suffers a concussion and faints. We have both the actus reus and mens rea of a crime. Yes ( ) No ( )

How did you fare? See the answers opposite.

Feedback

In all but question 3 your answer should be (Yes). The reason is that in question 3 B's mens rea would have been invalidated by A's death prior to the commission by B of the actus reus. He would not have caused the event of A's death! Revise the definition of criminal liability in Smith and Hogan, cited above.

Elements of the actus reus

In our definition of the actus reus, we mentioned certain components of it. To refresh your memory, we will repeat them here. Actus reus (conduct) includes acts and omissions, consequences and surrounding circumstances (states of affairs). We will look at these components now.

Acts and omissions

It is true to say that a commission or an omission may be deemed an actus reus. For example, some action of mine may lead to a result forbidden by the criminal law, but yet that action is not my 'act', in a legal sense. To him my 'act' must be proven to be a voluntary, conscious movement by me, of my muscles. Thus, as we shall see on the next page, there is a defence of 'automatism'. In this instance, the commission is not my will.

Hill v. Baxter [1958] 1 All ER 193, [1958] 1 WLR 76, [1958] 1 QB 277

Here A, the accused, was stung by bees while driving, as a result of which he lost control of the vehicle, which hit and killed D. There was no actus reus on A's part, resulting in D's death.

R v. Burgess [1991] 2 QB 92, [1991] 2 All ER 769, [1991] 2 WLR 1206

Here A, who suffered from apoplexy, while under an attack of the illness, hit B. A's action was held to be involuntary. (See also Bratty v. AG for Northern Ireland [1963] AC 386, [1961] 3 All ER 523, [1961] 3 WLR 965.)

These two cases show instances when an act or omission is not an actus reus. Now, we will look at some instances of omission.

Omissions may occur where, for example, a statute imposes a duty, such as that to report an accident, under the Road Traffic Act, or to pay taxes, under the Income Tax Act.

An omission may also render one criminally liable at common law in the following situations:

Contractual duty

In R v. Pittwood (1902) 19 TLR 37, P, the keeper, was liable for failing to close the gate at a railway crossing before the train came, resulting in the death of D, the driver of a vehicle that attempted to cross the line. P was found guilty of manslaughter.

By virtue of holding office, professional responsibility

In R v. Adomako [1995] 1 AC 171, A, an anaesthetist, was found guilty of manslaughter for failure to perform on time a procedure during surgery, resulting in the patient's death. He had failed to discover a disconnected endotracheal tube, even though an alarm went off after the disconnection to which A should have been alerted. The House of Lords upheld the decision of the Court of Appeal where it was asked in relation to gross negligence that 'in cases of manslaughter by criminal negligence not involving driving but involving a breach of duty is it a sufficient direction to the jury to adopt the gross negligence test set out by the Court of Appeal ... without reference to the test of recklessness as defined in R v. Lawrence [1982] AC 510 ...?' Their Lordships answered in the affirmative, adding that a trial judge may use the word 'reckless' in his exposition of law, as the circumstances of the case warrant.

Undertaking to care for another

Where one undertakes to care for an aged or infirm person, or someone with physical or learning difficulties,...', one may be found liable for failing to discharge that undertaking.

In R v. Stone and Dobinson [1997] the parties, an unmarried couple, had an elderly relative (sister of one of them) living with them. She later became incapable of caring of herself and the couple did nothing to assist her as her condition deteriorated, as a result of which she died. The couple was found guilty of manslaughter.

By virtue of relationship

Parents or persons in loco parentis have a duty to care for their child. In R v. Gibbins and Proctor (1918) 13 Crim App Rep 134, a father and his girlfriend were found guilty of murder where they neglected to feed the father's child, as a result of which the child died.

Duty to minimise own act

Where A's actions lead to a state of affairs, A may incur liability even if A acted innocently. This occurs where the act might cause harm and A does nothing to avert it. In R v. Miller [1983] AC 161, D went to sleep with a lighted cigarette in his hand. He awoke to find his mattress smouldering, but did nothing about it, going into an adjoining room where he went to sleep. The house caught fire and D was convicted of arson. D had a duty to make an effort to put the fire out.

Consequences of one's action

As we saw earlier, the consequences of one's action is a part of the actus reus.

In R v. Shivpuri [1987] AC 1, [1986] 2 WLR 988, [1986] 2 All ER 334, S was convicted for attempting to be knowingly involved in dealing with a prohibited drug, contrary to statute. S was arrested by customs officials while in possession of a suitcase. The suitcase contained material, which S said he knew to be a prohibited drug. It turned out that the substance was not a prohibited drug but something similar to snuff. By attempting to bring about an illegal consequence, S was guilty of a criminal offence.

Another instance when the consequences of A's action can lead to criminal liability occurs where that action results in the injury or death of B, who takes evasive action to save himself from A. This was the case in R v. Lewis [1970] Crim LR 647, where D, fearing her attacker A, jumped out of a window and was injured. In a subsequent case R v. Williams and Davies (1991) 95 Crim App Rep 1, [1992] 2 All ER 183, [1992] 1 WLR 380, it was established that in these instances, there are two criteria that must be fulfilled. The first is whether a reasonable and responsible man in the assailant's position could foresee the consequences of his action. The second, applicable only in fatal cases, is whether the unlawful act is such as to raise in a sober and reasonable person a recognition that the person attacked would suffer harm, albeit not serious harm.

If a third party reacts reasonably to an accused's threat, the accused will be liable for the consequence. An example of this was seen in R v. Paget and Pemberton (1983) 76 Crim App Rep 279. There, while armed with a shotgun, the accused held a pregnant girl hostage using her as a shield while he fired at the police. The police fired back, killing the girl. The accused was found guilty of manslaughter. His appeal on the ground that it was the police's action, a novus actus interveniens, and not his action, which resulted in the girl's death, was unsuccessful.

What if the victim receives improper medical treatment after being injured by an assailant, resulting in the victim's death? An accused must take his victim as he finds him. The court will look at the cause of the victim's death. See R v. Cheshire [1991] 3 All ER 670, [1991] 1WLR 844. In R v. Malcherek [1981] 2 All ER, 422, where the victim's life support was turned off, resulting in the victim's death, an appeal against conviction for murder was dismissed. Turning off the life support in a situation where the deceased was brain dead did not break the chain of causation.

Where the victim's religious belief forbids him to take a blood transfusion, there is no break in the chain of causation if he dies. This was decided in R v. Blaue [1975] 3 All ER 466, [1975] 1 WLR 1411. The accused was found guilty of murder.

Surrounding circumstances of states of affairs

Lastly, we look at surrounding circumstances. In these cases, the accused's willed action is not the issue. The existence of the state of affairs or the surrounding circumstances is enough. It is sufficient that the accused is 'found' or is in 'possession'. These are usually statutory offences. Therefore, in R v. Larsonneur (1933) 24 Crim App Rep 74, the accused who had been refused leave to enter the UK, was convicted of 'being found' in the UK after being brought there from Ireland by the police.

In Winzar v. Chief Constable of Kent (1983) The Times, 28 March 1983 (reported at pages 46–7 of Smith and Hogan, 6th ed.), the accused was

Example

1 A is driving a car when she is attacked by a swarm of bees. The car goes out of control, hitting and killing D, who is standing by the roadside. According to Hill v. Baxter (1958), there is no actus reus on A's part, resulting in D's death.

2 During a fight, X stabs Y in the chest. Y does not die immediately, but is taken to hospital. He refuses to have a blood transfusion for religious reasons, and dies a few days later. Here, according to R v. Blaue [1975] X is liable. There is the actus reus of murder.

taken to a hospital on a stretcher, and being found to be drunk was told to leave. He was seen slumped in a chair in the corridor and was apprehended by the police to a car stationed outside the hospital. He was convicted for 'being found' drunk in the highway. (Both this case and Larsonneur have been criticised by Smith and Hogan as 'peculiarly offensive' because of the involvement of the police (page 47).)

A Privy Council decision is that 'remaining' in a country, contrary to statute, is not an offence where the accused is ignorant of the prohibition (Lim Chin Aik v. R [1963] AC 160, [1963] 1 All ER 223).

You will no doubt conclude that the actus reus of a crime is not always a straightforward issue. Let's look at some scenarios to seek to determine whether or not there is the actus reus.

Elements of the mens rea

We have already examined how the actus reus affects criminal liability. In this section we will look at the mens rea in much the same way.

First, we should revise our definition of the mens rea. The mens rea refers to the accused's state of mind and includes intention, recklessness, gross negligence and knowledge, that is, the accused's 'defined state of mind' must have 'caused the event'.

We will be looking at the following elements of the mens rea:

- intention
- recklessness
- negligence
- blameless inadvertence.

Intention and the mens rea

We refer to some crimes as 'crimes of specific intent'. These include murder, theft, burglary and wounding with intent. By the nature of these crimes, the accused apparently sets out to do something and takes steps to do it, achieving the result or the probable consequence. For example, A intends to shoot to kill B and fires a gun in B's direction, killing or wounding him. Either consequence can arise from that action, and A will be regarded as having the mens rea of the crime. This is referred to as 'direct' intent.

On the other hand, A intends only to frighten B and approaches him with a gun. B sees A approach him and screams before trying to wrest the gun from A. The gun goes off, injuring B. In such a situation, A is said to have 'oblique' intent. A trilogy of cases in 1985 and 1986 examine the questions that a jury must consider to determine whether the accused could have foreseen that consequence from which his intention can be established. The cases are R v. Moloney [1985] 1 AC 905, [1985] 1 All ER 1025, R v. Hancock and Shankland [1986] 1 AC 455, [1986] 1 All ER 646 and R v. Nedrick [1986] 3 All ER 1, [1986] 1 WLR 1025.

In R v. Nedrick, N, who threatened to 'burn out' P against whom he had a grudge, poured paraffin through the letter-box of her house and set it alight. P's child died and N was convicted of murder. His conviction was quashed and a verdict of manslaughter substituted. Lord Lane CJ identified two questions, which a jury must ask themselves. These are:

1 How probable was the consequence, which resulted from the defendant's voluntary act?
2 Did he foresee that consequence?

You may also wish to look again at Hyam v. DPP [1975] AC 55, [1974] 2 All ER 41.

Recklessness and the mens rea

Recklessness arises where A, not intending to cause a certain harm, takes an unjustifiable risk in causing it to occur. Emphasis is on the word 'unjustifiable'. There are two types of recklessness; subjective and objective.

Subjective recklessness

R v. Cunningham [1957] 2 QB 396, [1957] 2 All ER 412 is the leading case. There, D tore a gas meter from the wall of the cellar of an unoccupied house, in order to steal money from it. He left the gas gushing out, with the result that it seeped into a neighbouring house, endangering P's life. D was convicted under section 23 of the Offences against the Person Act 1861, for 'maliciously administering a noxious thing so as to endanger life'. The judge at first instance misdirected the jury that 'malicious' meant 'wicked'. The Court of Appeal quashed the conviction on the basis of the misdirection. The court laid down two essential elements to determine recklessness; relying on an earlier principle of the law:

1. The accused must have demonstrated 'an actual intention to do the particular kind of harm that in fact was done'.
2. The accused demonstrated 'recklessness as to whether such harm should occur or not. (That is, the accused has foreseen that the particular kind of harm might be done and yet has gone on to take the risk of it.) It is neither limited to, nor does it indeed require, any ill-will towards the person injured.'

Objective recklessness

Here, the considerations of the reasonable man are crucial. Would a reasonable man have acted as the accused did? The case in point is R v. Caldwell [1982] AC 341, [1981] 1 All ER 961. In this case, D who held a grievance against P, the proprietor of a residential hotel, got himself very drunk and decided to set the hotel on fire. Some 10 guests were resident in the hotel at the time. The fire was discovered and extinguished before serious harm was done. Lord Diplock laid down two tests in determining whether the accused had been reckless:

1. The accused 'does an act which in fact creates an obvious risk that property would be destroyed or damaged'.
2. The accused, 'when he does the act he either has not given any thought to the possibility of there being any such risk or has recognised that there was some risk involved and has nevertheless gone on to do it'.

Objective recklessness does not apply to offences against the person. Look at the following case, for example:

DPP/R v. Parmenter [1992] 1 AC 699, [1991] 4 All ER 698, [1991] 3 WLR 914 and R v. Savage [1991] 4 All ER 698, [1991] 3 WLR 914

In Parmenter, the accused was convicted on four counts of unlawfully and maliciously causing grievous bodily harm to his infant son from the time of the baby's birth on 8 February 1988 to 11 May 1988. In his defence, P said that he was not aware that his manner of handling the child would have resulted in the injuries caused.

In R v. Savage, S, who held a grudge against another woman, B, made her way through the crowd in a pub and approached B, who was sitting with friends, and emptied a glass of beer on her. The glass fell from S's hand and B's wrist was cut by broken glass. In her evidence S denied that she had let the glass slip purposely. At first instance, the jury was directed that S's deliberate action of throwing the beer on B constituted an assault and that if she unintentionally let go of the glass so that it caused the wound, she was guilty. The Court of Appeal quashed S's conviction in relation to the wound, holding that S would be guilty only if she foresaw that some physical harm would result from her act. The court substituted a conviction for assault occasioning actual bodily harm.

Both these cases went before the House of Lords on appeal and were considered together with another case, R v. Spratt [1991] 2 All ER 210, [1990] 1 WLR 1073.

In R v. Spratt, S fired an air pistol from his flat into the square below. A young girl playing in the square was injured by two pellets, which hit her. S's defence was that he was aiming at a sign on a rubbish chute and he did not know anyone was there, and that he would not have fired the pistol had he known someone was there. On appeal against sentence, S having pleaded guilty to assault occasioning actual bodily harm, the Court of Appeal allowed D's appeal, holding that he was not guilty of the offence unless he foresaw that he would occasion actual bodily harm. In his guilty plea, his counsel said it was based upon recklessness.

Before their Lordships' House, the question was whether the accused persons were properly convicted on the directions given on the law of recklessness. Their Lordships discussed the leading cases of Cunningham, Caldwell and Mowatt and concluded that the appeal in Savage would be dismissed. Parmenter was allowed in part, their Lordships substituting another charge. Significantly, they held that:

> '[It] is quite unnecessary that the accused should either have intended or have foreseen that his unlawful act might cause physical harm of the gravity described [in section 20 of the Offences Against the Person Act] that is, a wound or serious physical injury. It is enough that he should have foreseen that some physical harm to some person, albeit of a minor character, might result.'

Negligence and the mens rea

We shall now consider negligence and its role in determining the existence of mens rea. The learned writers of Smith and Hogan suggest that the law in this area has become more uncertain since the decision in R v. Caldwell. 'Negligence' in this sense connotes 'gross negligence'. The issue is whether a reasonable man would have acted as A did.

Cases involving manslaughter are usually those considered under this head, as in R v. Adomako [1994] 3 All ER 79, [1994] 3 WLR 288, [1995] 1 AC 171, which we looked at earlier. The anaesthetist in this case was convicted of manslaughter on the basis that his conduct had fallen way below that of a reasonable man (meaning a reasonable anaesthetist!).

Blameless inadvertence

We come now to the fourth important element of the mens rea, blameless inadvertence. This refers to those situations in which the accused reasonably failed to foresee the consequences of his action or where statute imposes a duty. There are two sides to this element, namely crimes of strict liability and transferred malice.

Strict liability

In relation to the actus reus crimes of strict liability do not require mens rea in the same sense that other crimes do. The cases reveal, however, that the courts still examine the accused's mens rea. Public policy is an important consideration and the burden of proof is on the accused, unlike in other cases when it is on the prosecution. They are usually creatures of statute and are sometimes referred to, infelicitously, as crimes of 'absolute liability'. Violations of road traffic legislation, dangerous drugs offences and violations of spirit licences are among the most common occurrences. A growing situation is that involving the protection of the environment.

Dangerous drugs

As you are no doubt aware, this issue is one of concern as traffickers present serious challenges to law enforcement personnel. In the Commonwealth Caribbean, all countries have legislation dealing with the nemesis of dangerous drugs. You should look at the legislation of your own State. Here are two interesting cases:

Sweet v. Parsley [1969] 1 All ER 347

D, a teacher, let to tenants rooms in a farmhouse of which she was a sub-tenant, retaining a room for herself. The tenants smoked cannabis on the premises. D was held liable for the offence; even though it was proved that she had no knowledge of it. Her conviction was on the ground that she was 'concerned in the management of premises used for the purpose of smoking cannabis'. The House of Lords quashed her conviction, based on the principle that the statutory provision required some element of mens rea. D had no such mens rea.

R v. McNamara (1988) 87 Crim App Rep 246

X was apprehended for being in possession of a box which he was carrying on the back of his motor cycle. The box contained a cannabis resin. His explanation was that he was delivering the box for a man, whose name he refused to give and that he thought the box contained pornographic material or private videos. He was charged under a relevant statute (Misuse of Drugs Act S. 5(3)). The trial judge had directed the jury to convict if they were "satisfied so that you are sure that he had possession of the contents of the cardboard box ... and knew that the box contained something, unless on the balance of probabilities he has proved that he neither knew, suspected nor had reason to suspect the contents of the box was any controlled drug". This direction was approved by the Court of Appeal and the accused's appeal against conviction was dismissed.

Pollution

The leading case is Alphacell Ltd v. Woodward [1972] AC 824, [1972] 2 All ER 475. There, D Ltd built and operated settling tanks, which had an overflow channel into a river and provided pumps to prevent an overflow. The pumps became obstructed with vegetation, and an overflow of polluted water occurred.

There was no evidence of negligence on D's part, nor that they knew that the pollution was taking place. Liability for the offence was strict.

Spirit licence violation

In Cundy v. Le Cocq (1884) 13 QB 207, D was convicted for selling intoxicating liquor to a drunken person, contrary to a statutory provision.

The relevant section did not include the word 'knowingly'. It was held that D was strictly liable, and there was no need to consider whether D knew, had the means of knowing or could with ordinary care have known, that the person to whom he served the drink was drunk at the time.

Transferred malice

In 'transferred malice' cases, we examine whether D is liable, having the mens rea of a particular crime, and then does something which causes the actus reus of that crime, even if the result is unintended. For example, D meaning to kill X, kills Y whom he believes to be X. D would be liable for Y's murder. R v. Latimer (1886) 17 QBD illustrates the point. In this case, D hit at X with his belt, hitting him slightly but wounding Y who was standing nearby. D was held liable for the injury to Y. The actus reus and mens rea of the same crime coincided, even though D had not set out to hit Y.

Where the mens rea and actus reus of the same crime do not coincide, D is not liable. R v. Pembliton [1874–80] All ER Rep 1163 demonstrates the principle. There, D who was involved in a fight outside a public house threw a stone at X. The stone missed X but broke a window. He was convicted at first instance for malicious damage. The conviction was quashed on the basis that he did not have the mens rea for the result. In other words, the actus reus of malicious damage had not coincided with the mens rea of the crime.

Example

Suppose X throws a bomb into a building, aiming at a room where he believes Y is sleeping. Y is not in the room but his son D who is asleep there is killed by X's bomb. Would X be liable for D's death? Obviously he would be. (See R v. Nedrick.) You will note that in Nedrick the accused's conviction for murder was reduced to manslaughter.

Activity 5.4

Recognising elements of the mens rea

This activity will assist you in recognising the elements of the mens rea. Identify the particular heading of the mens rea under which each fact situation falls, citing a case.

1 Mallards Sugar Ltd operates a refinery in Endeavour. From time to time residents have complained that effluent from the factory has been allowed to contaminate the Endeavour River. The Environmental Agency conducts a survey and finds that effluent is in fact coming from the factory and prosecutes them. They are convicted under the relevant statute.

   a Issue: Pollution (strict liability offence)

   b Case: Alphacell Ltd v. Woodward

2 Barry is driving his car with a group of friends who have come down from Canada to the Caribbean for the holidays. They are on their way to the beach and come upon a roadblock mounted by the police, who stop Barry and search his car. At the bottom of a backpack in the boot of the car the police found two sticks of crack cocaine and arrest Barry and all the occupants of the car. The backpack belongs to one of the visitors and Barry does not know what is in their bags.

   a Issue:

   b Case:

3 X throws a stone at Y who shies away from it. The stone lands in the windscreen of Z's Mercedes Benz, breaking it.

   a Issue:

   b Case:

4 A, a diabetic, is admitted to hospital in a coma. B, a private nurse assigned to A, fails to give A insulin at the times ordered by Dr D and A dies.

   a Issue:

   b Case:

5 Abbot tells Sheriff 'I am going to get even with you'. Abbot sets fire to Sheriff's house. All of Sheriff's family and Sheriff escape, except his wife, who is burnt to death.

a Issue:

b Case:

Let's see how well you did. The answers are opposite:

Feedback

2 Issue: Being in possession of dangerous drugs, contrary to applicable statute (strict liability offence)

Case: Sweet v. Parsley, R v. McNamara

3 Issue: Transferred malice

Case: R v. Latimer, R v. Pembliton

4 Issue: Negligence

Case: R v. Adomako

5 Issue: Recklessness

Case: R v. Cunningham, R v. Caldwell

Activity 5.5

Understanding the elements of the mens rea

The first one has been done for you.

1 A direct intent is where an accused has the intent or desire of making something happen. True (√) False ( )

2 Objective recklessness does not apply to offences against the person. True ( ) False ( )

3 In subjective recklessness, there is no requirement that the accused bore ill will towards the victim. True ( ) False ( )

4 In crimes of strict liability the accused will always be convicted as the law is applied strictly. True ( ) False ( )

5 In cases of negligence, resulting in death, the accused will be convicted of manslaughter, not murder. True ( ) False ( )

6 Large corporations are always convicted for reports of environmental breaches. True ( ) False ( )

7 In transferred malice, a defendant will be convicted even if the actus reus of the crime, which results, is different from the mens rea of the crime intended. True ( ) False ( )

8 Theft is a crime of specific intent. True ( ) False ( )

9 Crimes of strict liability are usually creatures of statute. True ( ) False ( )

10 Recklessness is the taking of an unjustified risk. True ( ) False ( )

Check the answers opposite.

Feedback

1 True (√)
2 True (√)
3 True (√)
4 False (√)
5 True (√)
6 False (√)
7 False (√)
8 True (√)
9 True (√)
10 True (√)

Offences against the person

Homicide – murder

Definition of murder

Crimes that result in death fall generally under the law of 'homicide'. 'Homicide' refers to murder and manslaughter. In this section we will discuss the law relating to murder.

With violent crimes, including murders, increasing in most Commonwealth Caribbean jurisdictions, citizens are demanding more punitive action. In fact, on the question of penalty for murder, there appears to be unanimity across the region that we should retain capital punishment. The issue inspires passionate debate and in a later section, we shall examine the equally convincing arguments put forward by those in support, and those against, when we come to examine sentencing practices in the region.

We will examine the definition of murder. Once again, we turn to Smith and Hogan Criminal Law, 2002. At page 353, of the 10th edition, they refer to Coke's 'classic definition of murder'. Notwithstanding its archaic wording and subsequent statutory interventions, Coke's definition stating the common law, is still essential. It is as follows:

> 'Murder is when a man of sound memory, and of the age of discretion, unlawfully killeth within any country of the realm any reasonable creature in rerum natura under the king's peace, with malice aforethought, either expressed by the party or implied by law, so as the party wounded, or hurt, etc. die of the wound or hurt, etc. within a year and a day after the same.'

To get a good grasp of Coke's definition, we will select the four key elements in the definition. These are:

1. 'A man of sound memory and of the age of discretion.'
2. 'Unlawfully killeth within any country of the realm any reasonable creature in rerum natura under the king's peace.'
3. 'With malice aforethought either expressed by the party or implied by law.'
4. 'So as the party, wounded or hurt etc., die of the wound or hurt, etc. within a year and a day after the same.'

Task: Examine the definition of murder in the Offences Against the Person Act, or equivalent legislation for your jurisdiction.

The nature of the crime

There are four main elements of the crime of murder, as our definition shows. We will look at each one in turn.

A man of sound memory and of the age of discretion

The accused, male or female, must be competent to form the mens rea of the crime. He or she must therefore be insane or be suffering from diminished responsibility. He or she must also not be a juvenile as defined by statute.

Task: Check the Juveniles Act or equivalent legislation for your jurisdiction.

'Unlawfully killeth within any country of the realm any reasonable creature in rerum natura under the king's peace'

Several important issues arise here:

1. The killing must be unlawful. A hangman or executioner, performing his duties in accordance with the laws of the State is not guilty of murder, neither is a person who kills another in self-defence where, had he not acted in his own defence, the deceased would have him killed.
2. The victim must be a human being. This raises important questions as to when a person begins or ceases to be one. This is important in respect of foetuses at one end, and at the other end, those who are considered 'brain dead' as against those who are 'heart dead'.

The foetus must have been expelled from the mother, and be alive at birth, at the time of the act causing its death, for a charge of murder to be laid. However, if the act against the foetus was committed before its birth but results in its subsequent death, after having been born alive, the prosecution may succeed with a charge of murder against an accused.

See AG's Reference (No. 3 of 1994) [1997] 3 All ER 936, the facts of which are stated in Smith and Hogan (2002), page 355.

On the issue of 'brain death' as against 'heart death', the law relies upon medical science to a great extent. It has been held in an American case, that brain death is sufficient for charge of murder. There it was held that the disconnection of a respirator following brain death was not the cause of death. The accused, who had attacked the victim and placed him in a coma, was guilty of murder (Commonwealth v. Goldston 366 NE 2d 744 (Mass. 1977)). As for who is 'under the king's peace' (at the present time, 'the queen's peace') this is regarded as anyone within the realm. This concept was more meaningful during imperial and colonial times, but is still valid in that it conveys the idea of universality, and is closely related to extradition laws.

'With malice aforethought' either expressed by the party or implied by law

The rather quaint expression, "malice aforethought", is a term of art and goes to the root of the mens rea of murder. It is not required that the accused had 'malice' towards the victim. Neither is it necessary that he had thought about the crime before committing it. The leading case of R v. Moloney has set out the two criteria for determining the existence of 'malice aforethought'. These are that the accused had an intention:

- to kill any person; or
- to cause grievous bodily harm to any person.

See R v. Moloney [1985] AC 905, [1985] All ER 1025; Hyam v. DPP [1975] AC 55; Frankland and Moore v. R [1987] AC 576, [1987] 2 WLR 1251 (PC).

See the Offences Against the Person Act of your State and study the definition of 'grievous bodily harm'.

According to Smith and Hogan, the terms 'express malice' and 'implied malice' must be taken, respectively, to mean (a) the intention to kill and (b) the intention to cause grievous bodily harm. The learned writers suggest that these terms do not offer much assistance (10th ed., page 360).

'So as the party ... die of the wound or hurt etc. within a year and a day after the same'

In England, the common law 'year and a day rule' has been abolished by the Law Reform (Year and a Day Rule) Act 1996, ceasing to affect homicides after 17 June 1996. Is there need for similar reform in our jurisdiction? The arguments for it are compelling.

This common law rule relates to the element of causation and provides a convenient cut-off point up to, or after which the victim's death can, or cannot be, attributable to the accused. This is what is referred to as the 'causal relationship' between the violator's act, which results in the victim's death. (See R v. Dyson [1908] 2 KB 454.) The issue of causation is a very important one, raising a number of complexities. Among these we find intervening and contributory events, the 'but for' principle and contributory cause. Let's look at these in turn.

Intervening acts or events: The Latin name for intervening or supervening events is 'novus actus interveniens'. Here are some examples:

- What if, after A inflicts an injury to D, D who is a diabetic, dies from a complication exacerbated by his diabetes? A must take his victim as he finds him.
- What if A shoots D who subsequently becomes depressed because of his slow recuperation and commits suicide? A would be found guilty, not of murder, but of manslaughter, his original act being an operating cause of D's death. (See Smith and Hogan, 10th ed., page 48.)

R v. Malcherek [1981] 2 All ER 422, [1981] 1 WLR 690

In R v. Malcherek doctors switched off the victim's life support after careful deliberation. The accused, who later appealed on the ground that it was the doctor's action and not his original felony that resulted in the victim's death, had his appeal dismissed and his conviction upheld.

R v. Jordan (1956) 40 Cr. App Rep 152

In this case A stabbed D who was admitted to hospital and died eight days later. Medical evidence showed that D died, not from the wound, which had substantially healed, but from a medicine administered to D to prevent infection. The Court of Appeal found that the medical treatment was 'palpably wrong' and allowed A's appeal. The wound must be shown to be a sine qua non direct.

Compare R v. Smith [1959] 2 All ER 193, [1959] 2 QB 35.

The 'but for' principle: By this is meant that A will not be liable where D's demise would have occurred in the same way without A's intervention. The prosecution must show that 'but for' (that is, 'were it not for') A's act, D's demise would not have occurred.

Contributory cause: Under this head, we make a distinction between a 'cause' and a 'substantial cause'.

There are a number of interesting cases, which explain the distinction, and we shall look at a few of them now.

In determining the 'cause' of death, the principle is that the wrongful act of the accused does not have to be the main cause. Compare R v. Benge (1865) (at page 43 of Smith and Hogan, 10th ed.) and R v. Dalloway (1847) (at page 44 of Smith and Hogan, 10th ed.).

In R v. Benge it was no defence that the negligent act of third parties played a role in the victim's death, when a flagman and an engine driver failed to perform their duties. A's original mistake in placing the flagman at a wrong distance, resulting in the flagman's death, was the primary cause, resulting in A's liability for manslaughter.

In R v. Dalloway, a three-year-old child was killed after it ran into the path of a cart drawn by a horse. The cart was being driven by A, who was not holding the reins, which were loose on the horse's back. The question was whether A caused the child's death. Could the child's death have been avoided if A had held the reins? This was the issue left for the jury.

The importance of identifying the 'substantial cause' of the victim's death is a necessary factor. The accused's act in contributing to the death 'must not be so minute that it will be ignored under the de minimis principle' (Smith and Hogan, 10th ed., page 44). Some weight is therefore placed on A's wrongful act vis à vis supervening events and whether those are in essence the cause of the wrong prescription or if D neglected to care for himself so that his condition deteriorated, resulting in his death.

Look also at R v. Holland (1841) (Smith and Hogan, 10th ed., page 321) and R v. Blaue [1975] 3 All ER 446, [1975] 1 WLR 1411.

Activity 5.6

Determining liability for murder

This activity will assist you in learning the definition of murder and to identify instances of liability for the crime.

Identify in each of the following sets of fact situations: (i) the element of the crime of murder which is raised and (ii) whether on these facts there is or is not criminal liability.

The first one is done for you.

Q: Donat and Eddie, both aged 10, are flying their kites, each boy determined that his kite should fly higher than the other's. All is going well until the string on Eddie's kite burst causing his kite to become entangled in a tree. He accuses Donat of tampering with the string earlier that morning. Donat denies it and the boys begin to fight. Eddie tries to escape, but Donat chases him, shouting 'Watch me and you today. I must kill you'. Eddie throws a large stone at Donat. The stone catches Donat in the head, wounding him seriously. He is admitted to hospital and dies a week later from an enormous swelling of his brain. Is Eddie liable for murder?

A: The main issue is Eddie's age. He is only 10 years old; therefore he is not 'of age of discretion'. You would need to look at the relevant provision of your own Juveniles Act. An infant of such tender years cannot form criminal intent as the statutory provisions show. Eddie would be dealt with as a juvenile and could, at the end of his trial, if found guilty of manslaughter (which on the facts, he would be), be placed in the care of the State.

Now attempt the following:

Q: Cindy is eight weeks pregnant and confides in her friend Regina that she wants to have an abortion. Regina decides to take Cindy to see Dr Mort who she says performed the procedure for her when she was pregnant. Dr Mort gives Cindy a milky substance, which she ingests, subsequently becoming very ill. She is hospitalised. When Cindy recovers, she is still pregnant and is now too scared to go ahead with the abortion. The baby is born prematurely with severe brain damage and dies six weeks after birth. The substance Cindy ingested is the cause of the brain damage.

What, if any, is the criminal liability of Cindy?

Feedback

First, you should identify whether or not there are statutory provisions making abortions illegal in your jurisdiction. (See the Offences Against the Person Act or other relevant legislation.) All three persons would be in violation of the statute. Secondly, you must ask yourself whether the damage done to the foetus, resulting in the infant's death, is sufficient to make them liable for the baby's death. The discussion must turn on who is capable of being a 'victim', in rerum natura. (AG's Reference (No. 3 of 1994) [1997] 3 All ER 936.)

How did you do? You will note that these fact situations required you to identify the issues and to support your answers with case law and statute, as appropriate. Ensure that you always follow this approach.

Activity 5.7

The issue of intervening or supervening events and their impact on an accused's liability always evokes great interest. No doubt you have your own views. The following exercises will assist you in identifying the legal approach.

Put an '√' in the correct box to indicate whether the statement is "true" or "false".

The first question is done for you.

1 The Latin term for intervening or supervening events is 'novus actus interveniens'. True (√) False ( )

2 A administers a lethal dose of poison to D. Before the poison takes effect D, who has a history of heart disease, dies from a heart attack. A is liable for D's death. True ( ) False ( )

3 A stabs D and believing D to be dead, throws D's body into a pond. D dies from drowning and would probably have survived, had he been able to swim. A is liable for D's death. True ( ) False ( )

4 A shoots B who is grievously wounded and is expected to die within an hour. B swallows poison and dies before the hour elapses. A is liable for B's death. True ( ) False ( )

Feedback

1 True (√)
2 False (√)
3 True (√)
4 False (√)
5 True (√)
6 True (√)

5 A hits B as a result of which B falls and hits his head, then lapses into a coma. B is given incorrect medication and dies from a heart attack. A is liable for B's death. True ( ) False ( )

6 C is diagnosed with a rare form of bone cancer. Her mother, X, does not agree with the doctor's advice that C should undergo some special treatment. Instead, X secludes C inside her religious community where she relies on faith healing and alternative medicines. C dies from the cancer. X is liable for C's death. True ( ) False ( )

In Jamaica, the Offences Against the Person Act was amended in 1995 to make a distinction between 'capital' and 'non-capital' murder. Examine the distinctions set out in section 2 of the Act and write notes.

Also, look at Alfred Flowers v. The Queen (Privy Council Appeal No. 54 of 1999).

Homicide – manslaughter

In the last section, we discussed one limb of the law of homicide, namely, murder. We shall now embark upon a study of the second limb, which is manslaughter.

What is 'manslaughter'?

In their case book, Criminal Law, Cases and Materials (2002, 8th ed.), Smith and Hogan refer to manslaughter as 'a complex crime of no less than five varieties'. The learned writers then go on to state the law, as follows:

> 'It covers three cases where the defendant kills with the fault required for murder but, because of the presence of a particular extenuating circumstance recognised by law, the offence is reduced to manslaughter. These cases are traditionally known as "voluntary manslaughter". The other cases – "involuntary manslaughter" – consist of homicides committed with a fault element less than that required for murder but recognised by the common law as sufficient to ground liability for homicide.'

The learned writers then summarise the circumstances in which a person is guilty of manslaughter, setting them out as follows:

1 A kills or is party to the killing of another with the fault required for murder (R v. Moloney [1985] 1 All ER 1025), but he would be convicted for the lesser offence on the grounds of:
   - a diminished responsibility
   - b provocation (R v. Camplin [1978] AC 705, [1978] 2 WLR 679)
   - c the act having been committed as part of a suicide pact.

2 A's voluntary intoxication results in his lack of the required mens rea (DPP v. Majewski [1976] 2 WLR 623, [1976] 2 ALLER 142.

3 A kills another:
   - a as a result of an unlawful and dangerous act (DPP v. Newbury and Jones [1976] 2 All ER 365) or
   - b being reckless whether or not his act will result in personal injury (R v. Caldwell [1982] AC 341, [1981] 2 WLR 509, [1981] 1 All ER 961)

Let us now examine the two key elements: voluntary manslaughter and involuntary manslaughter.

Voluntary manslaughter

A person is guilty of voluntary manslaughter where the facts reveal that he had the necessary mens rea and actus reus for murder, but the circumstances are such that he is partially excused. The factors that will lead to his partial excuse are:

- provocation
- diminished responsibility.

Provocation

Two important elements for an accused in seeking to satisfy the court that he was provoked into committing the homicide are:

1 that he acted on a sudden impulse, that is, without pre-meditation
2 that he acted as any reasonable person would have acted.

Let's take these elements in turn.

Sudden impulse: Suppose A, a care-giver, is goaded by D over a period of time into killing him because D is suffering from a serious illness. A does not oblige but, one day, after D's urging, A asphyxiates D. A tells the police that 'It was the last straw'. Can A rely on provocation in his defence? In R v. Cocker [1989] Crim LR 740, upon which these facts are based, the Court of Appeal found that A did not meet the necessary criteria. Consider, what are the necessary criteria?

In R v. Duffy [1949] All ER 932n, Devlin J, as he then was, gave what the Court of Criminal Appeal described as a 'classic direction', the common law definition of provocation, thus:

> 'Provocation is some act, or series of acts, done by the dead man, to the accused, which would cause in any reasonable person, and actually causes in the accused, a sudden and temporary loss of self-control, rendering the accused so subject to passion as to make him or her for the moment not master of his mind.'

These factors were not present in Cocker.

We will look at another case, R v. Ibrams and Gregory (1981) 74 Cr. App R 154, for another example. Here, the deceased had bullied the accused persons over a period of time. They had not been able to secure effective police protection. Anticipating that the deceased would have continued with his usual behaviour, the parties conspired with a young woman to get the deceased into a drunken state and then to encourage him to take her to his bed. The accused would then come into the room and break the deceased's arms and legs. The plans were duly made and carried out, and the deceased was killed. These events took place a week after the deceased's last aggression. The accused appealed against their conviction for murder on the ground that the trial judge had not put the defence of provocation to the jury. Their appeal was dismissed, the Court of Criminal Appeal finding that there was no sudden loss of self-control of the type required in the Duffy definition. Cumulative acts by the deceased may lead to the accused's successful defence of provocation, although there were provocative acts in the past. There must be some act, which triggers the accused's response, however minor. This was the view of the Court in R v. Ahluwalia [1992] 4 All ER 89, [1993] Crim LR 63.

Here, their Lordships said:

> 'We accept that the subjective element in the defence of provocation would not as a matter of law be negative simply because of the

> delayed reaction in such cases, provided that there was at the time of the killing a "sudden and temporary loss of self-control" caused by the alleged provocation. However, the longer the delay and the stronger the evidence of deliberation on the part of the defendant, the more likely it will be that the prosecution will negative provocation.'

There is much discussion on how the court's position affects 'slow burn' in post-traumatic stress syndrome, or battered woman syndrome. Is there a preference shown towards male accused persons? (See Bandali [1992] Crim LR 715.) See also R v. Thornton, below.

R v. Thornton [1992] 1 All ER 306

A, who had a history of mental problems, married D, in 1988, knowing him to be a heavy drinker and that he was jealous and possessive. She was the victim of domestic violence during the marriage. In 1989, D was charged for violence against her. A month later, the abuse continued and A was heard to say that she would kill him. Two days after saying this, A and D quarrelled and he called her a whore. A went to the kitchen and took a carving knife, which she sharpened. A then invited D to bed, but D refused and said he would kill her when she was asleep. She replied that she would kill him first and D dared her, sarcastically. A killed him, stabbing him in the stomach. A called an ambulance and the police but told the police not to bother to try and save D, later telling them that D had threatened to kill her, and that she intended to frighten, but not kill him.

The Court of Criminal Appeal dismissed her appeal. Submissions on her behalf that there was a long course of provocative conduct negating the 'sudden impulse' requirements were unsuccessful.

Phillips v. R [1969] AC 130, [1969] 2 WLR 581, (1968) 53 Cr. App R 132 (A Jamaican Appeal to the Privy Council)

In Phillips v. R, the appellant and the deceased had been involved in a recently ended relationship. On the day of the killing, the deceased and the appellant's mother were involved in a quarrel during which the appellant was present but not involved. The deceased spat at the appellant's mother and the appellant pulled a machete from a bag his mother was carrying and used it to chop at the deceased six times, killing her. His defence was provocation. The trial judge directed the jury to convict if they found that the appellant had not acted as a reasonable man. He had claimed to have acted on sudden impulse and that he had spun around to punch her with his hand. The Privy Council upheld the trial judge's directions and the subsequent conviction. The Court of Appeal had allowed the appeal regarding the trial judge's direction, but had not disturbed the sentence.

The reasonable person/'the reasonable man': Would a reasonable person have responded in a manner similar to the accused? Who is the reasonable person? He or she was previously defined in English law as 'the man on the Clapham omnibus'. Cultural changes have redefined him/her, so that he/she is not homogenous and might be on the Castries or Basseterre omnibus (or. more likely, minibus). In other words he/she has metamorphosed.

The leading case is DPP v. Camplin [1978] 2 All ER 168, a decision of the House of Lords. You should read this case and must check on cases in your own jurisdiction, where available.

In Camplin, a 15-year-old boy killed a middle-aged man whom he claimed had seriously sexually assaulted him then laughed at him. He had told the police a different story about the circumstances of the deceased's death. He did not succeed with a defence of provocation. Their Lordships described the reasonable man, thus:

> '... a person having the power of self-control to be expected of an ordinary person of the sex and age of the accused, but in other respects sharing such of the accused's characteristics as they think would affect the gravity of the provocation to him ... not merely whether such a person would in like circumstances be provoked to lose his self-control but also would react to the provocation as the accused did.'

The previously regarded authorities of Mancini v. DPP [1942] AC 1, [1941] 3 All ER 272, Holmes v. DPP [1946] AC 588, [1946] 2 All ER 124, Bedder v. DPP [1954] 2 All ER 801, [1954] 1 WLR 1119 were held to be no longer authorities on the law of provocation. You may wish to look at these cases. However, their Lordships' views in Camplin about them, will indicate to you how much the law has evolved to place value on words spoken. The decision in Camplin modifies the previous requirement that the mode of resentment, such as the weapon used to kill the deceased, must bear a reasonable relation to the violence resulting from the provocation.

See also R v. Doughty (1986) 83 Cr. App R 319.

Diminished responsibility

Diminished responsibility is not the same as insanity where the accused has a 'defect of reason' as stated in the M'Naghten Rules. It has been referred to as a type of 'partial insanity', as in R v. Byrne [1960] 3 All ER 1. In this case, the court set out the requirements, which the accused must show, to succeed with the defence. These are as follows:

> 'That he was suffering from abnormality of mind; and that such abnormality of mind (i) arose from a condition of arrested or retarded development of mind or any inherent causes or was induced by disease or injury and (ii) was such as substantially impaired his mental responsibility for his acts in doing or being a party to the killing.'

The gruesome facts of the case are that A strangled a young woman and after her death, committed horrifying mutilations on her dead body. The facts of the killing were not in dispute, the accused making an admission in a long statement. His defence was diminished responsibility. He was convicted and appealed.

Medical experts were called to give evidence on behalf of the accused. Their evidence was to the effect that the appellant was a sexual psychopath, and they provided examples of how such a mind works. Further, the doctors all argued that although the accused was not insane within the definition of the M'Naghten Rules, he could be described as partially insane. The basis of the appeal was that the learned trial judge had erred in directing the jury that the defence of diminished responsibility was not available to the appellant, within the relevant provision of the Homicide Act 1957, which would have the effect of reducing the charge to manslaughter.

The Court of Criminal Appeal allowed the appeal but confirmed the sentence. Their Lordships said:

> 'The evidence of the revolting circumstances of the killing and the subsequent mutilations, as of the previous sexual history of the appellant, pointed, we think plainly, to the conclusion that the appellant was what would be described in ordinary language as on the border-line of insanity or partially insane.'

The defence of diminished responsibility is one about which the decision is to be made by the jury and not by doctors. The jury must be satisfied that the accused's impulse substantially impaired his responsibility.

Involuntary manslaughter

We will now examine those situations, which give rise to involuntary manslaughter. These homicidal offences are committed without malice aforethought, that is, without the mens rea for murder. The headings under which the offence is considered are: constructive manslaughter and reckless manslaughter or manslaughter by gross negligence. We shall look at each one in turn.

Constructive manslaughter

In law, we make a distinction between an 'actual' and a 'constructive' act. The 'actual' act in the present context would indicate the presence of the mens rea for a particular actus reus. It is a bit more difficult in the case of a 'constructive' act in which event the mens rea is implied from the actus reus, that is, the accused is deemed to have intended a particular result arising from a particular conduct. In homicide, the rule was strictly viewed by learned writers who saw such 'constructive' conduct as making an accused liable for murder. The Homicide Act 1957 removed the doctrine of constructive murder, thereby imposing liability for constructive manslaughter instead.

Three elements must exist for constructive manslaughter. These are: (i) there was an unlawful act; (ii) the act was dangerous in that a reasonable person would have realised the risk of injury; and (iii) it resulted in death.

We will examine some cases, which illustrate the principle. We start with an old case, R v. Franklin (1883). In this case, A threw 'a good sized box' into the sea, hitting D who was swimming, resulting in D's death. The jury found A guilty of manslaughter. It was sufficient that D died as a result of A's dangerous act. A reasonable person would have realised the likelihood or risk of injury from such an act in a place where someone is likely to be.

Compare these two interesting cases:

R v. Larkin [1943] 1 All ER 217

Here, A found his live-in companion D, at a party with another man with whom she was having a sexual relationship. A was upset when he saw D with the man and went away, returning with a razor. He inflicted a wound to D's throat, causing her death. In his defence, A stated that he intended only to frighten the other man and not to kill D who, he said, was groggy with drink, swayed against him and had her throat cut by accident. A was convicted of manslaughter and appealed. The Court of Criminal Appeal dismissed the appeal, upholding the position of the learned trial judge that the act of the accused in approaching the deceased and another with a naked razor was dangerous in that it resulted in D's death. A was therefore appropriately convicted.

R v. Church [1965] 2 All ER 72

The appellant, A, took the deceased, D, to his van for a sexual encounter. He was unable to satisfy her and she reproached him, slapping his face. They fought and he knocked her out. Unable to revive her, having made efforts to do so, A threw D into a river where she died from drowning. The trial judge directed the jury that if D was alive when she was thrown into the river, whether or not A knew it, he would be guilty of manslaughter. A was convicted and appealed. His appeal was dismissed.

In all of these cases, you will note that the three elements to which we referred earlier are present. An accused will not be guilty of manslaughter if, for example, death occurs from a lawful act. If D dies as a result of an accident in a dangerous sport such a motor racing or boxing, no liability would arise. However, if a parent or guardian drives fear into a child so that the child, in escaping, falls downstairs, breaks his neck and dies, that parent or guardian is liable for constructive manslaughter. These are the facts and the result in R v. Mackie [1973] Crim LR 54 and 438.

What if death occurs as a result of a prank, jest or horseplay? The answer may be found in R v. Lamb [1967] 2 All ER 1282. In that case, A pointed a revolver at his friend. The revolver had five chambers, bullets being in two of the chambers, neither of which was opposite the barrel. A thought it was safe to pull the trigger and his friend D was treating the situation as a joke. They did not understand how the revolver worked. A pulled the trigger and D was shot. A was found guilty of manslaughter, the trial judge having directed the jury that the mere pointing of the gun and pulling the revolver, resulting in D's demise, was a dangerous act, even if there was no intent to harm D, there being no need to consider whether there was an assault. D appealed. The Court of Appeal found that even though there was sufficient evidence of criminal negligence, the defects in the trial judge's direction warranted that the appeal be allowed.

Note: If the judge had directed the jury properly, the result would have been different. The answer to the question then, about whether one can be convicted for constructive manslaughter where death occurs as a result of a prank, jest or horseplay is: Yes. Public policy, not to mention the law (look again at the three elements), could not have it otherwise!

Reckless manslaughter or manslaughter by gross negligence

This area of the law has been the subject of much discussion, some of it having to do with whether the standard by which the accused is to be judged is an objective or subjective one. In addition to this, there has been debate in the House of Lords as to the use of certain epithets such as 'gross', 'wicked', 'complete' to describe the nature of the accused's recklessness or negligence. It appears that these issues have been settled to some extent by the decision of the House of Lords in R v. Caldwell [1981] 1 All ER 961 and in the case of R v. Lawrence [1981] 1 All ER 974.

We looked at the case, R v. Adomako [1995] 1 AC 171, [1994] 3 All ER 79, [1994] 3 WLR 288, in discussing the actus reus. A five-stage test was set out there for determining when an accused would be liable for manslaughter by gross negligence. These are as follows:

1 The ordinary principles of the law of negligence apply in determining whether the defendant was in breach of a duty of care towards the victim.
2 Did the defendant's breach of a duty of care result in the victim's death?
3 If (2), should the defendant's breach be characterised as gross negligence and therefore a crime?
4 The answer to (3) will depend on the defendant's breach of duty in the defendant's circumstances at the time the breach occurred.
5 The jury will consider whether or not the defendant's departure from the standard of care placed upon him involved a risk to the victim with the result that it caused the victim's death.

You will note the importation of some aspects of the law of negligence in the cases. See, for example, a case which we looked at previously in our discussion of the actus reus: R v. Stone and Dobinson [1977] 2 All ER 341. See also R v. Seymour [1983] 2 All ER 1058.

In R v. Seymour, A was convicted for manslaughter in the death of D, a woman with whom he had been living. Following a quarrel between them, A, who was driving a lorry, met D who was driving her car in an opposite direction. There was a slight collision and D got out of her car and approached the lorry. A, drove his lorry violently towards D's car, moving it 10 to 20 feet and forcing off one of its tyres. D was crushed between the two vehicles and sustained severe injuries. She died a week later. A contended that he had only intended to push D's car out of the way. A appealed against his conviction. Their Lordships dismissed his appeal, Lord Roskiill accepting the direction in R v. Lawrence and going on to say that 'it is appropriate also to point out than in order to constitute the offence of manslaughter the risk of death being caused by the manner of the defendant's driving must be very high'.

Compare the Privy Council decision Kong Cheuk Kwan v. R (1985) 82 Cr. App R 18. Here, their Lordships sought to settle the law and remove the 'confusion' they identified. The appellant was in command of one of two hydrofoils, which collided, in fine weather. Two passengers were killed. The appellant was among officers convicted of manslaughter. The Hong Kong Court of Appeal upheld his conviction and he appealed to the Privy Council. In delivering the judgment of the Board, Lord Roskill said:

> 'The model direction suggested in R v. Lawrence, and held in R v. Seymour to be equally applicable to cases of motor manslaughter, required first, proof that the vehicle was in fact being driven in such a manner as to create an obvious and serious risk of causing physical injury to another and second, that the defendant so drove either without having given any thought to the possibility of there being such a risk or having recognised that there was such a risk nevertheless took it.' (author emphasis)

While a vast number of the cases in this area are motor manslaughter cases, the same criteria mentioned in Kong Cheuk Kwan are relevant generally. See, for example, R v. Stone and Dobinson (op. cit).

Activity 5.8

1 We started out with Smith and Hogan's reference to manslaughter as 'a complex crime of not less than five varieties'. The learned writers then set out the instances when a person is guilty of manslaughter. Q. What are the circumstances when a person is guilty of manslaughter? (5 marks)

2 These five varieties of the law of manslaughter fall under two key elements, namely (a) voluntary and (b) involuntary manslaughter. Q. Write a definition of (a) Voluntary manslaughter and (b) Involuntary manslaughter. (5 marks)

3 Provocation is a good defence in reducing liability for murder to manslaughter. Q. Identify one case in which provocation is (a) successfully pleaded, and (b) not successful, and the reasons for the decision. (5 marks)

4 'Diminished responsibility' is one of the limbs of voluntary manslaughter. Q. Define 'diminished responsibility', and refer to one case in which it was successfully pleaded. (5 marks)

5 What are the three elements of constructive manslaughter? (5 marks)

6 What do you understand by 'reckless manslaughter' or 'manslaughter by gross negligence'? Refer to two cases to illustrate your answer. (5 marks)

Feedback

Set out below are model answers to the exercise you have just completed. Check your answers against the model and see how you have done.

1 a A person is guilty of manslaughter where his act results in the death of another and although he has the fault required for murder, there are mitigating circumstances, which result in his conviction for the lesser offence. These circumstances are: (i) diminished responsibility; (ii) provocation; (iii) he was a party to a suicide pact.

b Voluntary intoxication by the accused, resulting in a lack of mens rea (state principle in Majewski)

c The accused's dangerous act results in the death of another, or where the accused was reckless as to whether the consequences or his act could lead to the personal injury of another.

2 a Voluntary manslaughter refers to those instances in which the accused possesses the malice aforethought (that is, the mens rea) for murder but mitigating circumstances (for example, provocation, diminished responsibility, suicide pact) reduce the liability.

b Involuntary manslaughter refers to those cases in which the accused does not have the malice aforethought for murder but his act is inherently dangerous (Newton and Jones) or he is reckless (Caldwell) as to whether his act could result in personal injury.

3 Cite the definition given by Devlin J (as he then was) in R v. Duffy. Note that this is usually a defence raised by the prosecution.

a Provocation was unsuccessful as a defence in R v. Cocker, R v. Thornton, DPP v. Camplin.

b It was successfully advanced in R v. Doughty (1986) 83 Cr. App R 319, where the Court of Appeal reduced the conviction from murder to manslaughter. The accused killed his 17–day-old son whose constant crying, he claimed, was a provocation resulting in his loss of self-control.

4 Diminished responsibility is an abnormality of mind, but it is not the same as insanity and does not fall within the M'Naghten Rules. A person who relies on this defence must show that his condition arose from a retarded development of his mind and that this condition impaired his mental responsibility for the killing of which he is accused. R v. Byrne is the case on point.

5 a An unlawful act

b Act was dangerous and a reasonable person would have realised the risk of injury

c The act resulted in death. See R v. Franklin, R v. Larkin, R v. Church.

6 'Reckless manslaughter' or 'manslaughter by gross negligence' occurs where A owes a duty to B, but arising from A's negligent act B dies. This means that A is in breach of his duty to B. See R v. Adomako and Kong Cheuk Kwan v. R.

Activity 5.9

Case studies

This activity presents you with fact situations that highlight aspects of the law of manslaughter. At the end of the activity you should have a good understanding of the various nuances of the law.

1 Jack and Jill are husband and wife. They have a very close relationship. Jack leaves his licensed firearm on the dresser and goes outside, after telling Jill that he had cleaned the gun and taken out the bullets. Jill sees the gun and takes it up. Just then Jack enters the room and sees her with it. He says 'Hey sharp shooter, you look like an expert with that'. Jill responds, 'I am', pointing the gun at him. Jack then says 'Good thing there are no bullets in that'. Jill pulls the trigger and, unfortunately, there is in fact a bullet in the inner chamber. Jack had not remembered it. He dies instantly. What is Jill's criminal liability, if any?
(20 marks)

2 Popeye and his live-in girlfriend Olive Oyl live in a flat by the sea. Popeye's sister, Bo-Peep, becomes ill and Popeye invites her to come and live with him, promising that he and Olive Oyl will take care of her. Bo-Peep sells her flat and comes to live with them, handing over all her accounts to them. Popeye and Olive Oyl are 'party animals' and go to at least one soca party every weekend leaving Bo-Peep to fend for herself. Bo-Peep's condition deteriorates and she is unable to walk. One night there is a power cut and Popeye and Olive Oyl are determined to go to a fete. They light a kerosene lamp and place it in Bo-Peep's room, place the phone beside her and tell her that if she has any difficulties, she should call the neighbour. Bo-Peep dies in a fire, which seems to have started from the overturned lamp. Her burnt corpse is found on the ground, beside her bed. The police theorise that she might have toppled the lamp, starting the fire. What, if any, is the criminal liability of Popeye and Olive Oyl?
(20 marks)

3 Dr Rumpel is a young surgeon who is widely regarded by his colleagues and patients as a 'shining star'. One night while Dr Rumpel is on duty, a young woman, Alice, is rushed to the hospital in a serious condition after a motor vehicle accident. Owing to Alice's serious condition, Dr Rumpel and his team quickly perform surgery on her, trying desperately to save her life. In their zeal, they do not notice that Alice is wearing an anklet, which bears a note stating that she is allergic to certain medications and that she is an epileptic. Alice recovers well from surgery, but four days later she develops complications after an attack of epilepsy. She dies later that night. It is discovered that Alice is allergic to one of the medicines prescribed by Dr Rumpel, and that it had triggered the epilepsy. Her family wishes to sue Dr Rumpel and the hospital for damages. What would your advice be concerning the criminal charge of reckless manslaughter?
(20 marks)

4 Ulysses, a mentally challenged young man of 22, has always been teased by members of the community in which he lives. Ever since childhood, he has been the butt of everyone's jokes. Ulysses is at a bar drinking with his friends when Cyclops, one of his main taunts, walks up to him and starts to call him names, including 'Mama's Boy' and 'Freak', which Ulysses resents. Others in the bar tell Cyclops to desist, but he persists, whereupon Ulysses reaches for an ice pick and stabs Cyclops who dies a few days later. What arguments can be advanced in defending Ulysses in respect of (a) self-induced intoxication and (b) diminished responsibility?
(20 marks)

Feedback

1 The issue here is Jill's liability for Jack's death. The law to be relied upon is that relating to involuntary manslaughter of the constructive type. See the relevant cases in this area and relate them to the facts here to arrive at your conclusion. Cite some of the following cases: R v. Franklin, R v. Larkin, R v. Church, DPP v. Newbury.

2 Here, the issue is the liability of Olive Oyl and Popeye for Bo-Peep's death – causing death by gross negligence or reckless manslaughter. You are required to examine their liability, or the lack of it, based on the fact of their legal duty of Bo-Peep. See the important cases of R v. Adomako, Kong Cheuk Kwan v. R, R v. Stone and Dobinson and R v. Seymour. Analyse these cases, distinguishing and applying the legal principles in relation to the present facts, as the case may be.

3 See the outline to question 2 above. Was Dr Rumpel negligent in not noticing Alice's anklet? See the factors, which must be considered, as set out in R v. Adomako.

4 Here the issue is 'diminished responsibility' and self-induced intoxication. See the cases, which deal with these issues, apply them to the facts stated, and advice Ulysses accordingly. Majewski and Byrne are leading cases. See also the Barbadian case that was decided by the Privy Council: Walton v. R.

5 Here the issue is 'provocation'; you first define provocation, emphasising its chief elements. Examine the cases in the area and come to a conclusion whether or not A could succeed with the defence of provocation.

5 A, a 46-year-old cook, marries D, a 20-year-old dancer. D goes on a short vacation in Cancun, Mexico, along with A. While there she meets C, a masseur at the hotel where she and A are guests. A and D develop a friendship with C and invite him to their home. A few months later C accepts the invitation and visits them. D soon becomes very close to C and they engage in sexual intercourse regularly when A is away. D taunts A about how old fashioned he is and tells him she intends to return to Mexico with C. One morning they have a violent quarrel and C moves out of their house to a nearby guesthouse. That night D again taunts A and he goes away for the night. Next morning he returns and stabs D to death. Can A succeed with a defence of provocation?

(20 marks)

Assault and battery

You will note that the syllabus refers to "assault". Here we refer to "assault and battery" as battery is becoming subsumed into assault in criminal law, as well as in tort, (see Kodilinye in Tort.) We have examined those offences against the person that result in death. Here we will be examining offences against the person, which do not result in death, but which cause physical injury or an apprehension of physical injury. This is the substance of the law of assault and battery, which are two different offences, usually taken together because of the way they overlap. We shall look firstly at assault and then at battery.

Assault

The mens rea of assault

In the commission of an assault, the defendant engages in an act against the complainant intentionally or recklessly. Provided we can identify the accused's intention and recklessness, coupled with the actus reus, he is guilty of the offence. In this context, recklessness must be of the R v. Cunningham variety, that is, subjective. (You will already be familiar with this case, but should look at it again: R v. Cunningham [1957] 2 QB 396, [1957] 2 All ER 412. Revise the objective standard in R v. Caldwell, and be reminded that objective recklessness does not normally apply to offences against the person.) The following case, decided before Caldwell, supports the Cunningham standard of recklessness:

R v. Venna [1975] All ER 788

The police were called to restrain the appellant and others who were creating a disturbance in the street. During a scuffle, as the police sought to arrest him, the appellant kicked out, resulting in the fracture of a hand of one of the officers. The appellant was convicted for assault and appealed. His appeal was dismissed, the Court of Appeal, Criminal Division, approving the direction of the judge at first instance who had found that the appellant had been reckless, as defined in Cunningham.

The actus reus of assault

What is assault? Can words constitute an assault? Must there be a particular degree of violence? These are among the questions that come readily to mind when one is seeking to define the actus reus of assault. The definition of 'assault' itself points us in the direction we should go.

Smith and Hogan in the 10th edition of their leading text, Criminal Law, define an assault as 'any act by which D, intentionally or recklessly, causes P to apprehend immediate and unlawful personal violence' (page 411). Two elements are significant; namely:

1 the accused must have acted intentionally or recklessly; and
2 the complainant must apprehend immediate and unlawful personal violence.

If, therefore, A sends a message to B to say that he has a gun that he is going to use to shoot her, A would not have assaulted B. B would be advised, though, to report A's threat to the police. It would be an assault, however, if A, points the gun at B and says 'Shut up or I'll blow your brains out!' The same words by A, without the pointed gun, would that be an assault? We will come to that shortly. On B's part she must apprehend the infliction of immediate and unlawful violence to her person. For her, it must be more than her being fearful of B because of a past event. The following cases illustrate the point.

In Logdon v. DPP [1976] Crim LR 121, D showed P a pistol in a drawer and declared that he would hold her hostage. His action constituted an assault. In Smith v. Superintendent of Woking Police Station (1983) 76 Crim App Rep 234, D looked through C's window while C was in her nightclothes. He intended to frighten her and succeeded in doing so. He was found guilty of an assault.

We will now look at whether or not words can constitute an assault. Relying upon an old authority, Meade and Belt (1823) where the trial judge directed the jury that 'no words or singing are equivalent to an assault', it has long been the view that mere words do not amount to an assault. The authority for this view is Tuberville v. Savage (1669). In this old case, D laid his hand on his sword and said, 'If it were not assize time I would not take such language'. This was held not to be an assault. Compare Light (1857). There, D was held to be guilty of an assault for raising a sword over his wife's head and saying, 'Were it not for the bloody policeman outside, I would split your head open'. Note that, here, D's words were accompanied by a menacing act.

The view among some scholars is that words can constitute an assault, but the courts are reluctant to agree, and take the traditional view that there must be some accompanying menacing act, as in the Canadian case R v. Byrne (1968). There, the appellant entered a bank and, having a coat draped over his arm, said to the teller, 'I've got a gun; give me all your money or I'll shoot'. As Smith and Hogan question, in Criminal Law: Cases and Materials, 8th ed., should the decision not have turned on the effect (author emphasis) of the appellant's words on the teller?

Battery

The mens rea of battery

Like assault, battery is a crime of basic intent, requiring either intention or recklessness. This was stated in a case we looked at earlier, R v. Venna [1975] 3 All ER 788, where the Court of Appeal said:

> '... the element of mens rea in the offence of battery is satisfied by proof that the defendant either intentionally or recklessly applied force to the person of another.'

In DPP v. Majewski [1977] AC 142, [1976] 2 All ER 142, it was said by the House of Lords that in crimes of specific intent, evidence of self-induced intoxication negating mens rea is a defence. It would not be a defence to a charge of battery. We will look at these issues later when considering defences.

The actus reus of battery

A battery is the infliction of unlawful violence by one person upon another. Smith and Hogan (Criminal Law, 10th ed., page 415) point out that 'it used to be said that every battery involves an assault; but this is plainly not so, for in battery there need be no apprehension of the impending violence'. The act of violence itself is the essence of this offence. It is, therefore, battery where D, hearing A approach, lets fly a trap door causing A to fall into a dungeon, but it is not battery where D stands in a narrow path blocking A's movement and, in diverting, A falls and breaks her wrist. In the second example, it is clear that D is acting unlawfully, but there is no 'violence' per se.

Assault occasioning or causing actual bodily harm

Having already examined the actus rea and mens rea of assault and battery, we now turn to the statutory offence of 'assault occasioning or causing actual bodily harm'. See the Offences Against the Person Act (or equivalent) of your jurisdiction. Some of the references are listed here, the model being the Offences Against the Person Act of England, section 47 of which provides that:

> 'Whosoever shall be convicted upon an indictment of any assault occasioning actual bodily harm shall be liable ...'

Similar provisions in Commonwealth Caribbean jurisdictions include:

The actus reus of the offence

The actus reus is the same as for common law assault (see above). In DPP v. Smith [1961] AC 290, [1960] 3 All ER 161, the House of Lords said that 'bodily harm' needed 'no explanation' and that " "grievous" means no more and no less than "really serious"." (This case has since been discredited for reasons that do not affect the principle stated here.)

The position is also set out in R v. Miller [1954] 2 QB 282, [1954] 2 All ER 529, where the court held that actual bodily harm includes a hysterical and nervous condition arising from an assault. Lynskey J said:

> 'There was a time when shock was not regarded as bodily hurt, but the day has gone by when that could be said. It seems to me now that, if a person is caused hurt or injury resulting, not in any physical injury, but in an injury to the state of his mind for the time being, that is within the definition of "actual bodily harm".'

The mens rea of the offence

The mens rea of assault occasioning or causing actual bodily harm is similar to that of assault and battery (see above), R v. Savage, DPP v. Parmenter. The accused is not guilty of the offence if he does not foresee that he might occasion actual bodily harm.

R v. Spratt [1991] 2 All ER 210

In R v. Spratt, the appellant fired an air pistol from his flat, hitting a young girl who was playing in the square below. He claimed to have been aiming at a rubbish chute and that he did not know anyone was there. His appeal against a conviction for assault occasioning actual bodily harm was successful, the court holding that he would be guilty only if he foresaw the result, which occurred.

We now turn two other offences under the assault and battery head, namely, wounding with intent and malicious wounding.

Wounding with intent

Wounding with intent is the more serious of the two offences and the statutory provisions indicate this clearly from the penalty prescribed. See the relevant statute for your own jurisdiction. We take an example of one, namely section 173 of the Criminal Code, Cap. 124 of the Laws of St Vincent and the Grenadines, which provides that:

> 'Any person who, unlawfully and maliciously, by any means whatever, wounds or causes grievous bodily harm to any person with intent so to do, or with intent to resist or prevent lawful apprehension or detainer of any person, is guilty of an offence and liable to imprisonment for life.'

See the relevant legislative provisions from your country.

Mens rea of wounding with intent

As you will have seen, the statutory provision refers to (i) the unlawful and malicious act of the accused and (ii) the effect on the victim of wounding or causing grievous bodily harm.

The crucial word in (i) is 'maliciously'. For 'unlawfully', the literal meaning is to be applied. By 'maliciously' is meant 'intentionally or recklessly'. Once again, the important case of Caldwell applies. Read also: R v. Belfon [1976] 3 All ER 46, [1976] 1 WLR 741. This case is helpful in defining the accused's 'intent'. It was said that, for this offence, intention means the same as intention for murder. The burden on the prosecution is to show:

> '(i) that it was D's purpose to cause grievous bodily harm or, if it was not his purpose (ii) that he knew that grievous bodily harm was a virtually certain consequence of his act.'
>
> Smith and Hogan, Criminal Law, 10th ed., page 443

Actus reus of the offence

Most importantly, for an accused to be guilty of this offence, there must be a wound. This may appear to be a simplistic comment, but in truth, it is not, as the cases show. The whole skin must be broken as was said in an old case, Moriarty v. Brookes (1834). If the inner skin remains intact, with the outer skin or cuticle having been broken, there is no 'wound', neither is the breaking of a collarbone, where the skin remains intact. If the victim's inner skin is broken when D takes evasive action from A's attack, even if A would have cut him, A is not guilty of causing the wound from D's evasive action. The wound must be directly inflicted whether from a battery or not.

We now turn to what is meant by 'causing or inflicting grievous bodily harm'. 'Causing' has a wider meaning than 'inflicting'. The House of Lords decided the issue in R v. Wilson and Jenkins [1984] AC 242, [1983] 3 All ER 448. It was said there that 'inflict' does not imply assault, having a narrower meaning than 'cause'. 'Inflict' implies a direct application of force.

In R v. Martin (1881) 8 QBD 54, D put out the lights in a theatre shortly before the end of a performance. He was convicted of causing grievous bodily harm to those who were injured in the panic.

In R v. Clarence (1888) 22 QBD 23, D, who knew that he was suffering from gonorrhoea, had sexual intercourse with his wife and infected her with the disease. The position previously held, arising from this case, that 'inflict' implies assault, has been overruled, though not the decision itself. It was held that though D caused his wife grievous bodily harm he had not inflicted it, as there was no assault. It is submitted that since Wilson, the decision on that ground would be different today on similar facts.

Malicious wounding

The statutory provision common to our various jurisdictions is equivalent to section 20 of the Offences Against the Person Act 1861, as follows:

> 'Whosoever shall unlawfully and maliciously wound or inflict any grievous bodily harm upon any other person, either with or without any weapon or instrument, shall be guilty of an offence ... And being convicted thereof shall be liable [to a term not exceeding five years].'

You will note that the penalty is less harsh than for wounding with intent.

Actus reus of malicious wounding

The comments made above concerning 'inflict' are helpful here. You should look at them again, as well as at those referring to 'malicious'. For this offence, there are two limbs, namely:

- inflicting grievous bodily harm; and
- unlawful and malicious wounding.
- We will look at each in turn.

Inflicting grievous bodily harm: See the comments made above in reference to the word 'inflicting'. 'Grievous' means 'really serious' as the cases show. See R v. Wilson and Jenkins.

Unlawful and malicious wounding: Again, refer to your notes above, with reference to the words 'unlawful', 'malicious' and 'wounding'. Read C (a minor) v. Eisenhower [1984] QB 331, [1983] 3 WLR 537. In this case, the victim was shot and an airgun pellet hit him near the eye. He sustained a bruise below an eyebrow and, for a period, the flint filling the front of the eye contained red blood cells. It was held that a wound is a break in the continuity of the whole skin. An internal rupturing of a blood vessel was not considered a wound.

Mens rea of malicious wounding

This is a crime of basic intent. You should re-read your notes above on the use of the word 'maliciously' and look at R v. Savage, DPP v. Parmenter. The accused must be seen to have had foresight that his action would have resulted in harm, however slight. The actual harm caused, however, must be serious.

Sexual offences

In this section, we will examine the law relating to two sexual offences, namely (i) rape and (ii) incest. It is important to understand, of course, that these are not the only sexual offences, but that they are the two required for study by your syllabus. (Others include prostitution, buggery and indecent assault, voyeurism and bestiality, pornography. Pornography, especially when it affects children, has fast become an area of very great concern.)

> **Activity 5.10**
>
> From this activity, your knowledge of, and familiarity with, the relevant statutory provisions of the law in your jurisdiction will be vastly improved.
>
> Look at the Offences Against the Person Act (or the equivalent statute of your jurisdiction) and identify the sections that are equivalent or similar to the Offences Against the Person Act 1861 (UK). Match your own statutory provisions with the following provisions from the UK Act: sections 18, 20, 38 and 47. You should note that there have been some amendments to the UK statute of 1861 by subsequent legislation.

Since 2009, two of our jurisdictions, Jamaica and Guyana, have each enacted a new Sexual Offences Act; Jamaica in 2009 and Guyana in 2010. In enacting these pieces of the legislation, both countries have introduced provisions which make substantial changes in the law relating to sexual offences. We shall therefore examine, in brief, some of the key provisions of both Acts, as we proceed in this chapter of your Study Guide.

Rape

The law relating to rape is by no means uniform throughout the Commonwealth Caribbean. As we shall see, some States no longer use the Offences Against the Person Act, having enacted legislation that more reflects current trends including a gender-inclusive approach.

Actus reus of rape

Definition

The actus reus of rape has undergone an evolution in its definition, beginning with the common law definition, some aspects of which are still reflected in statutes, even those statutes that were enacted in the late 1980s and early 1990s by States in the region, such as Trinidad and Tobago, Barbados and now, Guyana and Jamaica. The common law definition of rape is 'unlawful sexual intercourse with a woman without her consent, whether by force, fear or fraud.' We will see from the cases and statutory provisions that the definition has widened to include anal intercourse, and includes rape of a male.

The Barbados legislation, the Sexual Offences Act, Cap. 154 (1992), at section 3(1), reflects the newer position and provides as follows:

> 'Any person who has sexual intercourse with another person without the consent of the other person and who knows that the other person does not consent to the intercourse or is reckless as to whether the other person consents to the intercourse, is guilty of the offence of rape.'

Compare this with the provision of the 1956 Sexual Offences Act in England, which provided that 'It is an offence for a man to rape a woman' and you will appreciate the movement from a male or female offence to the more gender-neutral, all-inclusive offence of 'any person'.

The earlier (and still current in those jurisdictions that have the Offences Against the Person or Sexual Offences legislation – namely, the majority) view of the penetration being conceived of as penile only, is widened to include penetration by the use of objects.

Section 3(6) of the Barbados legislation demonstrates this widening of the concept, by providing that:

> 'For the purposes of this section "rape" includes the introduction to any extent, in circumstances where the introduction of the penis of a person into the vagina of another would be rape,
>
> (a) of the penis of a person into the anus or mouth of another person; or
>
> (b) an object, not being part of the human body, manipulated by a person into the vagina of another.'

The Sexual Offences Act of Guyana follows the approach taken by the Barbados Act and uses even more gender inclusive language, as for example, in section 2 where "penetration" is defined. It provides as follows:-

S.2 "penetration" means any intrusion, however slight and for however short a time, of any part of a person's body or of any object into the vagina or anus of another person, and any contact, however slight, and for however short a time, between the mouth of one person and the genitals or anus of another, including but not limited to sexual intercourse, cunnilingus, fellatio, anal intercourse and female to female genital contact.

- **i** and where the penetration is by the penis the emission of seminal fluid is not necessary to prove the penetration;
- **ii** penetration is a continuing act from entry until withdrawal.

Despite its modernity, the Jamaican legislation is more traditional in its approach and gender reference. This is indicative of a reluctance to define rape as possible otherwise than between a male and a female. Hence, the offence of "grievous sexual assault" which is created in section 4 of the Act.

Section 3 of the Sexual Offences Act, Jamaica, provides as follows:

– A man commits the offence of rape if he has sexual intercourse with a woman –

- **a** without the woman's consent; and
- **b** knowing that the woman does not consent to sexual intercourse or recklessly not caring whether the woman consents or not.

Consent is treated as not existing where sexual intercourse is induced by extortion, physical assault, or threats or fear of physical assault to the complainant or a third party. Neither these situations nor one in which sexual intercourse is obtained by a false and fraudulent misrepresentation as to the nature of the act or the identity of the offender, will amount to consent.

Section 4 describes the offence of "grievous sexual assault" which is committed by penetration of the vagina or anus, other than by a penis. It can be by an object manipulated by the accused or when such acts are committed with the encouragement of another person, and includes oral sex.

Elements of the actus reus

Penetration

Penetration, however slight, is an essential element of the actus reus of rape. In one case, the question turned on when the act is 'complete'. This case is also important in demonstrating that if the withdrawal of consent is made at any point after penetration and the aggressor continues the act, it is an act of rape.

Kaitamaki v. The Queen [1958] AC 147 (Privy Council)

K penetrated V, believing that she consented. During intercourse he discovered that she did not consent, but continued the intercourse nonetheless. He was convicted of rape and appealed. His appeal was dismissed, the Privy Council dismissing the point argued for the appellant as to the meaning of the word 'complete'. The applicable statutory provision contained a provision that 'sexual intercourse is complete upon penetration'. Lord Scarman who delivered the Committee's judgement said:

> '"Complete" is used in the statutory definition in the sense of having come into existence, but not, in the sense of being at an end. Sexual intercourse is a continuing act which only ends with withdrawal.'

One of their Lordships, Lord Brightman, said in the course of the argument before them that the statutory provision refers to 'complete' and not to 'completed.'

Consent

As you would have probably concluded, both Guyana and Jamaica legislations address the matter of consent. See again the definition of "rape" as well as of "grievous sexual assault" in the Jamaican Legislation where consent, or the lack thereof, is a key element of the mens rea of the crimes.

In the Guyana Act, persons with a learning disability or mental disorder cannot be deemed to consent to unlawful sexual intercourse. A similar provision is in the Jamaica Act. Both Acts have abolished the presumption of incapacity, referring to the previous position at common law, that a boy under 14 years was incapable of sexual intercourse.

Consent, when or not it is given, remains the most controversial issue, as the cases show. It is also important in relation to the mens rea of the crime, as we shall see.

Earlier, we saw in the common law definition a reference to 'force, fear or fraud'. These are still considered when examining what vitiates the victim's consent – and these three factors do. Where, therefore, any of these factors leads to submission, there is no consent.

R v. Olugboja [1982] QB 320

L raped V, then took her companion, K, into an adjoining room, intending to rape her. L's companion, O told K that he was going to have intercourse with her and told her to remove her trousers, which she did, out of fear. She did not struggle or resist O when he had intercourse with her. O's appeal against conviction was dismissed by the Court of Appeal. Dunn LJ said:

> 'They (referring to the jury) should be directed to concentrate on the state of mind of the victim immediately before the act of sexual intercourse, having regard to all the relevant circumstances, and in particular the events leading up to the act and her reaction to them showing the impact on her mind. Apparent acquiescence after penetration does not necessarily involve consent which must have occurred before the act takes place.'

For the impact of force and threats in vitiating consent, see R v. Jones [1861] 4 LT 154.

The well-known case, R v. Clarence (1888) 22 QBD 23 is a good example of the proposition that consent is not vitiated by a mere suppression of the truth. In Clarence, the facts were as follows: C had sexual intercourse with his wife while he was suffering from gonorrhoea, as a result of which she contracted the disease. It was found that had she been aware, she would not have consented. C's appeal against conviction for assault occasioning and for unlawfully and maliciously inflicting grievous bodily harm was allowed.

Their lordships examined a number of cases where the truth was withheld or tricks used to induce consent.

Impersonation of a spouse in circumstances where the victim willingly has sexual intercourse with an impersonator will also give rise to a conviction for rape. There is no consent in such circumstances, consistent with the view expressed in the cases, such as the dictum of

Dunn L J in Kaitamaki referred to on page 114, in which he said that consent is aligned to the victim's state of mind.

R v. Elbekkay [1995] Crim LR 75

E had sexual intercourse with V, she believing that he was her boyfriend. E was convicted of rape, upon V's complaint. He appealed.

In dismissing E's appeal, the Court of Appeal agreed with the position taken by the trial judge that the law must reflect 'modern attitudes and values ... where possible', thereby making no distinction between a wife and her husband, and a girlfriend or fiancée with her regular partner. Mr McCowan LJ said, in reference to the trial judge's finding and in espousing the view of the court:

> 'We wholly agree. Indeed, we think it would be extraordinary for us to come to any other conclusion in 1994. How could we conscientiously hold that it is rape to impersonate a husband in the act of sexual intercourse, but not if the person impersonated is merely, say, the long-term, live-in lover, or in the more modern idiom, the "partner" of the woman concerned?'

Not only were their lordships prepared to adopt the more modern idiom, but they were also prepared to accept the change in spousal relationships. They saw no conflict between this approach and the law, McCowan LJ going on to say:

> 'The vital point about rape is that it involves the absence of consent. That absence is equally crucial whether the woman believes that the man she is having sexual intercourse with is her husband or another.'

We move on to another area, which has undergone quite a bit of change in recent times, the issue of marital rape.

Can a man rape his wife?

In 1992, the House of Lords came to the decision that a man can rape his wife. This position was confirmed by an amendment to the Sexual Offences Act 1956. The case is R v. R [1992] 1 AC 599, [1991] 4 All ER 481, [1991] 3 WLR 767.

Smith and Hogan (13th ed.), 2011, regard this case as a watershed, describing its effect as follows:

> 'In 1991, in R, the courts decided that there was no rule that a husband cannot be guilty of rape of his wife and that the word, "unlawful" in section 1 of the 1976 Act was "surplusage". It is arguable that this decision flouted the will of Parliament but, as is now generally recognised, the result was highly desirable ...'

The learned writers' view is consistent with their earlier position, taken prior to the quotation mentioned, that the common law rule, with a few exceptions, that a husband could not be convicted of raping his wife, was 'based on an absurd fiction'. This 'absurd fiction' was authoritatively expounded by Hale in his The History of the Pleas of the Crown (1736).

Although R v. R is not binding in the Commonwealth Caribbean – a point the student must note with caution – it is still to be reckoned with as part of the law's development. Here are the facts: The parties were married in 1984 and separated for a short period in 1987, later resuming cohabitation. They separated in 1989 when the wife left the matrimonial home to live with her parents. They were contemplating divorce, and each made this position known to the other, but they had not initiated proceedings. Less than two months after W had removed to her parents' home, H forced his way into her place of abode and attempted to have sexual intercourse with her, squeezing her neck with both hands in the process. H admitted his actions to the police. H and W later divorced. At H's trial for rape, the trial judge ruled that whatever implicit general consent for sexual intercourse existed during the marriage was extinguished when W moved out of the matrimonial home. His appeal against conviction was dismissed and the question being put to the House of Lords, for certification, 'Is a husband criminally liable for raping his wife?'

The House of Lords answered the question in the affirmative, taking the law further than what had been the previous position in England, and still is the law in the Commonwealth Caribbean region. Lord Keith indicated that the status of women had changed, marriage in these times being 'regarded as a partnership of equals, and no longer one in which the wife must be the subservient chattel of the husband'. He went on to say:

> 'Hale's proposition involves that by marriage a wife gives her irrevocable consent to sexual intercourse with her husband under all circumstances and irrespective of the state of her health or how she happens to be feeling at the time. In modern times any reasonable person must regard that conception as quite unacceptable .... On grounds of principle there is now no justification for the marital exemption of rape.'

Prior to R v. R, in England, and still Commonwealth Caribbean law, the position was, and is, respectively, that marital rape could, and can, occur in the following circumstances (all of which are mentioned in R v. R):

1 a non-cohabitation order by the court
2 the granting of a decree nisi
3 a non-molestation undertaking by a husband (for example, in domestic violence proceedings)
4 formal separation agreement.

Section 3(4) of the Barbados Sexual Offences Act 1992 specifically makes it an offence for a husband to engage in sexual intercourse by 'force or fear of fraud' in all of the four situations just mentioned. The Sexual Offences Act (1986) of Trinidad and Tobago does not incorporate the common law exceptions. Section 5(1) of that Act provides that a husband can be found guilty of sexual assault but there is no provision for marital rape, even within the confines provided by the Barbados legislation.

The mens rea of rape

The Sexual Offences Act of Jamaica provides that a man can rape his wife. Section 5 sets out the circumstances in which this can take place. Sub-section 1 of the section provides that: A husband commits the offence of rape against his wife if he has sexual intercourse with his wife in any of the circumstances specified in subsection 3

a without her consent; and
b knowing that she does not consent to sexual intercourse or recklessly not caring whether she consents or not.

Consent is not applicable in the following circumstances. Section 5 (2) states that: For the purposes of subsection (1), consent shall not be deemed to exist where the apparent agreement to sexual intercourse:

a extorted by physical assault or threats of physical assault to the wife or to a third person: or

b obtained by false and fraudulent representation as to the nature of the act or the identity of the offender.

(3) The circumstances referred to in subsection (1) are that:

a the spouses have separated and thereafter have lived separately and apart within the meaning of the matrimonial causes Act;

b there is in existence a separation agreement in writing between the spouses;

c proceedings for the dissolution of the marriage or for a decree of nullity of marriage have been instituted;

d there has been made or granted against the husband an order or injunction, as the case may be, for non-cohabitation, non-molestation or ouster from the matrimonial home for the personal protection of the wife; or

e the husband knows himself to be suffering from a sexually transmitted infection.

This latter point on sexually transmitted infection can be illustrated in the case of R v Mohammed Dica.

You will also note that the Guyana legislation, while not as expansive on the subject as the Jamaican legislation also makes provision for marital rape. Section 37 of the Sexual Offences Act of Guyana recognises marital rape by stating as follows:

"Unless where specifically stated in this Act, a marital or other relationship, previous or existing, is not a defence to a charge of any offence under this Act."

By what standard is the accused deemed to have the mens rea for this crime? In trials for rape, the defence is often that the woman gave her consent or that by her conduct she led the accused on, or that even her past indicates that she must have, or would have, consented to sexual intercourse with this person, on this occasion.

The decision by the House of Lords in DPP v. Morgan [1975] 2 All ER 347, [1976] AC 182, [1982] 2 WLR 913 has been generally followed in the Commonwealth Caribbean. The facts of that case are set out below. M, a member of the Royal Air Force, invited three men of junior rank to go with him to his home where all of them would have sexual intercourse with his wife. At first, the young men were reluctant but M persuaded them, telling them of his wife's sexual aberrations, including that if she resisted, it was merely a pretence, as it meant that she was really excited. M provided them with condoms. Later, he denied the conversation.

W's account was that she was asleep in a room she shared with one of her children. She was dragged out of the room by M and the other men into another room where the men took turns in having sexual intercourse with her, the last to do so being M. She said she screamed, struggled and called out to M to tell the men to stop.

At the trial the three men gave evidence that from W's response she was evidently consenting. M gave evidence that W had consented prior to the intercourse with the men, and that her only complaint was that one of them was not wearing a condom.

The three younger men were convicted of rape and of aiding and abetting rape, while M was convicted of aiding and abetting rape. The trial judge directed the jury that the men were guilty of rape even if they believed she was consenting, if their belief was not based on reasonable grounds.

The men''s appeal was dismissed by both the Court of Appeal and the House of Lords. Lord Hailsham of St Marybone said, in part:

> 'Once one has accepted, what seems to me abundantly clear that the prohibited act in rape is non-consensual sexual intercourse, and that the guilty state of mind is an intention to commit it, it seems to me to follow as a matter of inexorable logic that there is no room either for a "defence" of honest belief or mistake, or of a defence of honest and reasonable belief and mistake ...'

In essence, Morgan decided that where D honestly believes that v. consents, whether or not D had reasonable grounds for so believing, D will not be convicted for rape. This is a matter to be left to the jury. The question is whether the test of reasonableness of D's belief is to be an objective one as in Caldwell or subjective, as in Cunningham. (Both cases were dealt with in chapter 4.) In R v. Satnam and R v. Kewal (1983) 78 Crim App R 149, both S and K appealed their convictions for rape on the ground that the trial judge erred in directing the jury on the meaning of 'reckless'. The judge had said (inter alia):

> '... if there was an obvious reason that the girl was not in fact willing to have sexual intercourse, that is to say, obvious to every ordinary observer, and the defendant either did not apply his mind to that reason at all, for whatever reason, but carried on having sexual intercourse with her, or trying to, that is recklessness.'

The decision in Morgan was approved in the Guyanese case of State v. Persuad [1975] 27 WIR 82. The facts are as follows:

V, then aged 15, was violently sexually assaulted by A on Christmas Day, 1973, on a beach on the Essequibo coast. V's account was that during her ordeal she scratched and bit V, evidence of such being found by a doctor who examined A who was taken to the doctor by the police, as part of their investigations. v. claimed that she managed to escape when the voices of men on the beach indicated that persons were approaching her and A. A claimed that v. had promised to have sexual intercourse with him and that he had run off when he heard the voices.

A was convicted of rape and appealed. At the trial, the judge had directed the jury that because of A's admission of sexual intercourse with V, there was no need for the corroboration of her story. The Court of Appeal, comprising Ev Luckhoo C, Persaud and Haynes JJA, allowed A's appeal on the basis that the jury had been misdirected on the question of corroboration. Their lordships also considered the issue of A's belief in V's consent to intercourse and concluded that A's honest belief in V's consent was the applicable standard. Their lordships referred to the then recently concluded decision in Morgan, approving Lord Hailsham's dictum that:

> 'Mens rea means "guilty or criminal mind", and if the mental element in rape was not knowledge but intent, then to insist that a belief must be reasonable to excuse was to insist that either the accused was to be found guilty of intending to do that which in truth he did not intend to do, or that his state of mind, through innocent of evil intent, could convict him if it were honest but not rational.'

Ev Luckhoo C, in approving this dictum, concluded that the test is a subjective one. He continued that if A held a bona fide belief that v. was consenting, based on her original consent, then he should have been acquitted.

The judgment of Haynes JA covers a wide range of cases on the question of corroboration in rape cases and the accurate test of 'honest belief', over 'reasonable belief' in such cases. You should obtain and read this case in its entirety. See also R v. Beckford [1988] AC 130 (PC) (Jamaica), on the applicability of 'honest belief' as the test in determining the accused's mens rea, to be discussed later under self-defence.

Incest

Incest is a crime prohibiting sexual intercourse between persons who are within certain degrees of family relationships, such as brother, sister, mother and father. These persons, within the 'prohibited degrees of consanguinity' as referred to under the Marriage Act, cannot in law marry each other. Section 3(3) of the Marriage Act of Jamaica sets out the circumstances when a marriage shall be void, providing as follows:

> 'If the parties to any marriage are within the prohibited degrees of consanguinity or affinity according to the law of England from time to time in force, the marriage shall be void.'

Actus reus of incest

The actus reus of incest is to be found in statutory provisions. You should see the Offences Against the Person Act or Sexual Offences Act of your jurisdiction. Smith and Hogan's Criminal Law (2002), page 482, points out that the law relating to incest is targeted towards 'a narrower range of relationships' than those contemplated by the Marriage Act.

Section 10 of the Sexual Offences Act 1956 sets out the prohibition as follows:

> 'It is an offence for a man to have sexual intercourse with a woman whom he knows to be his grand-daughter, daughter, sister or mother.'

Subsection 2 of the same section defines 'sister' to include 'half-sister' and extends the inclusion within incestuous relationships to those 'not traced through lawful wedlock'.

Section 11 makes it an offence for 'a woman of the age of 16 or over to permit a man whom she knows to be her grand-father, father, brother or son to have sexual intercourse with her by consent'. The section defines 'brother' to include 'half-brother' and, as in section 10, includes those relationships as set out which are 'not traced through lawful wedlock'.

See the relevant statutory provision applicable to your jurisdiction.

In England, the common law rule that a boy aged 14 cannot commit an offence involving sexual intercourse has been repealed. The decision in R v. Pickford [1995] 1 Cr. App Rep 420, would now be decided differently, as a result of this change in the law. There, the court held that it was not an offence for a boy under 14 to commit incest with his mother.

See also R v. Dimes [1911] 7 Cr. App Rep 43.

The mens rea of incest

You will recall the earlier reference to State v. Persuad where the court cited with approval Lord Hailsham's dictum in DPP v. Morgan that mens rea means 'guilty or criminal mind'. This is no less so in this area of the law.

In R v. Carmichael [1940] 1 KB 630, [1940] 2 All ER 165, it was held that it was a defence where D had sexual intercourse with his wife's daughter as he believed the girl to have been fathered by an adulterer. Such a belief, however honest, would not now be the law, if one renders a true meaning and effect of sections 10 and 11 of the Sexual Offences Act 1956, which extends the offence to include stepbrother and stepsister. Would it not be applicable to stepdaughter or other step-relative whose affinity, were it within the blood relationship, is prohibited? Certainly it would be applicable, as the same sections extend the offence to relationships 'not traced through lawful wedlock'.

Smith and Hogan's Criminal Law (2000) suggests that the retention of some aspects of the law of incest raises something of a debate because it:

> 'imposes a relatively slight restriction on liberty – it excludes the right to have intercourse, not altogether, but only with close relatives; and it applies to everyone.'

What do you think? What are your views on the position put forward by the learned writers that, in any event, Parliament will have to 'provide protection for persons under 21 from the lustful attentions of other members of the family?'

Should age be a barrier?

Activity 5.11

The debate

This exercise should stimulate your thought processes, enabling you to examine critically whether the reforms taken over the past 50 years have gone far enough. Is there not an urgent need for reform of the law in our region? Ask yourself, has the Barbados model satisfied this need?

Moot: 'Be it resolved that the law relating to rape and incest has not kept pace with modern realities.'

You are the first speaker for the opposition. Conduct your research and prepare your speech. You will speak for 10 minutes. If you are able to do group work, you and your companions could develop this into a full-fledged debate, presenting arguments for the proposition and opposition sides. You could make the activity more interesting by asking someone to assess the presentation, and determine a winner.

Feedback

Here are some suggestions: You are required to examine the law as presented in this chapter. Is there a case for harmonising the law relating to sexual offences? A Barbados model maybe? For example, there is much to be said for a modern definition of rape and for a wider inclusion of family relationship beyond 'degrees of consanguinity' to keep pace within modern realities of family structures. If you do not feel that there is need for reform, could you not argue that the old law has served us well and is still adequate? Do not the modern statutory provisions merely codify the common law, which is dynamic? Should a man be able to be convicted of raping his wife or partner? Go ahead and prepare your arguments for either side.

How did you do? You will find that there are equally convincing arguments on both sides. Your improved understanding and wider knowledge are your sure reward!

Activity 5.12

Applying the law

We will begin with an example:

This exercise presents you with an opportunity to relate fact situations to the law and to make your conclusions accordingly.

Examine the following fact situations, identifying the issues and refer to a case or statutory provision in support of your conclusion

1 A agrees to go to a secluded beach with X, a popular cricketer. She does not intend to have sexual intercourse with him, as she has a boyfriend and knows X to be a philanderer. While at the beach, X overpowers A and has sexual intercourse with her, despite her protests and struggles. X says that by going to the beach with him, he believed A meant to have sex with him and he thought her protests and struggles were fake. X is guilty of rape.

Yes (X) No (   )

Issues: (a) Consent (b) Honest belief

Case and statutory provision: DPP v. Morgan, State v. Persaud, Sexual Offences Act or Offences Against the Person Act of your jurisdiction

2 A agrees to have sexual intercourse with X. Unable to have an erection, X tells A not to worry, as he will use a sex toy. A objects and tries to escape, but X restrains her telling her to shut up as she had already agreed. He engages in anal intercourse using the toy. Has X committed an offence?

Yes (   ) No (   )

3 Barbie, aged 29, marries Ken, a widower, aged 65. Ken has a son, Randy aged 25, with whom Barbie engages in regular sexual intercourse. Are Barbie and Randy guilty of incest?

Yes (   ) No (   )

4 Chaunty has recently separated from his wife Perty. One rainy evening he passes by the matrimonial home to collect his personal belongings. Perty is making soup and offers Chaunty some of it. He accepts and, after eating, tells her that he has been longing for her. He pushes her against the sofa and has sexual intercourse with her. Is Chaunty guilty of rape?

Yes (   ) No (   )

5 Billie Jean is asleep naked in her upstairs bedroom on a hot July night. She leaves her window open. Michael climbs up on a ladder, peeps in and sees her there. He enters the bedroom. Billie-Jean, whose boyfriend, Paul, often climbs up to her bedroom to have sex with her, awakens to find Michael in the room and believes his to be Paul. She beckons him over and has sex with him. Is Michael guilty of rape?

Yes (   ) No (   )

Feedback

The first one was done for you.

2 Yes (X) No ( )

Issues: Consent or withholding consent, whether there is liability for other than penile penetration, recklessness as to consent.

Cases: DPP v. Morgan, R v. Satnam, R v. Kewal

Relevant statutory provision: Definition of rape

3 Yes (X) No ( )

Issues: Does the 'step' relationship fall under the law of incest?

Cases: R v. Dimes, R v. Carmichael

Relevant statutory provision: Provisions of Marriage Act in relation to 'prohibited degrees of consanguinity'. Law in relation to changes in, for example, England and Barbados as against the older provisions of the common law.

4 Yes ( ) No (X)

Issues: Is the law relating to marital rape, as decided in England, applicable in the Commonwealth Caribbean?

Cases: DPP v. Morgan, R v. Satnam, R v. Kewal

Relevant statutory provision: For example, Barbados and Jamaica, stating the circumstances when marital rape is applicable.

5 Yes (X) No ( )

Issue: (a) Is this a case of sexual intercourse through fraudulent frustration or trickery? (b) Consent.

Cases: R v. Olugboja distinguished, R v. Elbekkay applied.

Relevant statutory provision: Sexual Offences Act, Offences Against the Person Act, as applicable.

Offences against property

Theft and larceny

If there is any area in the criminal law that is a veritable minefield, then this is it! In England, the Theft Acts of 1968 and 1978 sought to create a new code to replace the Larceny Acts of 1861 and 1916, which aimed, according to Smith and Hogan, in Criminal Law (2002, page 511), 'to re-state the common law and numerous statutory additions and amendments in a convenient and accessible form.'

Here in the Commonwealth Caribbean, there are still several states that have in force the Larceny Act, patterned on the 1916 English legislation. Barbados has enacted the Thefts Act 1992–9, patterned on the English Theft Act of 1968 and 1978. Similar enactments have been made in other States such as St Vincent and the Grenadines. Jamaica, Guyana and Trinidad and Tobago have Larceny Acts. You should study the relevant provisions of the applicable legislation for your jurisdiction.

We shall look first at the law of theft and then at larceny to see where they overlap and what distinctions there are. This will enable you to analyse both and conclude for yourself on the need for reform.

Theft

In the Theft Act of Barbados theft occurs where one:

> 'Dishonestly appropriates property belonging to another with intention of depriving the other of that property.'

This is similar to section 1(1) of the Theft Act 1968.

The actus reus of theft

There are three elements of the actus reus of theft. These are: (i) appropriating; (ii) property; (iii) belonging to another.

Appropriation

Section 5(1) of the Barbados Theft Act contains similar wording to section 3 of the Theft Act 1968 and provides as follows:

> '5(1) (a) … a person appropriates property belonging to another when he assumes the rights of an owner.
>
> 5(1) (b) … he appropriates when he has come by the property, innocently or not, without stealing it, if he later assumes a right to the property by keeping or dealing with it as owner …'

A quartet of cases decided by the House of Lords has supplied authoritative discourse on the history and meaning of appropriation. The most recent case follows:

R v. Hinks [2001] 2 AC 241, [2000] 4 All ER 833, [2000] 3 WLR 1590

You should endeavour to read Hinks, which discusses in detail the judgments in the other three cases: Lawrence v. Commissioner of Police [1972] AC 626, [1971] 2 All ER 1253, R v. Morris [1938] 3 All ER 288, [1984] AC 320 and DPP v. Gomez [1993] AC 442, [1992] 3 WLR 1067.

In Hinks, H, a woman aged 38, who claimed to be a care-giver to D who was proven to be mentally challenged, and easily taken advantage of, received over £60,000.00 which D transferred from his building society account to H's account. It was also proven that D understood the concept of ownership. He also gave H a television set. H was convicted on four counts involving the money and on one count with respect to the television. H appealed. Rose LJ, in dismissing the appeal said:

> '… in relation to theft, one of the ingredients for a jury to consider is not whether there has been a gift, valid or otherwise, but whether there has been an appropriation. But a jury should not, in our view, be asked to consider whether a gift has been validly made.'

H's appeal to the House of Lords was dismissed. Lord Steyn approved the position in R v. Gomez, which, he said, 'gives effect of section 3(1) of the 1968 Act by treating "appropriation" as a neutral word comprehending "any assumption by a person of the rights of an owner".'

The right of an owner was therefore found, amounting to appropriation in the following circumstances:

- Where a taxi-driver, without objection from his passenger, an Italian student who did not know the correct fare, over-charged the passenger: Lawrence v. Commissioner of Police.
- Where the defendant replaced the price tag on a joint of meat in a supermarket by a lower price tag obtained from another joint: R v. Morris.
- Where D assisted B to obtain goods with the use of fraudulent cheques, D in so doing having represented to his boss that the cheques were 'as good as cash': R v. Gomez.

We can now move on to the second limb of the actus reus of theft, namely property.

R v. Kelly [1998] 3 All ER 741

K, an artist, had permission to draw anatomical specimens used by surgeons in training. With the help of a technician, he removed some of the body parts. Some of the parts were found buried in a field. A leg was found at K's flat and other parts at the home of one of his friends. He was convicted of theft and appealed. A ground of K's appeal was that the body parts were not 'property'. Their lordships considered the common law rule of over 150 years that a corpse or part of it cannot be stolen. They found that the body parts had been in the 'possession' of the College of Surgeons, within the meaning of section 5(1) of the Act. They could therefore be stolen.

Property

See section 4 of the Theft Act 1968 of England and section 4 of the Barbados Theft Act; where property includes real and personal property.

This is a very important area, especially in these days when property in intangible things is increasingly becoming a problem, for example in the case of intellectual property, including property in one's likeness. Technological advancements have certainly added much to the excitement of this area.

Smith and Hogan, Cases and Materials (2002, at page 596) indicate how vast this area is by stating that 'almost anything may be property, and, if it is possessed or owned by someone, it "belongs" to him.' The only exception, they point out, 'is the human body or parts of it.' The following case, however, illustrates that there is 'ownership' of a human body or parts by an institution, though not by you and me, of our bodies and body parts. They cannot be stolen from us, thankfully!

Compare the following case about a cheating student:

Oxford v. Moss [1979] Crim LR 119

M, an engineering student, acquired the proof of an examination paper. It was held that confidential information is not a form of intangible property while the paper itself was. M was charged with stealing intangible property belonging to the Senate of the University. The prosecutor appealed, but his appeal was dismissed.

In Chan Man-sin v. AG of Hong Kong [1988] 1 All ER 1, a Privy Council decision, C, an accountant of two companies, deposited the proceeds of cheques forged by him from his employer's accounts into the account of a company he owned. He was charged with theft of the debts (that is, a chose in action) of the amounts owed by the employer's banks, and was convicted. He appealed, on the ground that there was no property in which there could have been an appropriation. His appeal was dismissed.

Belonging to another

See section 5 of the Theft Act 1968 of England and section 5 of the Barbados Theft Act where 'belonging to' means having possession or control of, or having a proprietary right or interest in something. Where property is with a bailee, while he is in control of it, the property belongs to him. The general rule is that one cannot steal from oneself, but as in the case of bailment where 'belonging to' extends to the bailee, in any circumstance where one's conduct indicates dishonesty, the court will find accordingly:

R v. Turner [1971] 2 All ER 441, [1971] 1 WLR 701 (CA)

T took his car to a garage to have it repaired. When the repairs were practically completed, the car was left on the road outside the garage. T, in breach of his promise to the garage owner that he would come to pay for the job and collect the car, used his spare key and took the car, unknown to the garage owner and without paying for the repairs. He was convicted of theft of the car and appealed. In his defence, he argued that he could not steal his own car.

T's appeal was dismissed. In the course of his judgment Lord Parker CJ said, in reference to section 5(1) of the Theft Act 1968:

> 'This court is quite satisfied that there is no ground whatever for qualifying the words "possession or control" in any way. It is sufficient if it is found that the person from whom the property is taken, or to use the words of the Act, "appropriated", was at the time in fact in possession or control ...'

Compare Turner with the next case.

R v. Meredith [1973] Crim LR 253

M left his car in a road while attending a football match. The police removed the car to a yard where they parked confiscated vehicles. M went to the yard and saw his car, on the steering wheel of which a police krooklock was placed. He removed the krooklock and drove the car away without the permission of the police. He did not pay the applicable fine. M was charged with theft of the car, the property of the police, for obstruction of the road and with not paying the applicable fine. M contended that he could not steal what was already his. M's contention was upheld.

Here is another interesting situation. What if A has conducted himself in such a way that B concludes that A has no interest in an item, but which B needs? The following case provides the answer:

R v. Woodman [1974] 2 All ER 955 (CA)

In this case, A and his son B went on to O's land to collect scrap metal. The scrap metal was in fact the remnant of similar material previously sold by O to X. After X left, there still remained some scrap metal in which O seemed to have no intention of removing at any time soon.

O placed a sign at the premises on which were the words 'Private Property, Keep Out'. O also installed a barbed wire fence. When A and his son went on to O's property and removed the scrap metal, did the scrap metal then 'belong' to O?

Did they 'dishonestly appropriate' the property belonging to another within the meaning of section (1) of the Act? Yes, it was held, O was still in control of the scrap metal when A and his son B removed it.

The mens rea of theft

We now move on to the mens rea of theft as conceived by the Theft Act 1968 and similar legislation where applicable, in our jurisdictions. Smith and Hogan in Criminal Law (2002) states that the law since the Theft Act has not changed materially from what it was under the Larceny Act 1916. Here you have a useful comparison of the two positions, by statute, giving you a foretaste of the law relating to larceny. At pages 547–8, the learned writers put it thus:

> 'The changes made by the 1968 Act in the mens rea of theft were less fundamental than the reform of the actus reus. The law of larceny required an intent to take or to convert property belonging to another and theft requires an intent to appropriate property belonging to another. Larceny required that the act be done fraudulently and without a claim of right made in good faith and with intent permanently to deprive the owner.
>
> It need not, however, be done lucri causa, that is, it was unnecessary to prove that D intended to make any kind of profit for himself or another. These characteristics are broadly preserved by the 1968 Act.'

You should pay close attention to this extract. In fact, it provides all you need to know in comparing the mens rea of theft with the mens rea of larceny. There is hardly any difference, as you will have seen.

See again the case referred to earlier of R v. Chan Man-Sin [1988] 1 All ER 1 (PC), where their Lordships found that there was 'ample evidence' that C intended permanently to deprive his employees of their credit balance. He therefore had the required mens rea for the offence.

Compare the following case:

R v. Lloyd [1985] 2 All ER 661, [1985] QB 829, [1985] 3 WLR 30 (CA)

In this case, L, who worked at a cinema, arranged with his accomplices to make copies of films for sale and profit. The reels were not away from the cinema for long, but L's action had the serious impact of depriving his employers of funds. He was convicted of theft but appealed successfully. Their Lordships found that L lacked the necessary mens rea, which is to intend to deprive the owner permanently of the item. Borrowing to return does not amount to stealing.

Larceny

As you will have already gathered, there are still a number of Commonwealth Caribbean jurisdictions in which the Larceny Act is the law.

Larceny is a complex, and intriguing, subject. We shall not attempt to cover all its areas as that is outside our scope. The most frequently arising areas of the subject are the ones we shall discuss.

At the beginning of this chapter you will have read a quotation from Smith and Hogan, Criminal Law, indicating the extent to which the mens rea of theft and the mens rea of larceny coincide. You will note, however, that the same is not true of the actus reus of theft and the actus reus of larceny. Larceny is deeply embedded in the common law, which it codifies.

As you read the following section on the actus reus of larceny, you should seek to identify those aspects of it which may be deficient in modern law enforcement, as you compare it with what you read earlier concerning theft.

The actus reus of larceny

We start with the definition of 'larceny' using the Jamaican legislation as a guide. (You may use your own legislation if applicable.)

Section 3 of the Larceny Act (J), which is a verbatim representation of section 1 of the Larceny Act 1916 of England, states as follows:

> 'For the purposes of this Act –
>
> (1) a person steals who, without the consent of the owner, fraudulently and without a claim of right made in good faith, takes and carries away anything capable of being stolen with intent, at the time of such taking, permanently to deprive the owner thereof:
>
> Provided that a person may be guilty of stealing any such thing notwithstanding that he has lawful possession thereof, if, being a bailee or part owner thereof, he fraudulently converts it to his own use or to the use of any person other than the owner.'

You will note that whereas appropriation is a key element in theft, fraudulent taking and conversion are the equivalent in larceny. The second element, 'anything capable of being stolen' is a somewhat vague term, lacking the precision of 'property' and the issue lends itself to vigorous debate especially in today's world and the recognition of value in intangibles, such as intellectual property. Is it merely a distinction without a difference? Another key element of the actus reus of larceny is depriving the owner of property. Let's look at each aspect in turn.

Fraudulent taking and conversion to own use

There are two limbs here, namely (i) fraudulent taking and (ii) conversion. For fraudulent taking to stick to an accused, he must be shown not to have been in rightful possession of the property. An American case is useful on this point.

Beside the fraudulent taking, the accused must have carried away the thing stolen. This would probably suggest that the property must be something tangible, but it is not so. That was the position at common law. Intangible property can also be 'taken away', as a result of statutory interpretation.

The technical term for carrying away is 'asportation'. The thing being taken away must have been attached.

If a thief removes items from a safe and places them on the floor but is caught before he takes them to a waiting vehicle, there is an asportation. The concept is an interesting one, as the following two cases show:

R v. Taylor [1911] 1 KB 674

The accused put his hand into T's pocket, seized T's purse and drew it to the edge of T's pocket. The purse lodged in T's belt enabling T to secure it. It was held that there was sufficient asportation amounting to larceny. The Court of Appeal found that the appellant was correctly convicted of simple larceny and dismissed his appeal.

R v. Lapier [1784] 1 Leach 320

The accused took hold of the prosecutrix's ear and pulled her diamond earring, causing her ear to tear. The earring was dislodged but upon arrival home, the prosecutrix found it lodged in her ear. There was held to be sufficient asportation.

Commonwealth v. Tluchak 70 A. 2d 657 (Pa. 1950)

Ds contracted to sell their farm to B. Certain chattels were included in the transaction. After the closing (or 'completion') B moved in to find that the chattels were missing. Ds were charged with larceny. It was held that the charge could not stand. At the time of the alleged misappropriation, the Ds were in lawful possession of the chattels. As they were to remain in possession until the Ds moved in, the taking and carrying away having occurred during this period, there was no larceny. (They were not charged for fraudulent conversion, which could have stuck.)

We end our discussion of the actus reus of larceny on the topics, 'larceny by trick', 'larceny by intimidation' and mistake. These are merely three of the ways in which the offence can be committed. (See relevant statutory provision, for example, section 3 of the Larceny Act (J).)

It must be shown that the accused obtained the property by trick or otherwise and without the owner's consent. Section 3(2) of the Jamaican legislation and section 1(2) of the 1916 English Act state as follows:

> '... the expression "takes" includes the possession –
>
> by any trick
>
> by intimidation
>
> under a mistake on the part of the owner with knowledge on the part of the taker that possession has been so obtained
>
> by finding where at the time of finding the finder believes that the owner can be discovered by taking reasonable steps.'

Set out below are cases under each heading:

Larceny by trick

R v. Bramley (1861)

X owned a colliery, which sold both coal and slack. Slack was cheaper than coal. The practice was to weigh the item and then make payment. A took a weight of coal, but on the way to the scales he put slack over the coal and indicated that what he had was a weight of slack. He paid for slack and left. He was convicted of larceny.

Larceny by intimidation

Any action on the part of the accused, which would have driven the owner to dispose of his property to the accused, will constitute intimidation and result in a conviction. Threats to damage one's reputation would be intimidatory.

R v. Lovell [1881] 8 QBD 185 (CCA)

The accused was given a job of grinding knives and agreed with the prosecutrix to pay a certain sum. When he completed the job he demanded, with threats, an amount four times the agreed sum. The prosecutrix, for fear of her life, paid the amount demanded. The jury found that the accused had obtained the money by menaces and he was convicted of larceny. His appeal against conviction was dismissed.

Mistake

Mistake may be as to the identity of the transferee or of the identity of what was delivered.

It is not larceny where A buys a book for $100.00 knowing it to be worth much more. But what if A expects to receive costume jewellery, a string of fake 'pearls', but receives instead a genuine string of pearls from B, in error. Would A be guilty of larceny if he keeps it? Yes, of course he would be!

R v. Middleton (1873)

A's savings balance was confirmed to him and he sought to withdraw some of it. The clerk made an error by referring to another balance and overpaid him. A took the excess and left. He was convicted of larceny, being found to have the animus furandi.

Anything capable of being stolen, that is, property

Trade secrets, copyrights and other intangibles are not included at common law, but the Larceny Act of 1916 changed that. You should check the relevant section in your legislation, if applicable. One cannot commit larceny of one's own property, but can do so in respect of property of which one is a co-owner. This is contained in section 3(1) of the Act, which is cited above.

Permanently depriving the owner

This is associated with conversion and points to any act on the part of the accused, which indicates that he had no intention of passing the property back to its rightful owner. If he can show that he was borrowing the item, to return it, there is no larceny. For example, X takes his employer's computer and printer to complete an assignment, which he is working on as part of his studies. The security guard at the gate stops him and searches his car, finding the items. Would a charge of larceny stick? No, it would not. The situation would be different if X was found selling the items. Needless to say, he would very likely be disciplined, even for the first part of the example, having borrowed without permission. It is not necessary for the accused to have taken the goods for his own benefit.

In R v. Wynn (1848), W, a postman, destroyed a letter after he found that he had made a mistake in sorting. This was held to be larceny.

Also, consider the following interesting case of R v. Hall (1849), where A, B's servant, took certain items belonging to B and brought them to B for sale, claiming that he had obtained them from C. A was found guilty of larceny. By his actions, A intended to permanently deprive B of the property, which B would only get back if he purchased what, indeed, was already his.

The mens rea of larceny

Refer to the quotation cited earlier from Smith and Hogan on the mens rea of larceny and of theft. The cases referred to on page 128 in relation to theft will also be helpful.

In our statutory provision we saw that the thief must 'intend' to deprive the owner of the thing stolen. Larceny can only be committed intentionally, not negligently or recklessly. The mens rea is often described as the 'animus furandi', which translates as 'intent to steal'.

There is an overlap here between theft and larceny as the Theft Act 1968 retains the words 'with the intention of depriving permanently'. There is a strict application of this 'intention'. Permanence is the key, therefore taking with an intention to return (that is, borrowing) does not amount to larceny or theft. The animus must exist at the time of taking:

R v. Ensom [1971] 2 QB 315, [1971] 3 WLR 82, [1971] 2 All ER 945

E took a handbag, searched it and, finding nothing to interest him, left it with its contents intact. The owner reclaimed it. E was convicted of theft and appealed successfully. The Court of Appeal held that there was no evidence that the accused was animated by an intention to deprive the owner of the contents of the bag.

See also R v. Lloyd (the cinema case), which we looked at earlier.

Beside the intention permanently to deprive the owner of the thing capable of being stolen, the accused must also be shown to have acted dishonestly. Three situations must exist in order for the accused to be deemed not to have acted dishonestly. These are:

- where he believes that he has a legal right to deprive another permanently of the property
- where he believes he would have received the consent of the owner had the owner been aware of the relevant circumstances
- where, after taking reasonable steps to find out, he concludes that the owner cannot be found.

If none of these situations exist, A will be found guilty of larceny.

The situation is different from that in Thurborn, where A finds something and keeps it, not caring to make an effort to locate the owner, for example, by reporting the find to the police. This would be a case of 'larceny by finding'.

R v. Thurborn (1849)

T found a banknote in the street. There was no form of identification on it. T had immediately resolved to keep the money as soon as he found it. Before he disposed of it, T became aware of who the owner was. Despite this, he disposed of the money. It was held that T was not guilty of larceny as at the time of finding the banknote he did not know who the owner was.

What if the finder believes that the thing has been abandoned? This is a question of fact and there must be shown to be a reasonable basis for such a conclusion.

See also the following interesting case:

R v. White (1912) Cr. App R 266

In this case A was convicted of feloniously receiving stolen property. The person from who he received it had been convicted of larceny. He appealed on the ground that the property had in fact been abandoned. The Court of Appeal so found and his conviction was quashed.

Robbery

The actus reus of robbery

Like theft and larceny, robbery is dealt with under both the Theft Act and the Larceny Act. The relevant provision in the Barbados Theft Act is similar to section 8 of the Act of England. It is contained in section 8 and reads as follows:

> (1) A person who steals any property, and immediately before or at the time of doing so, and in order to do so, uses force on any person or puts or seeks to put any person in fear of being then and there subjected to force is guilty of robbery.
>
> (2) A person who assaults another with intent to rob is guilty of an offence.
>
> (3) A person who is guilty of robbery or of an assault with intent to rob is liable on conviction on indictment to imprisonment for 15 years.
>
> The Larceny Act (J), section 37, states that robbery is a felony for which, when committed using an offensive weapon or violence upon conviction, an accused can be imprisoned for a term not exceeding 21 years. The felony is committed where:
>
> '37(1)(a) (a person) armed with any offensive weapon or instrument, or being together with one other person or more, robs, or assaults with intent to rob, any person;
>
> (b) (a person) robs any person and, at the time of or immediately before or immediately after such robbery, uses any personal violence to any person ...'

Section 24(1) of the Trinidad and Tobago legislation is similar.

Where the felony is committed without an offensive weapon or instrument, or is committed by assaulting the victim, the penalty is a term not exceeding 15 and 10 years, respectively.

Force is the key factor in the actus reus of robbery. Robbery may be referred to as an aggravated form of stealing. Note that the force must be applied 'immediately before or immediately after' the robbery. If, then, X commits a theft, then uses force to escape, X's theft would not be a robbery. Below are two interesting cases. In the first, the application of force is the issue before the House of Lords; in the second, the question turns on the extent of the force.

Smith v. Desmond [1965] AC 960, [1965] 1 All ER 976 (HL)

D and E used force in their stealing of money from an office at a bakery. The two persons against whom D and E directed force were the night watchman and maintenance engineer, in whom was the custody of the company's property. By placing the workers in fear of being subjected to force, D and E were held to have been correctly convicted for robbery.

R v. Hale (1978) 68 Cr. App Rep 415, [1979] Crim LR 596 (CA)

H and M entered Mrs C's house, wearing stocking masks. H put his hand over Mrs C's mouth to prevent her from screaming. M went upstairs and stole her jewellery box. Both men tied up Mrs C and, upon leaving, threatened to harm her child if she called the police. H was convicted of robbery and appealed. H's appeal was dismissed. The court's position is seen in the following extract from the judgement of Eveleigh LJ where he said:

> '... the act of appropriation does not suddenly cease. It is a continuous act and it is a matter for the jury to decide whether or not the act of appropriation has finished. Moreover, it is quite clear that the intention to deprive the owner permanently, which accompanied the assumption of the owner's rights, was a continuing one at all times. This Court therefore rejects the contention that the theft had ceased by the time the lady was tied up. As a matter of common sense the appellant was in the course of committing theft; he was stealing.'

The mens rea of robbery

What was said earlier about the mens rea of theft and larceny would apply here.

An honest belief that one is entitled to the property taken will suffice, as this next case shows:

R v. Robinson [1977] Crim LR 173 (CA)

D ran a clothing club to which P's wife owed £7.00. D met up with P and, along with others, threatened him. A fight ensued during which a £5.00 note fell from P's pocket. D took the money, telling P that he was still owed £2.00.

D's conviction for robbery was quashed. It was held that he only needed to show that he had an honest belief that he was entitled to the money and not that he honestly believed that he could have taken it in the way he did.

Burglary

Section 9 of the Theft Act 1968 sets out the actus reus of burglary. See the equivalent section in the Barbados Theft Act. The English Act provides as follows:

> 'A person is guilty of burglary if –
>
> he enters any building or part of a building as a trespasser and with intent to commit any such offence ...
>
> having entered any building or part of a building as a trespasser he steals or attempts to steal anything in the building or that part of it or inflicts or attempts to inflict on any person therein any grievous bodily harm.'

The Larceny Act contains a provision, which deals with burglary, but it is far less expansive than that in the Theft Act. Section 39 of the Larceny Act (J) provides as follows:

> '39. Every person who in the night –
>
> breaks and enters the dwelling-house of another with intent to commit any felony therein; or
>
> breaks out of the dwelling-house of another, having
>
> entered such dwelling-house with intent to commit any felony therein; or
>
> committed any felony in such dwelling-house,
>
> shall be guilty of felony called burglary ...'

One of the most striking limitations of the provision of the Larceny Act is its confinement to 'dwelling-house' as against 'building' in the Theft Act. Another is the limitation to 'at night' under the Larceny Act. This certainly restricts the ability of law enforcement to seek the conviction of those who, say, break and enter a supermarket. This is covered under housebreaking in section 40. The definition of 'dwelling-house' is extended under the Theft Act to include a vessel. In one case, the court extended the meaning to include a motor vehicle. The limitations of the Larceny Act are stark when comparisons are made.

The actus reus of burglary

Under the Larceny Act the breaking and entering of the dwelling house of another at night and the breaking out after having entered a dwelling house constitute the actus reus of burglary. Under the Theft Act, the actus reus of the offence comprises the entry of a building as a trespasser and stealing or attempting to steal anything in that building. Look at the definition again and note the particulars of the offence under the statutes.

If the householder leaves a door or window open, there is no burglary, neither is there burglary where the accused was invited into the building or house. What if he strays into a part of the house to which he was not invited and breaks and enters that part?

Here's an interesting case, which you will remember from the section on sexual offences:

> **R v. Collins [1972] 3 WLR 243, [1973] 1 QB 100, [1972] 2 All ER 1105 (CA)**
>
> D, a lustful and drunk 19-year-old, went at night to the home of X, a girl he knew slightly. He climbed up a ladder and saw X asleep naked on her bed. In his evidence,

D said that he stripped and then noted that X held out her arms to him in welcome. He entered the room and had sexual intercourse with her. She had thought D was her boyfriend but became suspicious, turned on the light and discovered it was not her boyfriend. D was charged with burglary with intent to commit rape.

D's conviction was reversed. He might have intended to commit rape but his belief that X welcomed him was an honest one. By X's welcoming him in, as he thought, D had not committed the necessary trespass for burglary.

This was a case decided under the Theft Act. It is submitted that a similar outcome would be reached under the Larceny Act, which requires 'breaking and entering'.

How much of the body must have 'entered' after the 'breaking' in? An old case answers this question:

R v. Hughes (1785)

Here, H, with intent to steal, inserted a centre bit into a door, near the bolt. The end of the bolt penetrated the door but no part of H's body entered the house. His indictment for burglary was dismissed.

In another old case, R v. Bailey (1818), it was said that insertion of any part of the body sufficed as an entry.

The mens rea of burglary

The accused must intend to commit the offence and must have broken and entered the dwelling house (Larceny Act) or entered as a trespasser with intent to steal (Theft Act). There can be no reasonable or honest belief that he should be there, unless he has permission. What if he used to live at the premises, and has moved, but had left personal property there? He goes back, and picks the lock to enter and is accosted by the police and charged with burglary. His protestations that he was going to tell the landlord in the morning and that he was going in to fetch his own property fell on deaf ears. The following case gives you an idea of how the court might deal with a situation such as the one raised hypothetically:

R v. Jones and Smith [1976] 3 All ER 54, [1976] 1 WLR 692 (CA)

J and S were convicted of burglary under section 9(1)(b) of the Theft Act 1968. In the 'dead of night' they entered S's father's house and stole two television sets. S's father had reported the theft to the police. At S's trial, the father gave evidence to the effect that he had given his son unreserved permission to enter his house, therefore S could not have committed the necessary trespass for burglary.

The Court of Appeal found that J and S had correctly been found guilty of burglary and dismissed their appeal. Their lordships approved the directions given to the jury at the trial where the judge said, inter alia:

> '... If you go in intending to steal, then your entry is burglary, it is to trespass because no one can give you permission to go and steal in the house ...'

His lordship had also said:

> '... if they went in there they must have gone in order to steal because they took elaborate precautions, going there at dead of night, you really cannot say that under any circumstances their entry to the house could have been other than trespass.'

Aggravated burglary

This, as the name suggests, is an aggravated form of the offence and occurs when the burglar carries with him and uses, or threatens with an offensive weapon, such as a gun.

Activity 5.13

Applying the law

Before you attempt this activity, look back through this section and make sure that you understand the distinctions between the Theft Act and the Larceny Act. Depending on the applicable statute in your own jurisdiction, this will be important to you as you apply the law to the fact situations presented.

The exercises that follow are aimed at ensuring that you are able to identify the nuances of the law of theft and larceny. At the end, you should be able to explain even the more difficult areas of the law.

In each of the following exercises you are presented with a set of fact situations. Read each problem and answer the questions, following the first example, which has been done for you.

1 Joseph, a local businessman, intends to give his brother Benjamin a golden goblet. As a surprise, he places the goblet in Benjamin's bag. He then decides to frighten Benjamin and tells the guards to detain Benjamin for stealing the goblet.

- a Is Benjamin liable for theft of the goblet or not?
- b Reason
- c Case and/or statutory provision
- a Benjamin is not liable for theft of the goblet.
- b There is an absence of both the actus reus and mens rea of theft and larceny.
- c Case: R v. Hinks (also Lawrence, Morris and Gomez). Statutory provision: section 5, Theft Act, section 3, Larceny Act.

2 Cain finds a ring, which he hides under his mattress, intending to sell the ring at a later date. He discovers that the ring belongs to Mrs Abel who got it as an anniversary present from her late husband. Cain decides to keep the ring.

- a Is Cain liable for theft and larceny or not?
- b Reason
- c Case and/or statutory provision

3 Moses, who is diagnosed as a schizophrenic, goes to the bank and signs over his bank account containing $2 million to his housekeeper, Miriam, who accompanied him. Miriam uses a part of the money to buy herself a small used car. Moses' son, Joshua, wants Miriam to transfer the funds back to Moses but she refuses.

- a Is Miriam liable for theft and larceny or not?
- b Reason
- c Case and/or statutory provision

4 Goliath, a hobo, picks up scraps of building material from a junkyard owned by David's family. He is arrested while putting the materials in a truck. David's family intends that the material be taken to the city dump.

- a Is Goliath guilty of theft and larceny or not?
- b Reason
- c Case and/or statutory provision

5 Sarah leaves a goat with Abraham, telling him to take care of it until she directs him what to do next. Abraham sells the goat and uses the money. Sarah is furious, even though she had intended to give Abraham the goat when it got bigger. She wants him to be arrested.

- a Is Abraham guilty of theft and larceny or not?
- b Reason
- c Case and/or statutory provision

6 Samson is owed $5,000.00 by his friend Aaron. His brother Ishmael sees Aaron and tells him that Samson now has a gun and 'will do anything to get his money'. Aaron, who has owed the money for a long time and has been avoiding Samson, becomes afraid, handing Ishmael $6,000.00, the excess to be taken as interest.

   a Is Ishmael liable for theft and larceny or not?

   b Reason

   c Case and/or statutory provision

7 Job decides to play a trick on Jeremiah his employer, who is very wealthy, but miserly. He hides in Jeremiah's closet, knowing that Jeremiah has gone to the theatre. Upon Jeremiah's entering the bedroom, Job who is wearing a mask, jumps from the closet with a toy gun in his hand. Jeremiah does not know that it is a toy gun and throws his wallet on the bed saying, 'Take it, take everything'. Job takes the wallet, which contains $20,000.00 and escapes, through an open window.

   a Is Job liable for robbery or not?

   b Reason

   c Case and/or statutory provision

8 One night, Esau and Jacob enter Isaac's house through an open upstairs window, using a ladder left in Isaac's garden. Isaac is their uncle. They intended to retrieve a coffee table they had left with Isaac some time ago, but which he has refused to hand over to them because they owe him money. Esau and Jacob take the table and also take a television set they believe is one belonging to their mother Rachel.

   a Are Esau and Jacob guilty of burglary or not?

   b Reason

   c Case and/or statutory provision

Feedback

2 Cain is liable in both theft and larceny. Under theft the issue is appropriation of property belonging to another. In larceny, he has the animus furandi. R v. Hinks (theft); R v. Middleton; R v. Thurborn (larceny).

3 Miriam is liable for theft. She 'appropriates' the property within the meaning given in R v. Hinks, also Lawrence, Morris and Gomez. The statutory provisions relating to appropriation would apply. The issue in larceny would be whether she fraudulently converts the property. See Commonwealth v. Tluchak.

4 The question is whether this is 'property belonging to another', which has been 'dishonestly appropriated'. R v. Turner; R v. Meredith; R v. Woodham. Section 5 of Theft Act (England) (B). Goliath is not liable for theft or larceny.

5 Abraham has appropriated property, which belongs to another. He is the bailee of the goat and is not expected to dispose of it. It is not yet his goat, even though Sarah intended to give it to him. The defence that he cannot steal his own property would not yet be available to him. Until Sarah tells him the goat is his, he cannot dispose of it without liability.He is therefore liable for larceny and theft. See cases and statutory provisions listed for question 4.

6 This is a clear case of larceny by intimidation and trick. Theft would also apply. R v. Bramley, R v. Lovell, R v. Hinks (also Lawrence, Morris and Gomez). See section 1, Theft Act (England), section 3(2), Larceny Act (J).

7 Job is not liable for robbery, even though it turns out that he was using a toy gun. He would be guilty of an aggravated assault. Smith v. Desmond, R v. Hale. Section 8, Theft Act (England) (B), section 37(1) (J), section 24(1) (TT), Larceny Act.

8 Esau and Jacob are guilty of burglary, as defined in both the Theft Act and the Larceny Act. See R v. Jones and Smith, R v. Collins, R v. Hughes. Section 9(1), Theft Act (England) (B), section 39, Larceny Act (J).

Inchoate offences

> The word "inchoate" means 'just begun', 'undeveloped', 'in the process of' or 'preliminary', 'rudimentary', 'unformed'.
>
> OED and Webster's

An essential element in inchoate crimes is an understanding of who are the parties to a crime. In two inchoate crimes, incitement and conspiracy, more than one party is usually involved. We will, therefore, begin with a brief discussion of the parties to a crime, and then proceed to examine each inchoate crime separately.

Parties to a crime

Where more than one person is involved in a crime, the question of the liability of each one will arise. Elliot and Wood, Cases and Materials on Criminal Law (1997, page 357), put it excellently, thus:

> 'The actual perpetrator of a crime or part of a crime, or one who effects it through an innocent agent, is guilty of the crime as principal. One who does not perpetrate a crime but participates in it is punishable as an accessory (author emphasis) if he aids, abets, counsels or procures (author emphasis) the principal offender to commit the crime.'

I have emphasised the two crucial elements: 'accessory' and 'aids, abets, counsels or procures'.

The accessory

As you will have gleaned from the quotation above, the principal and the accessory are equally guilty, though their roles are distinct. The accessory is punishable for his role before, or after, the fact, that is, of the crime committed. However, if the offence for which the accessory is charged would not make the principal liable, the accessory will not be guilty. Here's a case to illustrate the point:

R v. Whitehouse [1977] QB 868

W was charged for inciting his 15-year-old daughter to commit incest with him. He pleaded guilty and was convicted. On appeal against his sentence, the Court of Appeal gave him leave to appeal against conviction as he had pleaded guilty to an offence unknown in law. The relevant provision under the Sexual Offences Act made it an 'offence for a woman of the age of 16 or over to permit a man whom she knows to be her ... father ... to have sexual intercourse with her by her consent'.

Here the accessory, the father, would not be guilty as the girl, the principal, could not commit the offence for which he was charged. The conviction was therefore quashed.

To 'aid, abet, counsel or procure'

There are many learned discussions to be had on this issue, but for our purposes, we need not indulge. Suffice it to say, that the legislation from

Activity 5.14

This activity is intended to assist you with your revision. At the end of it you should have clarified in your mind the technical issues in the law.

1 Re-read your notes and write short notes on: (a) theft and (b) larceny.
   - a Write short notes on the distinction between theft and larceny.
   - b Are the distinctions ones without a difference? Write the reasons for your answer.

which the offence arises, the Accessories and Abettors Act 1861, uses the terms coterminously, stating that:

> 'Whomsoever shall aid, abet, counsel or procure the commission of any misdemeanour, whether the same be a misdemeanour at common law or by virtue of an Act passed, shall be liable to be tried, indicted and punished as a principal offender.'

The ordinary dictionary meaning of each word indicates that although they each convey a separate meaning, when used together as in the section just quoted, they form a chain of action, intricately interwoven to constitute the offence. The following case, a Privy Council decision from Trinidad and Tobago, indicates that it is not a requirement that all four words should apply for liability to arise. Here, the operative words were 'aiding' and 'abetting':

Mohan v. R [1967] 2 AC 187 (PC)

D was in a quarrel with M. R, D's father, intervened and attacked M with a cutlass. While R was chasing M, D went and obtained a machete. D and R struck M many times. M collapsed and was found bleeding. He died subsequently. It was found that the cause of M's death was a wound to the leg. D and R were convicted of murder. Both appealed on the ground that there was no evidence of a prearranged plan by D and R to attack M; neither was there evidence of who had struck the fatal blow.

The appeals were dismissed, the Board finding that there was evidence of a common intention and that it did not matter who struck the fatal blow, their aiding and abetting each other being the issue to contend with, and which was present. (Note that 'counselling and procuring' were not present. You will see how these operate in incitement and conspiracy, when we move next to the details of inchoate crimes.)

Incitement

Incitement is a common law offence, a misdemeanour. If I tell you that I wish you to commit a crime, it does not matter if you decline, in order to determine my criminal liability. I am liable for incitement, even though you, by declining, would not be guilty of any offence. You and I would be guilty if I incited you to incite C to commit murder and you complied, whether or not C himself complied.

The actus reus of incitement

Here's an interesting case the demonstrates the offence:-

Invicta Plastics Ltd v. Clare [1976] RTR 251 (Q/BS)

Invicta Plastics manufactured a device called 'Radatec' and advertised it for sale. It was not illegal to own the device, but it was illegal to use it, its purpose being for drivers to detect police radar. It was held that the advertisement incited readers to commit an offence. The court approved Lord Denning's dictum in an earlier case:

An old case illustrates Lord Denning's words, pointing to the fact that it is from words spoken or written that liability arises in incitement. In that case A encouraged others in various foreign countries to assassinate their Heads of State. He did so in certain publications and was found guilty of incitement: R V. Most (1881) 7 QBD 24.

The mens rea of incitement

As we saw in R v. Whitehouse, on page 135, to be liable the incitor, or principal, must incite the incitee, or accessory, to commit an offence, which would be a crime by him. If you look back at strict liability offences, you would see another angle to this – the statutory provision creating the offence must be seen to have been breached. It is the same kind of principle here. In R v. Curr [1968] 2 QB 944 (CA), the court said that a defendant could only be guilty of incitement if the woman who was purportedly incited knew that the action she was asked to perform knew it to be an offence. The facts are set out below:

C lent money and in return took family allowance vouchers as security. Borrowers signed their vouchers over to C. He got a woman to cash the vouchers at the Post Office. She did not know that she was committing an offence. C was charged, among other things, with soliciting the woman to commit an offence. C was convicted and appealed. His appeal was allowed for the reason stated above, that is, that the woman did not know she was committing an offence.

Conspiracy

Conspiracy is no longer a common law offence in England, but it still is in our independent jurisdictions. We shall look at the offence at common law. The position at common law was expressed in the well-known dictum of Willes J in Mulcahy v. R (1868) where he defined conspiracy as 'the agreement of two or more to do an unlawful act, or to do a lawful act by unlawful means'.

The statutory provisions in England have expanded those at common law, and have changed them, to some extent, the elementary principles still being applicable.

The actus reus of conspiracy

The act described as a conspiracy must be seen to have been agreed between the alleged conspirators the end being the commission of a criminal offence. The conspirators need not have taken steps to commit the offence; the agreement is the key element. At common law, the commission of the crime by any of the conspirators is also sufficient, and all of them need not carry it through. Here is an interesting case from Jamaica. This case also deals with the important issues of (a) conspiracy to defraud and (b) what happens when the agreement to commit the crime is made in one jurisdiction but the crime occurs in another jurisdiction:

R v. James Smith (1990) 27 JLR 469 (CA)

The appellant was a former Cabinet Minister who had portfolio responsibility for the Ministry of Labour. The Farm Work programme fell under his portfolio. He was convicted on the case made by the prosecution in the Resident Magistrates' Court for Kingston, that, inter alia:

1 He induced his Permanent Secretary to embezzle money in Farm Work programme from funds which came from the United States and Canada for the benefit of farm-workers in a compulsory saving scheme.

  The monies originated abroad but were embezzled in Jamaica, where both men were based.

Among the issues on appeal were that the object or purpose of the conspiracy was to obtain money outside of Jamaica and, therefore, whether the matter was indictable in Jamaica.

At trial, the former Minister gave no evidence, exercising his right to remain silent. The Permanent Secretary pleaded guilty and both men were convicted.

Race Relations Board v. Applin [1973] QB 815 (CA)

A sent a circular to W's neighbours complaining about W's taking non-white foster children. A wanted W to take white foster children only. The question was whether A's action contravened the relevant provision of the Race Relations Act 1968. It was held that A's actions constituted an incitement of W.

Lord Denning said, at page 825:

> '[It was suggested] that to "incite" means to urge or spur on by advice, encouragement or persuasion, and not otherwise. I do not think the word is so limited, at any rate in the present context. A person may "incite" another to do an act by threatening or by pressure, as well as by persuasion.'

Yip Chin-Cheung v. R [1995] 1 AC 111 (PC)

D was convicted of conspiracy to traffic heroin contrary to common law and the Dangerous Drugs Ordinance. He had entered into an arrangement with an American undercover agent of the Drug Enforcement Agency (DEA), with whom D agreed to meet in Hong Kong and to deliver the contraband to the agent there. This was a 'sting' operation and the authorities were fully aware of it. D proceeded with the deal as planned and D was arrested and subsequently convicted. The agent had, however, missed his flight and the actual delivery did not take place. D's point of appeal was that he was improperly convicted as the agent lacked the required mens rea for the offence. His appeal was dismissed. In the judgment of the Board, Lord Griffiths said that the facts of the case represented a common occurrence in which undercover agents enter into an arrangement by which they agree to commit a crime in order to prevent the wider perpetration of that crime. While the agent would not expect to be arrested, the same principle would not extend to the co-conspirator, who would, as you can see, have the necessary mens rea, in any event.

Shaw v. DPP [1961] 2 All ER 446, [1962] AC 220, [1961] 2 WLR 481 (HL)

Shaw and others produced a booklet, The Ladies' Directory, in which prostitutes advertised their services. Shaw was charged with and convicted of conspiracy to corrupt public morals. He appealed unsuccessfully.

Upon the appellant's appeal before the Court of Appeal, it was held, inter alia, as follows:

2 At common law the indictable misdemeanour of conspiracy is complete by the agreement of two or more persons who agree to carry into effect an unlawful act, and depends not merely on the intention of two or more, but in the agreement of two or more to do an unlawful act or to do a lawful act by unlawful means.

Where two or more persons engage in the common enterprise, the acts and declarations of one in pursuance of that common purpose are admissible against the other. (Note: The Permanent Secretary cooperated with the police and testified against the former Minister.)

3 The mere agreement to commit the act having been made in Jamaica, even though the object of the agreement concerned persons outside of Jamaica, would not have rendered the men guilty. It was sufficient here that there was evidence of other overt acts in furtherance of the agreement, such acts having been committed both in Jamaica and abroad.

Rowe P said in his judgment that it is essential to identify 'the true object of the conspiracy', and said:

> 'In our view in the instant case the object of the conspiracy was to defraud the Government's farm-workers programmes administered by the Ministry of Labour and the further activities of Aitken (the Permanent Secretary) and the appellant were the means employed to that end.' (at page 484)

The mens rea of conspiracy

As we saw earlier, the agreement is the essential element in the crime of conspiracy. We also saw that not all the conspirators need actually to perpetrate the crime to be held liable. The following case, which involves a 'sting', shows, however, that even if there is a deliberate attempt to entrap one who has a criminal intent, it is no excuse for that person that his 'co-conspirator' did not have the mens rea for the offence. The co-conspirator was here carrying out his duties in crime prevention.

Conspiracy to corrupt public morals and outrage public decency

There is an offence known as conspiracy to corrupt public morals and outrage public decency, as the following two well-known cases indicate.

In both these cases, we see that an individual may engage in an activity, by himself, and the nature of that activity is such as to lead the court to conclude that there is a common law conspiracy. Here are the facts of both cases:

Both cases are of great interest on the subject of morality and the law. You should make an effort to read the judgments.

You will also note that even though an agreement is essential for a conspiracy to take place, these cases suggest that the agreement need not take place before the crime is committed, nor do the parties need to know each other. Mere publication by way of inducement constitutes the 'agreement'!

Attempts

We will be examining the common law offence. Attempt is an indictable misdemeanour. Smith and Hogan's Criminal Law: Cases and Materials (2002, at page 414) describes the offence thus:

'An attempt to commit a crime is itself an offence. Often it is a grave offence. Often it is as morally culpable as the completed offence which is attempted but not in fact committed. Nevertheless it falls within the class of conduct which is preparatory to the commission of a crime and is one step removed from the offence which is attempted.'

On the question of the actus reus and the mens rea of the crime, the learned writers say:

'It is clear that on a charge of attempt, intention is required as to any result in the definition of the actus reus even though it is not required on a charge of committing the complete crime.' (page 45)

The crime is not without its uncertainties, as these cases will show.

The actus reus of attempt

The 'proximity test' formulated by Parke B in R v. Eagleton (1855) was approved by the House of Lords in the well-known case, DPP v. Stonehouse [1978] AC 55, but the test is not without its own challenges. Parke B had said:

'The mere intention to commit a misdemeanour is not criminal. Some act is required and we do not think all acts towards committing a misdemeanour are indictable. Acts remotely leading towards the commission of the offence are not to be considered as attempts to commit it, but acts immediately connected with it are ...'

Numerous academic writers have criticised the formulation by Parke B as they see it as somewhat flawed. In DPP v. Stonehouse, Lord Diplock, in approving Parke B's dictum, said:

'The constituent elements of the inchoate crime of an attempt are a physical act by the offender sufficiently proximate to the complete offence. Acts that are merely preparatory to the commission of the offence such as, in the instant case, the taking out of the insurance policies, are not sufficiently proximate to constitute an attempt. They do not indicate a fixed irrevocable intention to go on to commit the complete offence unless involuntarily prevented from doing so.'

Here are the facts of that well-known case, which caused quite a stir in the media of the day:

DPP v. Stonehouse [1978] AC 55, [1977] 2 All ER 909, [1977] 3 WLR 143 (HL)

Stonehouse was a well-known legislator. He engaged in a series of deceptive behaviours intended to give the impression that he had drowned off the coast of Miami. He did all this, including purchasing insurance policies on his life, in favour of his wife, in order to escape to Australia to live a new life with another woman. His wife never attempted to claim the insurance. S was eventually extradited to England and was convicted of 13 offences of dishonesty and 5 for attempting to deceive. His appeals were dismissed by the Court of Appeal and the House of Lords.

Their Lordships found that, on the date in 1974 in Miami, when S faked his death by drowning, he had 'crossed the Rubicon and burnt his boats' (per Lord Diplock). His Lordship said, further:

'In my opinion it is quite unarguable that, given the necessary intention, those acts were not sufficiently proximate to the complete offence of obtaining property by deception to be capable in law of constituting an attempt to commit the offence.'

Knuller Ltd v. DPP [1973] AC 435, [1972] 3 WLR 143, [1972] 2 All ER 898 (HL)

The appellants published a magazine entitled Males. Most advertisements in it were by male homosexuals with a view to attracting fellow homosexuals. The magazine had a circulation of over 30,000. The appellants were charged for conspiracy to corrupt public morals and for conspiracy, through the advertisements, to induce readers to engage in homosexual practices 'with intent thereby to debauch and corrupt the morals as well of youth as divers other liege subjects of Our Lady the Queen'. The appellants were convicted on both counts and appealed to the Court of Appeal, which dismissed their appeal. Their appeal to the House of Lords was dismissed on the first count, but allowed on the second.

R v. White [1910] 2 KB 724, [1910] 4 Cr. App Rep 257, [1908–10] All ER Rep 340 (C Cr. Ap)

The appellant's mother was found dead sitting on a sofa. Beside her was a glass with a drink in which was found a poison, two grains of potassium cyanide. She died from heart failure and not from the poison, no evidence being revealed that she had imbibed any of the drink. It was also found that even if she had taken that quantity of poison seen in the glass, it would not have been sufficient to kill her.

The appellant was indicted for murder but was convicted of attempted murder.

The court found that there was sufficient evidence upon which the appellant had been convicted for attempted murder, albeit that his effort would not have resulted in his mother's death. Bray J said:

> '... the completion or attempted completion of one of a series of acts intended by a man to result in killing is an attempt to murder even though this completed act would not unless followed by other acts, result in killing.'

Two further interesting cases in this area are R v. White and R v. Jones, one before, the other after, Stonehouse. Here are the facts of each:

Compare the next case, which leans more towards the 'series of acts test', which in itself may be regarded as an expanded approach to the proximity test. At what point are acts 'merely preparatory' and the 'last act' committed? Consider this question as you read:

R v. Jones [1990] 3 All ER 886, [1990] 1 WLR 1057, (1990) 91 Cr. App R 351 (CA)

In 1985, Jones, a married man, started an affair with Ms Gresley, with whom he lived in Australia in 1986. In 1987 they were both back in England and Ms Gresley began a relationship with the victim, Freeman. However, she continued to see J for whom she still had feelings. Later in 1987 G sought to break off the relationship with J and told him so, refusing all his advances.

In January 1988, J applied for a shotgun licence and purchased two guns at first, then two more. He shortened the barrel of one of the guns and test fired it twice.

J told his colleagues at work that he would be away in late January. He told his wife that he was going to Spain to do some work on their chalet. On the morning of the incident he left home dressed as if for work.

On that fatal morning, F, G's current lover, took his daughter to school by car. J, who had been waiting for him, went into G's car (as F stopped to let off his daughter) and told him to drive. J had covered his face. In the course of the encounter, J pointed the sawn-off gun at F and used words to the effect 'You are not going to like this'. F managed to wrestle the gun from J and threw it outside. J then tried to strangle him with a string. F escaped and called the police. J drove away in F's car.

In F's car the police found a bag belonging to J containing money and a sharp knife, a hatchet and some cartridges. The question for appeal turned on whether this was a situation of attempted murder.

Their Lordships reviewed the authorities, including Byrne J's dictum in Eagleton and its approval in Stonehouse. They also referred to 'the other test', meaning that enunciated by Stephen's Digest of the Criminal Law (5th ed., 1894) where the learned writer said:

> 'An attempt to commit a crime is an act done with intent to commit that crime, and forming part of a series of acts which would constitute its actual commission if it were not interrupted.' (art. 50)

Do you see a conflict in these two tests? It is submitted that they complement each other. What is your view? In R v. Jones, J's appeal was dismissed.

The mens rea of attempt

Smith and Hogan's Criminal Law, 2002, adopts an enlightened approach. The learned writers choose to discuss the mens rea of attempt, before they discuss the actus reus, because, they write 'as has often been remarked, the mental element assumes paramount importance in attempts' (page 328). They go on to say that even though an 'actus reus may be a perfectly innocent and harmless act as where D, intending to murder P, puts sugar in his tea, believing that it is not sugar but a deadly poison', D may still be liable for the criminal offence of attempted murder (pages 328–9). R v. White (1910) aptly illustrates this point.

In England, where there is a Criminal Attempts Act, there is a statutory offence of 'intent to commit an offence'. The term was held to mean the same as 'intent' at common law. The following case is helpful:

R v. Mohan [1976] QB 1, [1975] 2 All ER 193, [1975] 2 WLR 859 (CA)

M drove his car directly towards a policeman who managed to jump out of the way. M was convicted of attempting to cause grievous bodily harm to the policeman as a result of his driving. The jury found that he had been reckless as to whether his driving would cause bodily harm. M appealed against his conviction.

M's appeal was allowed.

James LJ's reasoning in support of the court's decision to allow M's appeal, really states the important questions to be answered in identifying the mens rea of an accused. His Lordship said:

> 'An attempt to commit a crime is itself an offence. Often it is a grave offence. Often it is as morally culpable as the completed offence which is attempted but not in fact committed ... The court must not strain to bring within the offence of attempt conduct which does not fall within the well-established bounds of the offence. On the contrary, the court must safeguard against extension of those bounds save by the authority of Parliament. The bounds are presently set requiring proof of specific intent, a decision to bring about, in so far as it lies within the accused's power, the commission of the offence which it is alleged the accused attempted to commit, no matter whether the accused desired that consequence of his act or not.' (author emphasis)

This dictum should be read closely.

See the following case:

R v. Khan and Others [1990] 2 All ER 783, [1990] 1 WLR 813

K and five other men were charged with rape and attempted rape of a 16-year-old girl. The girl had accompanied some of them to a house. They had all been at a discotheque. Three youths succeeded in having intercourse with her, but others were unsuccessful. The girl did not consent to sexual intercourse. Those who were convicted of attempted rape appealed unsuccessfully. The Court of Appeal upheld the position that the appellants were guilty of attempted rape, even if they did not know if the girl was consenting and were reckless whether or not she consented.

Russell LJ said that the intent of the defendant is the same in rape as in attempted rape. His Lordship continued:

> 'A man does not recklessly have sexual intercourse, nor does he recklessly attempt it. Recklessness in rape and attempted rape arises not in relation to the physical act of the accused but only in his state of mind when engaged in the activity of having or attempting to have sexual intercourse.'

These pronouncements very clearly enunciate the position. Read them again, carefully.

Let's now move on to our activities. Hopefully, you found this discussion of inchoate crimes an interesting one!

Activity 5.15

Revision time

At the end of the following exercises, you should have done plenty of revision and should have a good grasp of the lesson.

Read the following short problems carefully, then answer the questions that follow, placing an 'X' in the box and citing at least one appropriate case. The first one is done for you.

1 Mandy, a nursing assistant, is tired of her job as a caregiver to Mr P, an old man of 92. Mr P abuses her every day and makes her life difficult. Mandy puts a deadly poison in Mr P's tea, approaches him and says, 'You old bastard, take this'. Mr P tries to box the cup from Mandy's hand, but falls off the bed, breaks his neck and dies.

   a Q: Is Mandy liable for attempted murder?
   b True (X) False ( )
   c Reason:
   d Cases: R v. White, R v. Jones

2 Peter agrees with Paul to break into Robert's warehouse to steal crates of sodas, which they plan to sell at a fair in the adjoining village. Peter, who is a security guard at the warehouse, disarms the electronic security system. He becomes ill that night and is unable to participate in the break-in. Paul takes Timothy with him and they successfully undertake their project.

   a Q: Is Peter liable for conspiracy, but not for the theft?
   b True ( ) False ( )
   c Reason:
   d Cases:

3 Elizabeth and Marie decide to start a call-in service and a brothel called House of Ecstasy. They print brochures in which they state the services to be provided and containing details of men and women willing to provide sexual favours.

   a Q: Are Elizabeth and Marie liable for conspiracy to corrupt public morals and outrage public decency?
   b True ( ) False ( )
   c Reason:
   d Cases:

4 Raj agrees with Sterling who, unknown to him, is an undercover agent, to deliver 3 kilos of cocaine at an overseas port. With the help of his confederates, Raj successfully places the drugs on board the designated flight but changes his mind about flying and sends Pete instead. Pete is arrested upon his arrival overseas.

   a Q: Are Raj, Sterling and Pete guilty of conspiracy?
   b True ( ) False ( )
   c Reason:
   d Cases:

5 Sati operates a variety store which is not doing well. She and her husband, Tyler, decide to torch the store and claim on their insurance. Sati's father Raju overhears the discussion and torches the store while Sati and Tyler are away on vacation.

   a Q: Sati, Tyler and Raju are guilty of a conspiracy.
   b True ( ) False ( )
   c Reason:
   d Cases:

6 Diego and Olivia are having problems in their marriage. Diego forms a new relationship with Constancia and decides to go abroad to live with her. Diego stages his death, but prior to doing so, he buys a large policy on his life, naming Olivia as the beneficiary. Before Olivia claims on the policy, Diego is found alive.

   a Q: Is Diego, but not Olivia, liable for attempt?
   b True ( ) False ( )
   c Reason:
   d Case(s):

Feedback

2 True ( ) False ( )

Reason:

Cases:

3 True ( ) False ( )

Reason:

Cases: Shaw v. DPP, Knuller v. DPP

4 True (X) False ( )

Reason: It does not matter that here there is an 'agreement' with a person whose purpose is not to commit a crime, but to prevent one. The agreement is sufficient.

Cases: Yip Chin-Cheung v. R, R v. James Smith

5 True ( ) False (X)

Reason: It is not clear that Sati and Tyler agreed with Raj to commit the arson. There must be agreement among all the parties.

Cases:

6 True (X) False ( )

Reason: Olivia would have had to take steps preparatory to the commission of the offence. There is no indication that she has taken any such steps. Diego is the only one who did.

Cases: DPP v. Stonehouse

Activity 5.16

Case study

D, a married man, is having an affair with W, who is also married. W's husband, C, who is terminally ill, is very distressed at W's lack of attentiveness towards him. At every opportunity, C bemoans the fact that he and W have been married since they were both 21 years old, over 35 years ago.

C's friend, X, a known gunman, visits C one day. C confides in X that he is quite angry with W.

'To be truthful', C confides in X, 'I really wish I could do something about my wife, but I don't have the strength'. 'Don't worry man', says X, 'I'll fix the wretch', to which C responds, 'I know I can depend on you'.

X leaves C and instructs one of his henchmen, Y, to 'get' D and W. Y takes with him, Z, to a secluded spot on the beach where D and W are known to frequent. Both Y and Z are armed.

Y beckons to Z to shoot at D and W who are seen sitting on the bonnet of D's car. Z panics and misses W. D and W try to escape from Y and Z, who both shoot at them. D dies and W is seriously wounded. It is Y who fires the fatal shots.

Discuss the criminal liabilities of C, X, Y and Z. You should support your answer by reference to decided cases.

Feedback

You have here an instance of each inchoate crime.

C incites X by his words, reckless as to what C might do. This is followed by a conspiracy to murder. Is C part of this conspiracy? What did you think? Remember, X is a known gunman, to whom C says 'I know I can depend on you'.

Z's attempt is foiled by his nervousness, but his culpability is not in doubt.

You would also be required to discuss the 'parties to the crime' and the nature and extent of their involvement.

You have a wide body of cases from which to find support for your conclusions.

Hopefully, you were on target. If not, re-read the section and attempt the question again.

Defences

At the beginning of our study of criminal law, we discussed the principle that criminal liability arises where the actus reus and mens rea converge. You will recall the maxim, 'actus non facit reum nisi mensit rea': if not, you should look it up now.

In this section, we shall be examining the defences available to an accused person. It should become apparent to you that in most, if not all, circumstances the essence of a defence is that there is no convergence of the actus reus and the mens rea. The effect of a defence is either to absolve the accused or to mitigate the punishment, which would have been imposed, otherwise.

In the discussions about defences, distinctions are sometimes made between those defences that are 'true defences' and those that are 'hybrid'. Underlying these distinctions is that a true defence is not merely an excuse, but points towards justificatory action. A hybrid defence would include those that are more of an explanation, such as alibi, mistake, infancy and insanity. For some defences it is even questioned whether they are really defences, such as necessity.

In this lesson we shall consider the 'defences' that appear in your syllabus. We will examine these defences under two headings, namely (i) special and (ii) general defences.

Special defences

You will have already dealt with provocation, one of the special defences, when studying the law of murder. Special defences are those an accused person claims, in cases of voluntary manslaughter. In such instances the accused is being charged for murder. These special defences are to be left to the jury and are: provocation; diminished responsibility; and suicide pact.

Provocation

We have already examined provocation and you should revise the section dealing with this topic now. You should pay close attention to the cases dealt with there, such as R v. Duffy (1949), where Devlin J, as he then was, set out the criteria for determining when the defence applies.

Diminished responsibility

The 1957 Homicide Act of England defines diminished responsibility as an 'abnormality of mind':

> 'Where a person kills or is party to the killing of another, he shall not be convicted of murder if he was suffering from such abnormality of mind (whether arising from a condition of arrested or retarded development of mind or any inherent causes or induced by disease or injury) as substantially impaired his mental responsibility for his acts and omissions in doing or being a party to the killing.'

The Act also provides that:

- it is the defence's duty to prove that the person charged should not be convicted of murder
- where the person charged advances the defence successfully, the conviction will be for manslaughter, not murder.

Key points to note about diminished responsibility:

- It reduces a charge of murder to manslaughter.
- The accused suffers from abnormality of the mind.
- The abnormality can arise from a birth defect, or may arise inherently or be induced by disease or injury.
- The abnormality impairs the accused person's mental responsibility.

Abnormality of mind

R v. Byrne [1960] 2 QB 396 (CCA) is the case that is often first cited under this heading. In this case, the appellant admitted murder but advanced the diminished responsibility defence. He was convicted and appealed on the basis that the judge had misdirected himself in the summing up on the defence. The appeal was allowed.

Lord Parker CJ said:

> '"Abnormality of mind", which has to be contrasted with the time-honoured expression in the M'Naughten Rules "defect of reason", means a state of mind so different from that of ordinary human beings that the reasonable man would term it abnormal.'

Byrne had strangled the victim in a YWCA hostel and grossly mutilated her body. Medical evidence was adduced to show that he was a violent sexual psychopath.

Here's a very interesting Privy Council decision from Barbados:

Walton v. R (1978) 66 Cr. App Rep 25, [1978] AC 788, [1978] 1 All ER 542, [1977] 3 WLR 902

The appellant was driving his girlfriend and her mother when he stopped the car suddenly. His girlfriend thought his actions were weird and flagged down another car. The appellant shot and killed a passenger in the car, which had stopped. His defence was diminished responsibility. He relied on medical experts and a psychologist but the jury, finding no history of mental impairment, convicted him. His appeal to the Court of Appeal of Barbados and to the Privy Council was unsuccessful.

The Privy Council approved the approach taken by Lord Parker CJ in Byrne.

R v. Tandy [1989] (CA) 1 WLR 350, [1989] 1 All ER 267

The appellant was an alcoholic. After a round of vodka, she strangled her 11-year-old daughter. She pleaded diminished responsibility. The judge directed the jury that if she voluntarily took her first drink, she could not claim that her abnormality of mind was due to the disease of alcoholism. She was convicted and appealed. Her appeal was unsuccessful. The Court of Appeal found that the alcohol had not in itself produced an abnormality of mind.

Finally, we look at another well-known case on the topic:

General defences

The defences to be examined here are insanity, automatism, intoxication, necessity, self-defence, mistake and consent.

Insanity

Historically, insanity was a frequently used defence in instances when the punishment for murder was hanging. As is the case today, the burden was on the accused to prove that the accused was insane. The locus classicus or pivotal case is M'Naghten's Case (1843), from which the well-known M'Naghten Rules are derived. The facts of that very important case are as follows:

M'Naghten tried to assassinate Sir Robert Peel, a leading politician. He killed, instead, Peel's secretary. He pleaded insanity and the jury so found. He was committed to life in a secure mental institution.

Following M'Naghten's acquittal, the House of Lords discussed the extent to which unsoundness of mind renders an accused person free of a charge of murder. So were the famous M'Naghten Rules formulated, based on questions posed to their Lordships. The test has been of wide application in common law jurisdictions, including the United States of America. They are as follows:

- It must be put to the jury that 'every man is presumed to be sane, and to possess a sufficient degree of reason to be responsible for his crimes, until the contrary be proved to their satisfaction.'
- 'To establish a defence on the ground of insanity, it must be clearly proved that, at the time of the committing of the act, the party accused was labouring under such a defect of reason, from disease of the mind, as not to know the nature and quality of the act he was doing; of if he did know it, that he did not know he was doing what was wrong.'
- If the accused claims to have laboured under a delusion as to existing facts, he 'must be considered in the same situation as to responsibility as if the facts with respect to which the delusion exists were true.' (Author emphases.)

Note the portions that have been underlined. These phrases hold the key to your understanding of the law in this area.

The main concepts that are usually examined, based on the M'Naghten Rules are:

- disease of the mind
- defect of reason, and
- uncontrollable impulse.

Let us take a look at each of these concepts.

Disease of the mind

R v. Kemp (1957) and R v. Sullivan (1984) are the authorities here. Of course, there are many other interesting cases as well.

In our discussion of automatism (on page 148) we shall observe Lord Denning's dictum in Bratty v. AG for Northern Ireland (1963).

Defect of reason

'Defect of reason' is a consequence of a disease of the mind, under the M'Naghten Rules. We will look at two cases:

R v. Clarke [1972] 1 All ER 219, (1972) 56 Cr. App Rep 225 (CA)

Clarke went into a supermarket and picked up a number of items, some of which she put into her bag. She was charged with stealing. Her defence was that she had no intent to steal and that she was a diabetic and had domestic problems. There was evidence that she had behaved absent-mindedly before this event and a psychiatrist gave evidence that she suffered from depression.

Their Lordships declined to find that the accused suffered from a definitive disease of the mind, a defect of reason. She had a temporary absent-mindedness.

R v. Windle [1952] 2 All ER 1 (CA)

Windle was married to a woman 18 years his senior. He was known to be a person of low intelligence. She was a depressed person who spoke of suicide. Windle's friends became tired of him talking about his wife's problems and of her suicidal wish. One of his friends told him, in apparent annoyance, to give his wife 'a dozen aspirins'. He administered some 100 aspirins to her, as a result of which she died. He later told the police he supposed he would be charged for it.

Windle's defence was insanity. Devlin J, who would later decide Kemp (1957), found that the decision would rest on whether or not the accused suffered from a defect of reason as to not know that what he was doing was wrong. His Lordship said 'wrong' meant 'wrong according to law'. He concluded that the accused knew that what he was doing was wrong according to law and his defence failed. Windle's appeal to the Court of Appeal was unsuccessful. Lord Goddard CJ said: 'A man may be suffering from a defect of reason, but, if he knows that what he is doing is wrong – and by wrong is meant contrary to law – he is responsible.'

Uncontrollable impulse

The issue of uncontrollable impulse arises where the accused is alleging that because of his defect of reason due to a disease of the mind, even though he appreciates the nature and quality of his act and knows his act to be wrong in law, he was unable to prevent himself from acting as he did. The Privy Council has held in two cases that where the accused puts in such a defence, the M'Naghten Rules apply, despite attempts to suggest that they are too unscientific in today's world. The cases are as follows:

Sodeman v. R [1936] 2 All ER 1138 (PC)

The petitioner, who was a labourer, took a young girl for a ride on his bicycle, strangled her, tied her hands behind her back, stuffed some of her clothing into her mouth, and left her for dead. The cause of death was suffocation. The petitioner had committed three previous murders in very similar ways. The petitioner's defence was that he was insane at the time. At the trial two Government prison doctors gave evidence in support of that defence. No expert evidence on that issue was tendered by the Crown. It was held:

- the law with regard to insanity was stated in M'Naghten's case, and there was not to be added to that statement another rule that where a man knew that he was doing wrong, but was forced to do the act by an irresistible impulse produced by disease, he could rely upon a defence of insanity.
- the burden in cases in which an accused had to prove insanity might fairly be stated as not being higher than the burden that rested upon a plaintiff or defendant in civil proceedings.

This case raises the question whether the rules in M'Naghten's case are quite consistent with modern medical theory. The Privy Council refused to depart from the rules there laid down.

R v. Kemp [1957] 1 QB 399 (Bristol assizes), [1956] 3 All ER 249, [1956] 3 WLR 724

The accused suffered from a disease known as arteriosclerosis or hardening of the arteries. He was charged with inflicting grievous bodily harm on his wife. It was shown that Kemp's illness did not cause him any mental trouble, but that when under an attack by the condition, he would suffer a temporary loss of consciousness, which was what occurred when he injured his wife. He did not plead insanity. There was evidence that he was a devoted husband.

Devlin J, as he then was, found that the M'Naghten Rules applied. He said that 'the law is not concerned with the brain but with the mind'. Kemp was found guilty, but insane. His temporary loss of consciousness was a disease of the mind. 'Mind', his Lordship said, meant the ordinary faculties of reason, memory and understanding.

R v. Sullivan [1984] AC 156, [1983] 3 WLR 123, [1983] 2 All ER 673 (HL)

In this case, the House of Lords approved Devlin J's definition of 'mind' in Kemp (referred to above). This was another case of grievous bodily harm. At the trial, the accused admitted the offence, but claimed to have been under an epileptic attack at the time of its occurrence.

The trial judge found that a defence of insanity rather than of insane automatism was applicable. Sullivan then changed his plea to guilty and was convicted. He failed in his appeal to the Court of Appeal and appealed to the House of Lords where the appeal was dismissed.

The distinction made between this case and Kemp was that the disease of the mind did not result in the accused's not knowing 'the nature and quality of the act he was doing'.

Attorney General for the State of South Australia v. Brown [1960] AC 432, [1960] 2 WLR 588, [1960] 1 All ER 734

The respondent, who had been taken on as a station hand at a sheep station in South Australia on 20 November 1958 went, at a time a little after 9.15p.m. on Sunday evening, 23 November 1958, to the bedroom where the station manager was in bed asleep and shot him through the head. No one at the sheep station had given the respondent cause for malice. Some days later the respondent, who had left the sheep station, gave himself up to the police. He admitted the shooting but said he was not responsible for his actions at the time. In answer to a question by the police whether he knew at the time when he shot the deceased that it was wrong to point a loaded rifle at a person and shoot him, the respondent replied, 'Yes. But I couldn't help myself'. The respondent was tried on a charge of murder. In a statement from the dock at his trial he said, 'I shot L., but I do not know why. I had no reason to shoot him'. His defence was insanity, medical evidence being tendered that the respondent had a schizoid personality. Irresistible impulse, however, formed no part of the defence at the trial, the issue being whether, at the time of the shooting, the respondent knew that what he was doing was wrong. In a summing up, which put the defence of insanity before the jury, the trial judge, among other matters, directed the jury that a defence of uncontrollable impulse was unknown to the law and that, if the jury thought that uncontrollable impulse was the true explanation of the respondent's act, he was guilty.

Held: The respondent's answer to the police and his statement in the dock justified the trial judge in explaining to the jury that the criminal law of South Australia did not recognise the defence of insanity on the ground of

Automatism

Automatism is regarded as a difficult defence to raise successfully. The tenet of the defence is that the accused seeks to show that the prosecution has failed to produce evidence that the actus reus of the offence was voluntary.

You will see from the cases that automatism and insanity share a close relationship and therein lies the difficulty at times as to which one the accused should plead. You will also find that a defendant pleads one or the other and the judge raises the defence not pleaded, as in Kemp.

Automatism is of two types, namely insane and non-insane automatism. Insane automatism arises from an internal factor, while non-insane automatism is external or self-induced.

Insane automatism

The leading case of Bratty v. AG for Northern Ireland [1963] AC 386, [1961] 3 All ER 523 (HL) is a good example of the overlap of the defences of insanity and automatism.

In Bratty, the accused strangled a girl. He told the police that 'a sort of blackness' came over him and that 'I didn't know what I was doing. I didn't realise anything'. At the trial there was medical evidence that he might have suffered from a condition called psychomotor epilepsy, which could cause him not to know the nature and quality of his act. He raised both the defences of insanity and automatism. The trial judge rejected the defence of insanity and his defence of automatism failed. He was convicted and his appeals to the Court of Appeal for Northern Ireland and to the House of Lords were unsuccessful.

In the House of Lords, Lord Denning said:

> 'It seems to me that any mental disorder which has manifested itself in violence and is prone to recur is a disease of the mind.'

The dictum was not followed in Sullivan (1984) (see on page 147), but was approved in Burgess [1991] 2 QB 92, [1991] 2 All ER 769, where the illness was hyperglycaemia (an excess of blood sugar).

The appeal was dismissed in Bratty where their Lordships all agreed that the defence of insanity, not automatism, was available to Bratty. Two very important reasons for so deciding can be gleaned from Lord Denning's judgments:

> 'If the involuntary act proceeds from a disease of the mind, it gives rise to a defence of insanity, but not to a defence of automatism.'
>
> There was no evidence of automatism apart from insanity.'

Non-insane or self-induced

Next, we look at a case, which shows how self-induced automatism failed as a defence.

R v. Hennessy (1989) 89 Cr. App Rep 10, [1989] 2 All ER 9, [1989] 1 WLR 287 (CA)

H was charged with driving while disqualified. In his defence, he claimed that he had not taken his dosage of insulin because of stress, anxiety and depression and that, at the time of the act, he was suffering from hyperglycaemia (excessive blood sugar) and was in a state of automatism. The trial judge found that

H's condition was a result of diabetes, a disease, so therefore his defence was insanity within the M'Naghten Rules. H then changed his plea to guilty and was convicted. H appealed against conviction on the ground that the judge's ruling was wrong and that his depression and marital troubles were important factors overriding his diabetes.

In the Court of Appeal, their Lordships dismissed H's appeal, relying on such cases as Hill v. Baxter and R v. Sullivan. Lord Lane CJ cited Devlin J in Hill v. Baxter where he said:

> 'For the purposes of criminal law there are two categories of mental irresponsibility, one where the disorder is due to disease and the other where it is not.'

uncontrollable impulse; nor did the trial judge's direction as to the respondent's guilt, if uncontrollable impulse was the true explanation, amount to a misdirection.

Intoxication

Intoxication is another interesting, even controversial defence, which applies to a criminal charge in very limited circumstances. It covers the effects of drugs and solvents, as well as alcohol. There are two types of intoxication, namely voluntary and involuntary intoxication. We shall look at each one in turn.

Voluntary intoxication

Voluntary intoxication is sometimes referred to as self-induced intoxication. Its effect on crimes of basic intent and crimes of specific intent was highlighted in the leading case of DPP v. Majewski (1977), which we will be examining shortly.

Intoxication, when self-induced by the taking of or misuse of drugs or imbibing of alcohol, is a defence negating mens rea in crimes of basic intent, but not in crimes of specific intent.

Revision flash

Do you remember the distinction between crimes of basic intent and crimes of specific intent? Look back at our lesson on the mens rea of a crime.

In DPP v. Morgan (1975), Lord Simon defined crimes of basic intent as those requiring 'a mens rea which does not go beyond the actus reus'.

Crimes of specific intent, such as grievous bodily harm and murder, are those that require a higher level of mens rea. Intoxication may be accepted as a defence to such crimes.

DPP v. Majewski [1975] AC 443, [1976] 2 All ER 142, [1976] 2 WLR 623 (HL)

M was convicted for occasioning bodily harm and assault of a police constable in the execution of his duties. M claimed to have been too drunk from the combined use of drugs and alcohol, negating mens rea. M was a drug addict and had consumed large doses of amphetamines and barbiturates, prior to an evening of drinking at a pub. He admitted to having 'gone paranoid' before, but said that this was the first time he had 'completely blacked out'. Medical evidence was adduced, indicating that such effect as M described was uncommon, and that it was more likely that a person so intoxicated would know what he was doing at the time, but to suffer an 'amnesic patch' later.

R v. Quick and Paddison [1973] QB 910, [1973] 3 WLR 26, [1973] 3 All ER 347 (CA)

The appellants were both psychiatric nurses accused of assaulting a patient. Quick presented medical evidence that he was a diabetic. He argued that at the time of the alleged assault, he was suffering from hypoglycaemia (a deficiency of blood sugar) and was unaware of his act. He had taken his insulin, a small breakfast, some whisky, some rum and no lunch. His defence of automatism was rejected, the court taking the line that insanity was the appropriate defence. He changed his plea to guilty and was convicted. So too was Paddison, who was found guilty as an abettor. Both appealed against conviction and were successful. In the judgement of the Court of Appeal:

> 'Quick's alleged mental condition, if it ever existed, was not caused by his diabetics but by his use of insulin prescribed by his doctor. Such malfunctioning of the mind as there was, was caused by an external factor and not by a bodily disorder in the nature of a disease which disturbed the working of his mind.' (per Lawton LJ)

The court concluded that the defence of automatism ought to have been left to the jury so that certain questions of fact could have been probed.

R v. Kingston [1994] 3 WLR 519, [1994] 3 All ER 353 (HL)

K, a paedophilic homosexual, was convicted of indecent assault of a 15-year-old boy. He had been drugged by one P who, seeking to blackmail K, had procured the boy who was also drugged. P then induced K to assault the boy. In his defence K argued that his drink had been laced and that he remembered seeing the boy on the bed, but remembered nothing afterwards. K's appeal to the Court of Appeal was allowed, but the Crown appealed to the House of Lords. The court had quashed K's conviction on the ground that the surreptitious administration of the drugs had the effect of negating any mens rea he could have formed.

Their Lordships allowed the Crown's appeal, Lord Mustill saying:

> '... where the intoxication is involuntary Majewski does not subtract the defence of absence of intent, but there is nothing in Majewski to suggest that where intent is proved involuntary intoxication adds a further defence.'

M's appeal against conviction was dismissed by both the Court of Appeal and the House of Lords. Their Lordships concluded that self-induced intoxication is no defence to a crime of basic intent, where the mens rea is assumed and need not be proven. Lord Elwyn-Jones LC said:

> '... it is no excuse in law that, because of drink or drugs which the accused himself had taken knowingly and willingly, he had deprived himself of the ability to exercise self-control, to realise the possible consequences of what he was doing or even conscious that he was doing it.'

Task: Look again at R v. Caldwell (1981) and read DPP v. Beard [1920] AC 479, [1920] All ER Rep. 21.

Involuntary intoxication

Involuntary intoxication is a defence both to crimes of basic intent and crimes of specific intent, in that it negates mens rea. Sane automatism may also be a defence in such instances. Where, for example, A 'laces' B's drink with an intoxicant, unknown to B, if B engages in an unlawful act due to his intoxication, B becomes an innocent agent and A the principal. See the following important case and note how this principle was distinguished by the court's approach to the situation in which the accused had the intent to commit the offence and cannot, therefore, rely upon involuntary intoxication as a defence:

Self-defence

We have come to the final of our defences and, perhaps fittingly, it is best left for last as it is so often raised, albeit without merit. Like other defences that are prone to abuse, the courts have applied rigid conditions. Firstly, the circumstances when it is acceptable must indicate that reasonable force is used at the particular time and for the particular purpose. Such reasonable force, meaning appropriate force at that point in time, is acceptable in the following circumstances:

- in defence of oneself and one's family
- in defence of one's property
- to prevent a crime
- to make a lawful arrest or detention.

There are two tests in determining the reasonableness of the force used. These are:

- the objective test, dependent on the circumstances
- the subjective test, dependent on the defendant's perception of the situation.

Research the case of R v. Gladstone Williams along with the following case:

R v. Owino [1996] 2 Cr. App Rep 128, [1995] Crim LR 74 (CA)

Here, O was convicted of assaulting his wife, occasioning actual bodily harm. In his defence, O advanced that he used reasonable force to prevent her from assaulting him.

He was convicted and appealed on the ground that the trial judge had failed to direct the jury that test of reasonable force was subjective. His appeal was dismissed. Collins J expressed the requirements of the tests of reasonableness as follows:

> 'The jury have to decide whether a defendant honestly believed that the circumstances were such as required him to use force to defend himself from an attack or a threatened attack ... But the jury must then decide whether the force used was reasonable in the circumstances as he believed them to be.'

Here's an example of when the courts will not consider the force use as reasonable:

R v. Clegg [1995] 1 All ER 334, [1995] 1 AC 482, [1995] 2 WLR 80 (HL)

C fired shots at a car, which approached a patrol of which he was a part, performing his duties as a soldier in Northern Ireland. The car came at great speed. C fired three shots at the windscreen and one after the car passed. This fourth bullet killed a passenger in the car and C was charged with murder. C's defence was that he fired the shot in defence of himself and a fellow soldier. He was convicted and his two subsequent appeals failed. Their Lordships held that the force used was excessive, Lord Lloyd holding that the degree of permissible force, were the same. It did not matter that C acted in the course of his duties.

Question: How does this decision measure against the use of force by the police in some of our own jurisdictions, in what are referred to 'extra-judicial killings'?

Here's another question: What if the defendant had time to think about what to do and could even have walked away? The Privy Council examined a defendant's reaction in cases of imminent danger and those that are in the form of revenge. In the latter situation, self-defence would not arise:

Palmer v. R [1971] AC 814 (PC)

This was an appeal from Jamaica based on the shooting to death of a man by P. P and a group of men went to buy ganja. A dispute arose and P and the others took the ganja and left without paying for it. They were chased and P used a gun he had with him to shoot the deceased. He appealed against conviction on the ground of self-defence. His appeal was dismissed.

Is the test of reasonable force the same in the Commonwealth Caribbean? Yes, as the two Privy Council decisions that follow, indicate:

Shaw v. R [2002] 1 Cr. App Rep 77, [2002] Crim LR 140 (PC)

This is an appeal from Belize. S was convicted for murder. His appeal was self-defence. The Board stated the common law of Belize to be similar to the common law of England and framed the test to be:

- Did the appellant honestly believe or may he have believed that it was necessary to defend himself?
- If so, and taking the circumstances and the danger as the appellant honestly believed them to be, was the amount of force he used reasonable?

Questions: (1) When the police are chasing armed persons or fear that they might be shot, should they shoot first? (2) What if they are mistaken and the person was not armed?

Beckford v. Regina [1988] AC 130, [1987] 3 WLR 611, [1987] 3 All ER 425 (PC)

In this appeal from Jamaica, the appellant was a policeman who, while investigating a report that a man was terrorising his family, shot and killed a man who ran from the back of his house. He was convicted for murder and his appeal to the Court of Appeal failed. He appealed to the Judicial Committee of the Privy Council. His appeal was allowed. Lord Griffiths reiterated that 'the test to be applied for self-defence is that a person may use such force as is reasonable in the circumstances as he honestly believes them to be the defence of himself or another'.

Compare this decision with R v. Clegg. You will then see how much the court places emphasis on the circumstances. Notwithstanding the volatility of the situation in Northern Ireland, especially at the time of the incident, the court held the view that Clegg used more force than was warranted.

Activity 5.17

Here are some brain teasers. Each of the following questions is intended for you to test yourself on how much you remember from this section. At the end, you will then be aware how much revision you need to do!

1. a How can intoxication be used as a defence?

   b What is the difference between voluntary and involuntary intoxication?
2. What are the elements of the M'Naghten Rules? Give a brief outline of each one.
3. What are the issues surrounding self-defence and prevention of crime? (See Beckford v. Regina and R v. Clegg.)

   Discuss the distinction between (a) insanity and (b) diminished responsibility. What is the effect of each as a defence?
4. What does the court consider in instructing a jury on provocation as a defence?
5. What is the difference between insane and non-insane automatism?
6. How does intoxication affect crimes of basic intent and crimes of specific intent?

Sentencing

We started out in this chapter by stating that the criminal law has always had an element of interest and excitement, much of this being ignited by fiction and television. When we have solved the mystery, we want to see the offender brought to justice. Sentencing is the means by which the State, taking into consideration a number of factors, decides by what means the offender rights the wrong against the State and its citizens.

You will have noted that prosecutions are undertaken by the Crown or the State. It is dispensed with only when the Crown or State grants a fiat to the private citizen to undertake the prosecution. We will look now at the aims of sentencing.

Sentencing in changing societies

Sentences have always been prescribed in different forms and degrees, dependent on the nature of the crime. They have evolved over the years to reflect changes in the norms and values of society. For example, legislation may be enacted to decriminalise an activity (such as homosexuality, in England, after the Wolfenden Report of 1957) or it may create an offence, such as in economic and anti-terrorist issues, in keeping with current trends.

Changes can be brought about by popular agitation, such as is the case being urged concerning the use of marijuana (ganja) for medicinal and religious purposes.

Changes can also be prevented by popular agitation, such as has been demonstrated by many of our own people on the subject of capital punishment.

Aims of sentencing

In the past, and still so in some cultures, gruesome forms of punishment were imposed for crimes considered heinous, such as murder, rape and theft. These crimes are very serious and our system of justice seeks to impose types of punishment that are consistent with the nature of the crime.

Theories of sentencing affect the way in which the Courts approach the issue. These theories are discussed below.

Retributive or denunciatory theory

This theory posits that the offender must be 'done by as he did'. It is akin to the Mosaic Law: 'An eye for an eye and a tooth for a tooth'. It is, therefore, based on proportionality and, though harsh, is not unfair as we understand unfairness, except on the basis that this type of sentencing is meted out in respect of the particular offence and does not take the offender's history into account. In this respect, it is not regarded as the most efficient type of punishment.

The general deterrence theory

This theory is a well-known one, which has received judicial support as, for example, in the 'Great Train Robbery' case of 1964 where the English court expressed its position on the sentences imposed against bandits, as follows:

> 'Severely deterrent sentences were necessary ... to demonstrate to others tempted to follow them into lawlessness on this vast scale that, if they were brought to trial and convicted, commensurate punishment will follow.'

Compare Lord Denning's dictum in the London Borough of Southwark case, where, in frowning on too much latitude being extended to the use of necessity as a defence, he said, 'necessity would open a door which no man could shut'. From this, you will appreciate how public policy considerations influence sentencing, especially along the lines of the general deterrence theory.

The specific or individual deterrence theory

Here, the emphasis is on the individual defender. The aim of this theory is to seek to deter the particular offender from committing another crime. In some respects, it is related to the rehabilitation theory in that such elements as monitoring or the imposition of a suspended sentence are possible approaches. Its treatment of the offender as an individual makes it a useful way in which the offender's own willingness to work with law enforcement can assist the process itself.

The preventive theory

This theory posits that the offender should be imprisoned for long periods in order to prevent him or her from committing further crimes. This approach is inconsistent with proportionality and could be unfairly implemented. It also does not place sufficient emphasis on the individual whose needs may require him or her to be given medical treatment instead of incarceration. It is, therefore, not a frequently used approach today.

The rehabilitation theory

This is an approach, which courts in our jurisdictions, as well as in Europe and North America, are using it at an increasing rate. It includes among its advantages:

- giving offenders a second chance
- affording offenders social and educational opportunities to enable them to be absorbed into society after serving time or, where time was not served, for them to give service to the community while, at the same time, having time to reconcile themselves to the community that has been violated
- easing the burden on the prison population by reducing numbers. It may conflict with the general and specific deterrence theories.

Parole is an important part of this theory. In the United States the issue is a provocative one with respect to sex offenders. You may wish to read up some more on this, with particular reference to 'Megan's Law', which arose from the abduction, sexual abuse and murder of a child in the state of New Jersey.

Factors which influence sentencing

In addition to the offender's background, previous records, if any, and the nature of the offence, the courts also take into account a number of other factors. These include the following:

- What is the seriousness and type of offence?
- Was the offender in a position of trust?
- Does the offender have any previous conviction?
- Was the offender on bail, parole or was he or she given a suspended sentence for which time has not expired?
- What are the offender's family and social circumstances?
- What is the offender's health status?
- What is the offender's age? See, for example, the principle of doli incapax, which states that children under 10 years of age are incapable of committing a crime. Note also the applicable law relative to juvenile offenders in your country, and the age of consent, which would have an effect on the accused's charge in sexual offences.
- What is the offender's financial situation? This is an issue that sometimes arises in discussions on the sentencing of wealthier members of society, as against poorer persons, in relation to the ability to pay for experienced counsel as versus legal aid, which is not always served by more experienced counsel. The financial question is also important in relation to an offender's ability to pay fines, which, when an offender cannot pay, his or her option is incarceration. The issue is also important in relation to an offender's admission to bail.

- Is a non-custodial or custodial sentence appropriate, having regard to the nature of the crime?

Types of sentences

These are usually prescribed by statute or a penal code:

- Imprisonment.
- A suspended sentence. Here the offender has been found guilty and the judge sentences him or her for a period, but the offender will not be incarcerated. It is, therefore, described as a non-custodial sentence. If the offender commits another offence for which he or she is found guilty during the period of the suspended service, a usual term of the sentence is that the offender serves the term that was suspended, plus the term of the new conviction with both terms running consecutively.
- Fines. These are usually within the range of the maximum provided by statute.
- Community service orders. These are being made increasingly and are useful for more minor offences. They may be combined with another sentence such as a fine.
- Probation orders. This order, like the community service order, usually involves the social services, which would undertake an investigation and submit a report to the court.
- Absolute or conditional discharge.
- Binding over to keep the peace.
- Death (on page 156).

You should pay close attention to:

- the treatment of young offenders
- reference by the courts of parties to mediation, especially in domestic disputes. This is an integral part of the justice system in some countries. Check on the situation in your own country.

A much discussed sentence

Two very important questions to consider as regards sentencing relate to:

a Juvenile offenders

b Capital punishment or life imprisonment?

You can find a great deal of literature on both areas and should endeavour to read as much as you can in order to broaden your perspectives.

Juvenile offenders

In each of our Caribbean jurisdictions there is legislation which you should look at so that you are aware of what obtains in your own country. For example, some of the relevant legislation include:

1. Juveniles Act (Jamaica)
2. .....
3. .....

You will observe that the trend is towards rehabilitation, rather than incarceration, even where the juvenile is place in an institution. This is desireable as the aim must be to assist the juvenile, through education and other forms of social intervention, which might also include probation, counseling, and in some instances, community service.

Where the juvenile is placed in detention, the better view is that they should be provided with recreational, educational and other facilities which will assist in their mental and physical development, with the effect of steering them away from becoming habitual, or even hardened criminals. The physical conditions of the centres in which juveniles are detained are also important considerations as an adjunct to sentencing practices. For example, they should be separated from adults, as provided in Rule 29 of the "United Nations Rules for Juveniles Deprived of Their Liberty", which states that "in all detention facilities, juveniles should be separated from adults."

Capital punishment or life imprisonment?

What should be the penalty against one who takes the life of another person? What constitutes the appropriate penalty continues to be a highly emotive subject.

With improved facilities to assist the course of justice, such as DNS and other forms of forensic, there are greater possibilities for ensuring that innocent persons are not convicted for crimes they did not commit.

You may be familiar with some recent cases in the United States of America in which DNA testing has resulted in a number of persons being released from prison after many years of incarceration, for crimes of rape and murder. This certainly points to the type of evidence adduced by the prosecution, instructions by judges to juries and sometimes incompetent representation in cases where accused persons are unable to afford experienced counsel. The same situations may arise in our jurisdictions from time to time.

You may also be aware that the United States of America is still one of the leading countries in the world where capital punishment is practiced. In September 2011, there was a huge outcry against the execution of a man in Atlanta who was eventually executed, despite the strong lobby, numerous appeals and the retraction by a witness of evidence given at trial. It is against cases such as this, that the arguments against the death penalty find strength.

Victims' families and supporters are often supportive of the death penalty. The matter came again to the fore following the Privy Council decision in Pratt and Morgan v Attorney General of Jamaica [1994] 2 AC 1. In that case, the Board ruled that the length of time (over five(5) years) taken for the men's appeals against the death penalty to be heard, following their conviction and sentences, constituted cruel and inhumane treatment in violation of their fundamental rights as provided by the Jamaican Constitution.

The European Union demonstrated its opposition to capital punishment in the following statement issued on the European and World Day against the Death Penalty on October 10, 2011:

"The European Union....."

Complete abolition

The United Nations has also considered the death penalty and in 2007 put a non-binding resolution to the vote, in proposing a moratorium and eventual abandonment of the death penalty. 99 countries voted in favour, 52 against and 33 abstained.

In voting against the resolution, the United States representative argued that capital punishment is not a human rights issue but more a matter of law enforcement.

You may want to do some research on "The death Penalty Project", a human rights project which operates out of the United Kingdom. It states its main objectives as being:

> "to promote the restrictions of the death penalty in line with international minimum legal requirements; to uphold and develop human rights standards and the criminal law; to provide free and effective legal representation and assistance for those individual facing the death penalty; and to create increased awareness and encourage greater dialogue with key stakeholders in the death penalty." (Quotation taken from inside cover page, *Prison Conditions in Jamaica*, a publication of the Project).

Among the cases with which the Project has been instrumental, some of which are familiar to you, and all of which you will find helpful, are the following:

- Pratt and Morgan v Attorney General of Jamaica [1994] 2 AC 1
- Lewis v AG of Jamaica [2002] 2 AC 50
- Reyes v The Queen [2002] 2 AC 235
- The Queen v Hughes [2002] 2 AC 259
- Fox v The Queen [2002] 2 AC 284
- Bowe and Davis v The Queen [2006] 1 WLR 1623.
- Boyce et al v Barbados (unreported case from Barbados which found that mandatory death penalty and prison conditions were found to be in violation of the American Convention on Human Rights)

You may also want to check on the work of the following international agencies:

United Nations Human Rights Committee

Inter American Commission on Human Rights

Inter American Court of Human Rights

In addition, check also on local human rights organizations in your country and elsewhere throughout the Commonwealth Caribbean.

Activity 5.18

Upon completion of this exercise you will have been exposed to some issue in the current debate on capital punishment and on sentencing considerations, generally.

1. Check the internet for information on the work of Amnesty International.
2. Read the United Nations Convention on Human Rights and ask yourself how it affects the treatment of offenders.
3. Examine other Human Rights Conventions to which some of our Commonwealth Caribbean States are signatories.

Feedback

Your references to the conventions and to Amnesty need not be detailed, but your basic knowledge of them will give you a broad perspective on the subject.

Activity 5.19

Revision

As you revise this chapter and previous chapters you will observe that sentencing is an important part of the continuum of the administration and maintenance of justice, and not merely the end.

1. Evaluate the relationship between law and morality in relation to sentencing.
2. Examine the role defences play in sentencing.

Feedback

All these questions require you to do some research and revision. You will no doubt conclude that sentencing is a major part of the continuum in the administration of justice. Among the cases you should find helpful for your research are:

- Shaw v. Director of Public Prosecutions [1962] AC 220, [1961] 2 WLR 897, [1961] 2 All ER 446
- Director of Public Prosecutions v. Knulher [1973] AC 435, [1972] 3 WLR 143
- London Borough of Southwark v. Williams [1971] 2 All ER 175

R v. Blake [1961] 3 All ER 125 was a case on spying. Hilberry J referred to the need to condemn such conduct and to hold it in 'utter abhorrence'. The sentence, he said, should have the threefold purpose 'to be punitive', 'to deter others' and 'to safeguard this country'.

Activity 5.20

1. Review any recent cases reported in your country on the sentences meted out by the court for any criminal offence of your choice and:
   - write down the offence
   - note the background of the offender
   - identify the main arguments advanced by the prosecution and defence
   - identify and critically analyze the response by the media or members of the public, where applicable.
2. Recently, in one country, a man was sentenced to three (3) months for stealing 45 pods of a fruit from the Governor General's garden. There was a great hue and cry about the sentence, that it was too harsh. Some persons argued that the punishment for white collar crimes, where accused persons can afford legal representation, when compared to this sentence, was disproportionate. The accused claimed to have stolen the fruit so he could sell them to buy food. At the time of the writing there is an appeal against the sentence. The sentence was within the provisions of the Larceny Act.

   Prepare for a debate in your class on the factors which should/should not be taken into account by a judge when sentencing a convicted person. You should pay close attention to those situations in which the convict is a juvenile. Should poverty matter as a consideration in mitigating punishment?

Suggested further reading

Walton v. R (1978) Cr. App R (Privy Council, Appeal from Barbados)

DPP v. Newbury and Jones [1976] 2 All ER 365

R v. Watson [1989] 2 All ER 865, [1989] 1 WLR 684

R v. Savage, DPP v Parmenter [1992] 1 AC 699, [1991] 4 All ER 698, [1991] 3 WLR 914

End Test

1 Mr Grumps is an old man of 89 who suffers from senile dementia. He lives in a nursing home. Sometimes Mr Grumps is very endearing, but at times he makes angry outbursts, swears at the staff and will not let anyone touch him. He accuses his family and his nurses of trying to kill him and get his property. When he is in a good mood, Mr Grumps sings hymns, talks about his past and tells everyone that he is an old man now, and 'ready to go home'.

Mr Grumps's family is distressed. His son, Felipe, who was always close to his father, is particularly concerned as he watches his father deteriorate. In conversation with a nurse, Antona, who tells him of his father's frequent expressions that he is 'ready to go home'. Felipe says 'I really hate to see him suffer. He was such a strong and proud man'. Antona who, unknown to anyone, has put other patients 'out of their misery', concludes that certainly Felipe would not mind if his father died. Later that night she administers a drug to Mr Grumps, as a result of which his body convulses violently. He falls from his bed, breaks his neck and dies.

Following investigations, the police arrest Felipe and Antona.

What advice would you give to Felipe and Antona as to their criminal liability?

(Time: 35 minutes)

2 Mr Jones is a pharmacist who resides in Torrie, a Commonwealth Caribbean country. Under the Exchange Control Act, any person found to be in possession of a sum of foreign exchange exceeding 'the prescribed amount' shall be liable upon conviction to a fine not exceeding $2,000,000 or six months' imprisonment at hard labour. Mr Jones, who is well respected in his community, has been a pharmacist for over 40 years. On one of his trips overseas, Mr Jones is questioned at the airport about the amount of money in his possession. He admits to having US$580 more than 'the prescribed amount' for business and commercial travel, which is US$3,000. Mr Jones explains that the additional sum is to enable him to buy a new pair of spectacles suitable for his impaired vision. He is arrested and charged for breaches of the Act.

Mr Jones's family seeks your advice. In no more than 150 words, explain to Mr Jones's family the law as it relates to crimes of strict liability. **(25 marks)**

3 On 17 June 1999, Robert and Pedro, two opposing gangsters, engage in a bitter quarrel about their turf. The men nearly come to blows and both men pull their guns but are parted by onlookers. In the course of their quarrel they both use insulting and angry words to each other. The next day, Robert pursues Pedro to a lonely road and shoots him. Believing Pedro to be dead, Robert then disappears. Pedro is not dead, but suffers serious brain damage by the time he is discovered. He is admitted to hospital where he undergoes surgery, but remains in a coma. All attempts by the surgeons to assist Pedro are futile and they conclude that there is nothing more they can do for him. They think his life support should be turned off.

Pedro's wife is grief-stricken and agrees with the doctors that they should turn off Pedro's life support. On 8 June 2000, they decide to turn off Pedro's life support. He dies on 16 June 2000.

Robert is arrested and charged for murder. You are retained to represent him. In no more than 300 words, citing relevant cases, prepare and present Robert's defence.

4 a Illustrate with reference to decided cases, the distinctions between (i) voluntary and (ii) involuntary manslaughter. **(10 marks)**

b X shoots at B and misses. B is upset by X's action and vows to 'teach X a lesson'. Two days later, B is at a football match where X taunts him telling him he is a coward and that he is lucky not to have been shot already. X and his friends laugh, but B does not respond. At the end of the game, B corners X in a washroom and stabs X, killing him. Discuss B's criminal liability, if any. **(15 marks)**

5 Bill and Archer are playing dominoes at Bill's house and are arguing about politics and race. They differ greatly and the conversation soon becomes quite heated. Bill decides to quit the discussion but Archer persists. Annoyed that Archer will not quit, Bill goes upstairs and takes up his son's toy gun. He comes back downstairs, brandishes the toy gun at Archer and says, 'Now this will keep you quiet'. Archer, believing that the gun is real, rushes down the veranda steps and falls, breaking his ankle. Archer is very upset at Bill 'for frightening me like that', even after he discovers that it was a toy gun. Bill apologises and agrees to pay all Archer's medical expenses, but Archer insists on taking legal action.

In no more than 250 words, give Archer your opinion on Bill's criminal liability, if any.

6 Anjay and Keisha grew up in the same village and attend the same school. Now both aged 19 and preparing to go to college next term, they have been spending a lot of time together during the summer holidays. Keisha's parents are unhappy with how much time she spends 'hanging out' with Anjay and warn her to be careful. They would prefer her to spend time with her girlfriends, as she used to do.

One evening, Anjay invites Keisha to his home. He does not tell her that his parents are away on a visit to his maternal grandmother. They play a game of scrabble and watch a movie, all the time very aware of their physical attraction for each other. Keisha has never objected to Anjay kissing her, but tells him she is not yet ready to go all the way.

Anjay tells Keisha how much he has been aching for her and, despite her protestations, he overpowers her and has sexual intercourse with her. Keisha is very upset and threatens to tell her parents. She tells Anjay that he has let her down, to which he tells her not to worry as he loves her and reminds her that he had used a condom. 'After all,' he tries to console her 'it was only a matter of time. Your mouth was saying "no," but your eyes were always saying "yes".'

You are Keisha's friend, a law student, to whom she turns for advice. How would you explain the law to her?

7 Richard and Edmund become involved in a brawl at a local bar where both are drinking with friends. The brawl occurs after Swaby, a well-known drunk, accused Richard of having an adulterous relationship with Edmund's wife.

Edmund is very upset but says nothing for a while. He buys a dozen beers and after drinking them, he attacks and wounds Richard and Swaby. Swaby dies a few days later.

Explain to Edmund whether the defences of (i) intoxication, (ii) diminished responsibility or (iii) provocation are available to him, giving reasons for your answer. You should cite relevant cases in support of your conclusions.

8 Matt and Condra are walking along Promenade Street when Matt sees a small new suitcase on a bench at a bus stop. The suitcase has an airline tag attached. Matt glances around furtively and, seeing no one, he hurries off in the direction of his home, which is close to the police station. Condra encourages him to hurry along so that they can see what is inside the suitcase.

On the way, while in the vicinity of the police station, Matt and Condra see Douglas, their friend, who asks them where they are going.

'We found this at the bus stop and are taking it to the police', say Matt and Condra, turning into the gate leading to the station. When Douglas leaves, Matt and Condra do not go into the station, but go back through the gate and head to Matt's home.

Matt and Condra open the suitcase and see inside several pieces of jewellery, a pouch containing a small box in which there is a diamond ring, $5,000 cash in United States currency, along with a few items of designer clothing.

'We'd better take these to the police', says Condra who is quite terrified. 'After all, there's a name on the tag.'

'Are you stupid?' says Matt. 'We'll never find such loot again, not in our lifetime. If you don't want a share, I'll keep it all for myself.'

Condra reluctantly agrees to take a share.

Advise Matt and Condra of their criminal liability, after they are arrested and seek your advice. Write down the advice you would give them, supporting your answer with the use of cases and by reference to relevant statutory provisions.

9 You are the first speaker (proposer) in a debate for which the moot is: 'Be it resolved that harsher penalties by the Courts are the only deterrents to crime and the sole means of restoring the confidence of the citizens of this country in the system of justice.'

You are allotted 10 minutes to speak.

Prepare your speech, ensuring that as you do so, you anticipate the points your opponents would make so that your speech not only advances your own position, but it rebuts the opposition.

End Test Feedback

1 You will be expected to discuss the coincidence of the actus reus and mens rea of the crime (murder). There is evidence of this coincidence on Antona's part, but none regarding Felipe whose words cannot reasonably be concluded as exhibiting the mens rea, and certainly he lacks the actus reus.

See Thabo Meli v. R. It is clear that Antona's action in administering the drug is intended to kill Mr Grumps.

2 The issue here is one of strict liability. You are expected to examine the cases and discuss whether Mr Jones is guilty of any offence. On these facts, it is suggested that he is guilty of breaching the Act.

3 Firstly, you should pay close attention to the definition of murder. The key issue here is the cause of Pedro's death. Is it Robert's infliction of grievous bodily harm, or is it as a result of a novus actus interveniens, namely, the doctors' turning off the life support? You would be expected to examine the cases and to present Robert's defence based on these cases.

From this exercise, you will realise that a defence is often a very real challenge!

4 a You have already made this distinction in your first activity and so should find this to be another opportunity for revision.

b Here the issue is 'provocation'. Can the defence avail B? Refer to the relevant cases, noting in particular, the need for the accused to have been affected by a 'sudden impulse'.

5 Questions, which require you to 'advise' or 'give your opinion', are intended for you to analyse the various issues with which you are confronted. You must present both sides of the issues, examining the points in support of either; your conclusion being based on the overwhelmingly stronger side.

The two issues here are (i) the assault (pointing of the gun and use of intimidating words) and (ii) the battery (the fall and resulting injury).

In answering the question, you should follow the method of identifying facts, law and cases in support and basing your conclusion on the law as it relates to the facts before you. Cite relevant statutory provision where applicable.

Cases to consider: R v. Cunningham, R v. Savage, DPP v. Parmenter, R v. Kimber, Smith v. Chief Superintendent of Woking Police Station, R v. Venna.

6 Firstly, you should define rape, in its common law and statutory context, and then indicate which is applicable to your jurisdiction. The main issue is

consent, or the lack of it. The leading cases of Morgan, Kaitamaki and Persaud will assist you in explaining the actus reus and mens rea of rape. You should also explain the standard of recklessness. Is Anjay reckless?

Upon completion of this assignment you should have a very good grasp of this interesting subject. How did you fare? Did you conclude that Anjay was not reckless? Did you think that by spending so much time with Anjay, Keisha had only herself to blame? An example of a similar case occurred involving the boxer Mike Tyson who was convicted in 1992 for the rape of a young woman who visited him in his hotel room late at night.

7 (i) The issue is the effect of self-induced intoxication.

On the authority of Majewski, self-induced intoxication is not a defence to crimes of specific intent, such as murder. It would be necessary to make a distinction between crimes of basic intent and crimes of specific intent and the effect of self-induced intoxication on either type. It should be pointed out to Edmund by way of your explanation, what is the type of intent in the crime of which he is accused, i.e. murder and wounding with intent to cause grievous bodily harm. As an explanation is required, you must indicate to the party the aspects of law involved, having regard to the nature of the charge, then indicate what is applicable to him, basing your conclusion on the facts before you and the law. Contrast Majewski with Kingston. See also Caldwell.

(ii) Diminished responsibility: Does it apply here? Indicate what are the elements of the disease, paying attention to the definition as set out in the 1957 Homicide Act. Look back at your notes. Cases such as Tandy, Byrne and Walton suggest that Edmund would not succeed with a defence of diminished responsibility.

(iii) Provocation: Your first task, of course, is to define 'provocation' and R v. Duffy is your guide on this. Can Edmund rely on the defence? Look back at such cases as DPP v. Camplin.

You should place some value on the fact that words can provoke. Would the reasonable man respond to an accusation such as Swaby makes? Is Edmund 'the reasonable man' in the context of these facts? Support your conclusion by relying on the cases and you should find the exercise very interesting! In a recent case, R v. Smith [2000] 4 All ER 289, the House of Lords held that, ordinarily the judge should direct the jury not to ignore the defendant's characteristic, with a caveat that 'obsessive jealousy is not acceptable for loss of self-control and must be ignored in relation to the objective test'. Can this help Edmund?

8 You are expected to discuss the actus reus and mens rea of theft or larceny, depending on your own jurisdiction. You should define 'theft' or 'larceny', as the case may be, relying on the statutory definitions.

For theft, the issues are: 'appropriation' and 'property belonging to another".

For larceny, you would be required to discuss: animus furandi, permanently depriving the owner and larceny by finding.

The statutory provisions relating to the above issues as well as several cases, which interpret the statutes, are all set out in this section.

Some cases that would be helpful when discussing theft are R v. Turner and R v. Lloyd. Regarding larceny, look at R v. Hall, R v. Wynn, R v. Thurborn and R v. White.

You should be able to find a wealth of material on the criminal justice system by researching in your library, reading newspapers and from the internet. You could also check with persons from different backgrounds in your community and get their opinions on the subject. The outcome of your presentation will depend on the quality of your research.

Tutor marked assignment

At the end of this exercise you should be able to demonstrate an understanding of the topic covered.

In no more than 150 words, discuss, with reference to decided cases, the principle in criminal law that the intention and the act must coincide to constitute a crime. (25 marks)

Marking criteria

Content	
Knowledge and skills:	
■ definition of actus reus and mens rea	4 marks
■ examples to explain definition	3 marks
■ analysis of cases to illustrate principle	8 marks
Structure	
■ Length	2 marks
■ Coherence, relating cases to principle	5 marks
Presentation	
■ Paragraphing, grammar, punctuation	3 marks
	Total 25 marks

Marking criteria

Content	
Knowledge and skills:	
■ definition of actus reus and mens rea	4 marks
■ examples to explain definition	3 marks
■ analysis of cases to illustrate principle	8 marks
Structure	
■ Length	2 marks
■ Coherence, relating cases to principle:	5 marks
Presentation	
■ Paragraphing, grammar, punctuation	3 marks
	Total 25 marks